Selecting Materials for Library Collections

Selecting Materials for Library Collections has been co-published simultaneously as *The Acquisitions Librarian*, Numbers 31/32 2004.

The Acquisitions Librarian Monographic "Separates"

Below is a list of "separates," which in serials librarianship means a special issue simultaneously published as a special journal issue or double-issue *and* as a "separate" hardbound monograph. (This is a format which we also call a "DocuSerial.")

"Separates" are published because specialized libraries or professionals may wish to purchase a specific thematic issue by itself in a format which can be separately cataloged and shelved, as opposed to purchasing the journal on an on-going basis. Faculty members may also more easily consider a "separate" for classroom adoption.

"Separates" are carefully classified separately with the major book jobbers so that the journal tie-in can be noted on new book order slips to avoid duplicate purchasing.

You may wish to visit Haworth's Website at . . .

http://www.HaworthPress.com

. . . to search our online catalog for complete tables of contents of these separates and related publications.

You may also call 1-800-HAWORTH (outside US/Canada: 607-722-5857), or Fax 1-800-895-0582 (outside US/Canada: 607-771-0012), or e-mail at:

docdelivery@haworthpress.com

Selecting Materials for Library Collections, edited by Audrey Fenner (No. 31/32, 2004). *A comprehensive overview of building, maintaining, and updating any library collection.*

Collection Development Policies: New Directions for Changing Collections, edited by Daniel C. Mack (No. 30, 2003). *An in-depth guide to building and maintaining effective policy statements.*

Acquisitions in Different and Special Subject Areas, edited by Abulfazal M. Fazle Kabir (No. 29, 2003). *Presents profiles, methods, and processes for acquisitions in specialized subject areas, including local and regional poetry, oceanography, educational information in electronic formats, popular fiction collections, regional and ethnic materials, and more.*

Strategic Marketing in Library and Information Science, edited by Irene Owens (No. 28, 2002). *"A useful overview of marketing for LIS practitioners in a number of settings, including archives, public libraries, and LIS schools." (Barbara B. Moran, PhD, Professor, School of Information and Library Science, University of North Carolina-Chapel Hill)*

Out-of-Print and Special Collection Materials: Acquisition and Purchasing Options, edited by Judith Overmier (No. 27, 2002). *"Offers inspiration and advice to everyone who works with a special collection. Other librarians and bibliophiles who read it will come away with a new appreciation of the challenges and achievements of special collections librarians. . . . Also valuable for teachers who address these aspects of library work." (Peter Barker, PhD, Professor of the History of Science, University of Oklahoma, Norman)*

Publishing and the Law: Current Legal Issues, edited by A. Bruce Strauch (No. 26, 2001). Publishing and the Law: Current Legal Issues *provides lawyers and librarians with insight into the main areas of legal change that are having an impact on the scholarly publishing world today. This book explores constitutional issues, such as the Communications Decency Act, showing how the First Amendment makes it virtually impossible to regulate the World Wide Web. This unique book includes a history of copyright law up through current international treaties to provide an understanding of how copyright law and the electronic environment intertwine.*

Readers, Reading and Librarians, edited by Bill Katz (No. 25, 2001). *Reaffirms the enthusiasm of books and readers as libraries evolve from reading centers to information centers where librarians are now also web masters, information scientists, and media experts.*

Acquiring Online Management Reports, edited by William E. Jarvis (No. 24, 2000). *This fact-filled guide explores a broad variety of issues involving acquisitions and online management reports to keep libraries and library managers current with changing technology and, ultimately, offer patrons more information. This book provides you with discussions and suggestions on several topics, including working with vendors, developing cost-effective collection development methods to suit your library, assessing collection growth, and choosing the best electronic resources to help meet your goals.* Acquiring Online Management Reports *offers you an array of proven ideas, options, and examples that will enable your library to keep up with client demands and simplify the process of collecting, maintaining, and interpreting online reports.*

The Internet and Acquisitions: Sources and Resources for Development, edited by Mary E. Timmons (No. 23, 2000). *"For those trying to determine how the Internet could be of use to their particular library in the area of acquisitions, or for those who have already decided they should be moving in that direction . . . this volume is a good place to begin." (James Mitchell, MLS, Library Director, Bainbridge-Guilford Central School, Bainbridge, NY)*

Gifts and Exchanges: Problems, Frustrations, . . . and Triumphs, edited by Catherine Denning (No. 22, 1999). *"A complete compendium embracing all aspects of the matter in articles that are uniformly well-written by people experienced in this field." (Jonathan S. Tryon, CAL, JD, Professor, Graduate School of Library and Information Studies, University of Rhode Island)*

Periodical Acquisitions and the Internet, edited by Nancy Slight-Gibney (No. 21, 1999). *Sheds light on the emerging trends in selection, acquisition, and access to electronic journals.*

Public Library Collection Development in the Information Age, edited by Annabel K. Stephens (No. 20, 1998). *"A first-rate collection of articles . . . This is an engaging and helpful work for anyone involved in developing public library collections." (Lyn Hopper, MLn, Director, Chestatee Regional Library, Dahlonega, GA)*

Fiction Acquisition/Fiction Management: Education and Training, edited by Georgine N. Olson (No. 19, 1998). *"It is about time that attention is given to the collection in public libraries . . . it is about time that public librarians be encouraged to treat recreational reading with the same respect that is paid to informational reading . . . Thank you to Georgine Olson for putting this volume together." (Regan Robinson, MLS, Editor and Publisher, Librarian Collection Letter)*

Acquisitions and Collection Development in the Humanities, edited by Irene Owens (No. 17/18, 1997). *"Can easily become a personal reference tool." (William D. Cunningham, PhD, Retired faculty, College of Library and Information Service, University of Maryland, College Park)*

Approval Plans: Issues and Innovations, edited by John H. Sandy (No. 16, 1996). *"This book is valuable for several reasons, the primary one being that librarians in one-person libraries need to know how approval plans work before they can try one for their particular library . . . An important addition to the professional literature." (The One-Person Library)*

Current Legal Issues in Publishing, edited by A. Bruce Strauch (No. 15, 1996). *"Provides valuable access to a great deal of information about the current state of copyright thinking." (Library Association Record)*

New Automation Technology for Acquisitions and Collection Development, edited by Rosann Bazirjian (No. 13/14, 1995). *"Rosann Bazirjian has gathered together 13 current practitioners who explore technology and automation in acquisitions and collection development . . . Contains something for everyone." (Library Acquisitions: Practice and Theory)*

Management and Organization of the Acquisitions Department, edited by Twyla Racz and Rosina Tammany (No. 12, 1994). *"Brings together topics and librarians from across the country to discuss some basic challenges and changes facing our profession today." (Library Acquisitions: Practice and Theory)*

A. V. in Public and School Libraries: Selection and Policy Issues, edited by Margaret J. Hughes and Bill Katz (No. 11, 1994). *"Many points of view are brought forward for those who are creating new policy or procedural documents . . . Provide[s] firsthand experience as well as considerable background knowledge. . . ." (Australian Library Review)*

Multicultural Acquisitions, edited by Karen Parrish and Bill Katz (No. 9/10, 1993). *"A stimulating overview of the U.S. multicultural librarianship scene." (The Library Assn. Reviews)*

Popular Culture and Acquisitions, edited by Allen Ellis (No. 8, 1993). *"A provocative penetrating set of chapters on the tricky topic of popular culture acquisitions . . . A valuable guidebook." (Journal of Popular Culture)*

Collection Assessment: A Look at the RLG Conspectus©, edited by Richard J. Wood and Katina Strauch (No. 7, 1992). *"A well-organized, thorough book . . . Provides the most realistic representations of what the Conspectus is and what its limitations are . . . Will take an important place in Conspectus literature." (Library Acquisitions: Practice & Theory)*

Evaluating Acquisitions and Collections Management, edited by Pamela S. Cenzer and Cynthia I. Gozzi (No. 6, 1991). *"With the current emphasis on evaluation and return on funding, the material is timely indeed!" (Library Acquisitions: Practice & Theory)*

Vendors and Library Acquisitions, edited by Bill Katz (No. 5, 1991). *"Should be required reading for all new acquisitions librarians and all library science students who plan a career in technical services. As a whole it is a very valuable resource." (Library Acquisitions: Practice & Theory)*

Operational Costs in Acquisitions, edited by James R. Coffey (No. 4, 1991). *"For anyone interested in embarking on a cost study of the acquisitions process this book will be worthwhile reading." (Library Acquisitions: Practice & Theory)*

Legal and Ethical Issues in Acquisitions, edited by Katina Strauch and A. Bruce Strauch (No. 3, 1990). *"This excellent compilation is recommended to both collection development/acquisition librarians and library administrators in academic libraries." (The Journal of Academic Librarianship)*

The Acquisitions Budget, edited by Bill Katz (No. 2, 1989). *"Practical advice and tips are offered throughout . . . Those new to acquisitions work, especially in academic libraries, will find the book useful background reading." (Library Association Record)*

Automated Acquisitions: Issues for the Present and Future, edited by Amy Dykeman (No. 1, 1989). *"This book should help librarians to learn from the experience of colleagues in choosing the system that best suits their local requirements . . . [It] will appeal to library managers as well as to library school faculty and students." (Library Association Record)*

Selecting Materials
for Library Collections

Audrey Fenner
Editor

Selecting Materials for Library Collections has been
co-published simultaneously as *The Acquisitions Librarian*,
Numbers 31/32 2004.

The Haworth Information Press®
An Imprint of The Haworth Press, Inc.

New York • London • Victoria (AU)
www.HaworthPress.com

Published by

The Haworth Information Press®, 10 Alice Street, Binghamton, NY 13904-1580 USA

The Haworth Information Press® is an imprint of The Haworth Press, Inc., 10 Alice Street, Binghamton, NY 13904-1580 USA.

Selecting Materials for Library Collections has been co-published simultaneously as *The Acquisitions Librarian,* Numbers 31/32 2004.

The development, preparation, and publication of this work has been undertaken with great care. However, the publisher, employees, editors, and agents of The Haworth Press and all imprints of The Haworth Press, Inc., including The Haworth Medical Press® and Pharmaceutical Products Press®, are not responsible for any errors contained herein or for consequences that may ensue from use of materials or information contained in this work. Opinions expressed by the author(s) are not necessarily those of The Haworth Press, Inc. With regard to case studies, identities and circumstances of individuals discussed herein have been changed to protect confidentiality. Any resemblance to actual persons, living or dead, is entirely coincidental.

Cover design by Brooke R. Stiles.

Library of Congress Cataloging-in-Publication Data

Selecting materials for library collections / Audrey Fenner, editor.
    p. cm.
    "Co-published simultaneously as The acquisitions librarian, numbers 31/32, 2004."
    Includes bibliographical references and index.
    ISBN 0-7890-1520-X (alk. paper) – ISBN 0-7890-1521-8 (pbk: alk. paper)
    1. Collection development (Libraries) 2. Libraries–Special collections. 3. Book selection.
4. Selection of nonbook materials. 5. Academic libraries–Collection development. I. Fenner, Audrey.
II. Acquisitions librarian.
Z687.S435 2004
025.2'1–dc22
                                                                    2003027736

Indexing, Abstracting & Website/Internet Coverage

This section provides you with a list of major indexing & abstracting services. That is to say, each service began covering this periodical during the year noted in the right column. Most Websites which are listed below have indicated that they will either post, disseminate, compile, archive, cite or alert their own Website users with research-based content from this work. (This list is as current as the copyright date of this publication.)

Abstracting, Website/Indexing Coverage . . . . Year When Coverage Began

- *CNPIEC Reference Guide: Chinese National Directory of Foreign Periodicals* 1996
- *Combined Health Information Database (CHID)* 1996
- *Current Cites [Digital Libraries] [Electronic Publishing]*
  [Multimedia & Hypermedia] [Networks & Networking]
  [General] 2000
- *Current Index to Journals in Education* 2002
- *Educational Administration Abstracts (EAA)* 1991
- *FRANCIS. INIST/CNRS <http://www.inist.fr>* 1997
- *IBZ International Bibliography of Periodical Literature*
  <http://www.saur.de> 1997
- *Index Guide to College Journals (core list compiled by integrating*
  48 indexes frequently used to support undergraduate programs
  in small to medium sized libraries) 1999
- *Index to Periodical Articles Related to Law <http://www.law.utexas.edu>* 1992
- *Information Reports & Bibliographies* 1992
- *Information Science & Technology Abstracts: indexes journal articles from*
  more than 450 publications as well as books, research reports, conference
  proceedings, and patents; EBSCO Publishing
  <http://www.infotoday.com> 1992
- *Informed Librarian, The <http://www.infosourcespub.com>* 1993

(continued)

* Exact start date to come.

Special Bibliographic Notes related to special journal issues (separates) and indexing/abstracting:

- indexing/abstracting services in this list will also cover material in any "separate" that is co-published simultaneously with Haworth's special thematic journal issue or DocuSerial. Indexing/abstracting usually covers material at the article/chapter level.
- monographic co-editions are intended for either non-subscribers or libraries which intend to purchase a second copy for their circulating collections.
- monographic co-editions are reported to all jobbers/wholesalers/approval plans. The source journal is listed as the "series" to assist the prevention of duplicate purchasing in the same manner utilized for books-in-series.
- to facilitate user/access services all indexing/abstracting services are encouraged to utilize the co-indexing entry note indicated at the bottom of the first page of each article/chapter/contribution.
- this is intended to assist a library user of any reference tool (whether print, electronic, online, or CD-ROM) to locate the monographic version if the library has purchased this version but not a subscription to the source journal.
- individual articles/chapters in any Haworth publication are also available through the Haworth Document Delivery Service (HDDS).

Selecting Materials
for Library Collections

CONTENTS

ABOUT THE EDITOR

Audrey Fenner, MLS, BMus, BMusEd, ARCT, is Head, Acquisition Department at Walter Clinton Jackson Library, University of North Carolina at Greensboro. A librarian since 1984, Ms. Fenner has held professional positions in academic, research, business, government, and public libraries in the United States and Canada. She has had experience in a wide variety of library settings, from a one-person branch library housed in a trailer in the Arizona desert, to the National Library of Canada, where she did both original cataloging and reference work in two languages. Ms. Fenner holds a Master of Library Science degree from the University of Western Ontario, London, Canada.

Preface

Practical, up-to-date library literature on selection is always needed, and it is hoped that this volume will be of real interest and help to working librarians. For selectors, whether librarians or bibliographers, knowledge of the literature of subject disciplines is essential. Familiarity with collection development processes and tools is also vitally important, and this is generally acquired through practice rather than training. The experience shared here by librarians active in selection work should provide a head start for others new to selection, and for those who have been assigned selection responsibilities in disciplines that are new to them.

It is obvious to users and librarians alike that library collections incorporate materials in a wide variety of formats. Print, non-print, and Internet selection resources are presented here, useful library-wide and also in acquiring materials for specialized collections within libraries.

Selectors need to know what they are collecting, for whom, and for what purpose. In an academic library, for example, the collection must support the institution's research and educational needs. From the resources made available, users determine what is of value to them. It is the library's responsibility to provide what is needed, as promptly as possible. Librarians may try to anticipate user needs by studying what users request, what they actually use, and what methods are most efficient in providing these materials. The results of such studies provide an overall understanding of users' expectations. This understanding must be combined with knowledge of the resources available for purchase, alternative formats, costs, and available funds.

The volume covers subject areas of interest in both academic and public libraries. The majority of writers focus on selecting materials in a specific subject area. These evaluate selection resources of all types, based on their use as selection tools.

[Haworth co-indexing entry note]: "Preface." Fenner, Audrey. Co-published simultaneously in *The Acquisitions Librarian* (The Haworth Information Press, an imprint of The Haworth Press, Inc.) No. 31/32, 2004, pp. xvii-xix; and: *Selecting Materials for Library Collections* (ed: Audrey Fenner) The Haworth Information Press, an imprint of The Haworth Press, Inc., 2004, pp. xiii-xv. Single or multiple copies of this article are available for a fee from The Haworth Document Delivery Service [1-800-HAWORTH, 9:00 a.m. - 5:00 p.m. (EST). E-mail address: docdelivery@haworthpress.com].

xiii

Some contributors use one discipline as an example of particular approaches to selection, or to illustrate concerns that may arise for selectors. In "Dilemmas in Balancing a University Literature Collection," David Isaacson argues against intellectual elitism or excessive delicacy in selecting library materials. Isaacson recommends reconsidering traditional collecting priorities and makes the point that academic library collections need to include representative examples of genre literature and pornography. Isaacson also discusses hypertext fiction and the difficulties this new format presents in the context of book collecting. If a text does not exist apart from its interpretations, Isaacson asks, how can a library preserve it in any definitive version?

Susan Herzog presents selection from the viewpoint of the librarian new to collection development, or the librarian with other responsibilities besides selection. Herzog emphasizes the importance of consulting library policies concerning collection development, gifts and weeding.

Other contributors have chosen one particular subject and present selection resources in this area of emphasis. Stephen Luttmann writes on selection of music materials. In music, he says, the selector must possess a considerable degree of subject competence as well as knowledge of the needs of the user group. Elizabeth A. Lorenzen discusses acquiring art materials, stressing the effect that new technologies may have on the way art librarians acquire resources. As technology changes the art world, parallel changes take place in art librarianship.

Deborah Lee introduces major selection tools in business and economics. She presents examples of collection development policies in these areas.

Several contributors discuss health-related resources and their selection. Eva Stowers and Gillian Galbraith describe the process of planning and building a collection to support a completely new academic program in dental sciences. When the University of Nevada, Las Vegas planned its dental school, few pertinent resources were held in the general library collection. A dental sciences collection had to be developed and incorporated into the university's library. Parts of the planning process in this instance are applicable in other academic libraries, such as reviewing the school's curriculum, and studying published standards to prepare for an accreditation team's site visit.

Janet W. Owens provides comprehensive coverage of selection resources in nursing, including tools useful for both current and retrospective selection and acquisitions. Susan Suess writes as a librarian at a medical school, emphasizing the need to incorporate materials in many formats in a balanced, broad-ranging collection.

Two writers present selection resources for interdisciplinary fields. Lisa Wallis has contributed a guide to selection tools in public health, and Patricia Pettijohn describes the crossing of subject boundaries in her article on selection for another broad field, mental health.

Mary Beth Allen, writing on selection in the areas of exercise, sport and leisure, describes the use to be made of reviews and other sources of information, such as professional organizations.

Several writers discuss selection in subject areas that may be unfamiliar to many librarians. Jane Brodsky Fitzpatrick provides an account of library work at a maritime college where very specialized disciplines are represented. Resources used in the selection of appropriate library resources are similarly specialized.

Rhonda Harris Taylor and Lotsee Patterson describe strategies and tools for selecting materials concerning Native Americans. Resources in several formats are considered, and the selection approaches the writers describe are valid in any library.

Karen Wei's topic is the acquisition of materials for academic collections supporting Chinese Studies programs. Wei provides guidance on identifying and purchasing materials from the People's Republic of China, Hong Kong, and Taiwan.

Some contributors have written on selection for collections to be used in a particular way. Arthur McClelland presents a description of a local history and genealogy collection in a large public library in Canada. The needs of the researchers who use this collection play an important part in the way the materials are selected and made available. Retrospective selection is the focus of a chapter on assembling a core collection of resources to be used chiefly for academic research. The writers, John Fenner and Audrey Fenner, have assembled a basic but representative title list for a New Thought core collection.

Information provided by some contributors is applicable to library selection and acquisitions in general, and does not focus on a specific subject field. Selection aids for acquiring media are presented by Mary Laskowski, who discusses the impact of new technologies on media collection development. Audrey Fenner's article on approval plans discusses the role of these plans in library collection development and management. As an adjunct to title-by-title selection, a well-planned approval profile can be the means of freeing selectors for work with a smaller but harder to find portion of a library's yearly acquisitions.

Collection development is a process continually in flux. Acquisitions budgets remain static or shrink, library programs and policies change, new and traditional formats gain or diminish in importance, and administrators call for accountability in spending. It is important that librarians do not allow themselves to be driven either by lack of time or by budgetary constraints into neglecting their responsibilities as selectors of library resources.

Audrey Fenner

Dilemmas in Balancing
a University Literature Collection

David Isaacson

SUMMARY. This essay explores some of the conflicts faced by the author, a liaison with book-selection responsibilities to a university English Department. These conflicts include: trying to fill gaps missed by profiles set up with our book vendor; trying to achieve a reasonable balance between canonical and non-canonical texts; between primary texts and the secondary works interpreting these texts; between works that might become classic versus those that are truly ephemeral; between controversial pornography and less controversial or non-controversial erotica; and between hypertext fiction and traditional print resources. *[Article copies available for a fee from The Haworth Document Delivery Service: 1-800-HAWORTH. E-mail address: <docdelivery@haworthpress.com> Website: <http://www.HaworthPress.com> © 2004 by The Haworth Press, Inc. All rights reserved.]*

KEYWORDS. Book selection, English literature, American literature, pornography, canonical works, hypertext fiction

THERE IS NO SCIENCE TO SELECTING LITERARY RESOURCES

Sometimes I wish library science actually were as rigorous, predictable and reliable as one of the "hard" sciences. If it were, then I could do my job better

---

David Isaacson is Assistant Head of Reference and Humanities Librarian, Reference Department, Waldo Library, Western Michigan University, Kalamazoo, MI 49008-5080 (E-mail: david.isaacson@wmich.edu).

[Haworth co-indexing entry note]: "Dilemmas in Balancing a University Literature Collection." Isaacson, David. Co-published simultaneously in *The Acquisitions Librarian* (The Haworth Information Press, an imprint of The Haworth Press, Inc.) No. 31/32, 2004, pp. 1-10; and: *Selecting Materials for Library Collections* (ed: Audrey Fenner) The Haworth Information Press, an imprint of The Haworth Press, Inc., 2004, pp. 1-10. Single or multiple copies of this article are available for a fee from The Haworth Document Delivery Service [1-800-HAWORTH, 9:00 a.m. - 5:00 p.m. (EST). E-mail address: docdelivery@haworthpress.com].

10.1300/J101v16n31_01

as the librarian most responsible for acquiring the best materials to support my university's Ph.D. program in English and American Literature and Creative Writing. An ideal library scientific method would imply there were reasonably predictable and reliable ways of obtaining most of the books we need. Our library does not have the budget to hire full-time bibliographers, so collection development perhaps relies too much on the selection criteria we establish with our book vendor. Through the collection profiles we set up with Blackwell's of North America, after discussing the subjects and publication formats with our subject specialist teaching faculty, we hope we acquire on approval most of the academic books necessary to support our undergraduate and graduate programs. As the Humanities Librarian and Liaison to the English Department I supplement these automatic book purchases by selecting other books offered each week as form selections from Blackwell's. To further supplement these selections I try to find time to scan book review sources and publishers' catalogs to choose books that are not part of Blackwell's inventory. A few bibliographically astute English Department faculty also order materials we don't own but which they need for their teaching and research.

Despite these careful procedures, I know that numerous potentially very useful books, videos, audio recordings, CD-ROMs, journals, and online resources are not being ordered. I am not referring to materials we know about but can't afford to purchase. More distressing are the materials we don't acquire because we simply don't know they exist or because we interpret our collection guidelines too narrowly. This essay discusses some of the types of English and American literature materials many academic libraries like my own do not regularly or thoroughly collect. My purpose is to suggest that we reconsider some of our traditional collecting priorities.

THE PROBLEM OF COLLECTING NON-CANONICAL WORKS

If we assume that a university library has a responsibility not only to collect resources immediately necessary to the curriculum but also to build a repository of materials for posterity, we may be paying too much attention only to established authors and canonical texts. There are many second tier, not yet fully established writers, who are either not represented or under-represented in traditional university literary collections. A selector like me is faced with a number of dilemmas concerning works by these authors.

Our first responsibility is to be as sure as the budget permits that we have as many of the primary and secondary resources as we can afford to support an accredited Ph.D. program in English. But after we have acquired the most recent and authoritative primary sources–the scholarly editions of Chaucer,

Shakespeare, and Hemingway, as well as the reliable secondary sources–the university press books and peer-reviewed journals devoted to interpreting these authors' works–there are still some gaps to fill.

DO WE HAVE TOO MANY SECONDARY WORKS ABOUT, NOT ENOUGH PRIMARY WORKS OF LITERATURE?

Before multi-cultural studies, Gay and Lesbian studies, Women's studies, African-American studies, Native-American studies, and Ethnic minority studies became popular, our collections were woefully deficient in these and other areas outside of the traditional canon. I know that we have been building much more thorough and representative collections of what used to be called "fringe" materials than in the past. My concern now is that, ironically, we seem to be collecting more of the secondary materials than the primary literature in these areas. And we may even be missing some important secondary resources on the canonical writers because we may be ignoring or at least missing some of the important non-mainstream books and journals discussing these writers.

Granted, it is often difficult to identify works by lesser-known or little-known authors which may have enough staying power to warrant inclusion in a university collection. It is also difficult to know which of the small presses and journals are publishing materials important to add to our collections. But I think libraries have a responsibility to try to fill in some of these gaps. Our English Department has a number of quite different, sometimes competing, and indeed, even sometimes nearly hostile constituencies within it. As the liaison to the whole department I try not to play favorites, but I have to acknowledge that the needs of a Milton scholar are often very different from a professor specializing in English education, and their needs, in turn, are quite different from a Women's Studies specialist or a poet teaching creative writing. Each of these specialists sees the library differently. They should. It is not the responsibility of English professors to build a comprehensive and balanced collection. That's the job of a Humanities Librarian like me in consultation with them. But can I be sure that I am being a reasonably objective, unbiased, and informed selector playing fair with all these different groups? This is not an easy question to answer.

If we are to build the collection to assist traditional scholars with their work, it is incumbent on a liaison like me to consult with English professors to make sure we have as many of the authoritative print and online resources as we can afford. If there is a new variorum edition of Henry James's work the library must acquire it. All the university press monographs and all of the reputable commercial press books about James published in the United States as well as many of them published in England, and some of them published in other countries, should also be acquired. However, I don't think we have any obligation to purchase works with questionable scholarly authority, such as most of the books published by the University Press of America.[1]

If we have to make hard choices among reputable books I hope the balance tips in favor of primary rather than secondary works. There's no question that we must have a new edition of Hemingway's *The Sun Also Rises*. But we don't have to acquire *every* study that is published about that novel. In addition to collecting all the works by and many of the works about a classic writer like Hemingway I think we should also acquire as many new books by the so-called small literary presses as possible. Many future Ernest Hemingways will not have their first novel published by a mainstream publisher like Scribner's. We would not have acquired Hemingway's first book, a collection of stories and poems, unless someone had the prescience in 1923 to acquire *Three Stories & Ten Poems* by a small press in Paris called Contact.

WE CAN'T ALWAYS PLEASE ALL THE COMPETING INTERESTS IN AN ENGLISH DEPARTMENT

Our creative writing students need as rich a selection of contemporary fiction and poetry as our literature students need of the established masters. As a matter of fact, the English literature majors have as much potential interest in the books and journals published by the small presses as the creative writing majors need copies of the established and classic authors' works. If a large book vendor like Blackwell's does not include some of the small press books, we should, if the budget permits, try to set up separate standing orders with these presses. In many cases, setting up standing orders for the limited number of titles of many of these presses makes more sense than selectively ordering individual titles, since a busy selector like me, who is not a full-time bibliographer, may not get around to ordering these books before they go out of print.

No library has an obligation, however, to try to purchase *all* of the small press books. Some of these publications are truly ephemeral, some little more than vanity press publications, and many of them may not be read by our users, or not read very often. But I would rather err on the side of the inclusion of the mediocre rather than the exclusion of the good or excellent. For every librarian with the exquisite good taste to recognize the genius of a first book of poems by the next T. S. Eliot there must be hundreds of us who have neither the time nor the reading knowledge to make such wise choices. Considering the relative low cost of most novels, story collections, poetry books, and plays compared to the average price of a book in the social sciences or the sciences, I think libraries can afford to waste a little money setting up standing orders which will bring in some literary works that may not have enduring literary value, in order to acquire expeditiously other books which we will be very glad later that we purchased as first editions.

ACADEMIC LIBRARIES SHOULD COLLECT SOME EPHEMERAL WORKS

In an ideal world, I would also like to see book selectors in positions like mine making a greater effort to collect at least some representative samples of genre fiction and other mass audience popular culture materials usually thought to be the province of public libraries. Unless there are regular classes studying such material, the library has no need to acquire a large cache of romance fiction, detective stories, horror fiction, or pornography. A university library has no more obligation to collect a comprehensive collection of bodice rippers than it does a similarly complete collection of Christian fiction. But if there is a legitimate research and teaching need for such materials, some of them need to be made available in the circulating collection. For a very extensive discussion of the numerous issues raised by collecting popular culture materials in academic libraries see "Popular Culture and Acquisitions," edited by Allen Ellis.[2]

THERE'S A PLACE FOR PORNOGRAPHY AS WELL AS PIOUS RELIGIOUS FICTION

Determining which popular books–and especially which scandalously popular books–should be added to an academic library's collection presents a book selector with some deliciously difficult dilemmas. It would, of course, be absurd for libraries to "balance" their collections by collecting a certain number of books of questionable taste to "offset" the classics. I am not a First Amendment purist nor a firebrand out to *epater le bourgeois*, but I do think many academic libraries have an obligation to have at least a few examples of wretchedly awful fiction in all of the popular genres if only so that students will then be able to distinguish, say, between hard and soft-core pornography, run-of-the-mill romance fiction versus classic Gothic literature such as *Wuthering Heights*, or between genre Christian fiction and a genuinely classic work of Christian piety with literary resonance, such as *Pilgrim's Progress*.

I'm making a libertarian, even an old-fashioned conservative argument as well as a traditional liberal argument in favor of a collection that includes both popular and elite literature. How can we tell the difference between so-called elite, classic, or canonical texts and popular, general audience fiction, not to mention pulp fiction, if we don't have examples of each to compare? We should also acknowledge the fact that some works of classic literature are quite offensive to some readers. The graphic depiction of sex and violence, not to mention the excremental details of some passages in Boccaccio, Chaucer, Dante, and Shakespeare should make mass market pornographers blush with shame for their lack of imagination. Real erotic literature is fanciful and liberating; true pornography is demeaning, ugly, and very unimaginative. D. H. Lawrence is persuasive when he argues, in his essay *Pornography and Obscenity*,[3] that the truly obscene is that which the ancient Greek dramatists chose only to allude to "off-scene" or away from the main action of the stage (Lawrence speculates that the Greek origin of "obscene" is "obskena" meaning off-the-main-scene, although the Oxford English Dictionary says the etymology is obscure). In the same essay Lawrence argues that pornography (literally, writing by prostitutes) confuses the creative and the excretory. Literature that honors the creative life-force (the kind Lawrence hoped he was writing) is nothing if not sensual and sexual. But pornography does just the opposite: it mocks and casts dirt upon true sensuality and the open expression of the sexual. Just look what prudes have done to dishonor the unabashed celebration of love-making in *The Song of Songs*, one of the most poetically intriguing books of the Bible.[4]

Only libraries with a special purpose like the Vatican Library's famous collection of prohibited books, or the Kinsey Institute for Sex Research Library at Indiana University, have the need for comprehensive collections of pornography, but genuine erotica may be a different matter. Although some people even in the rather privileged world of academe may find some of Henry Miller's writing pornographic, a strong case can be made that his work is more accurately described as erotica. We simply cannot have a representative collection of English literature without including controversial writers like Miller. We surely need to try to have all the works of William Burroughs as well. But I don't think we must have every book that Howard Stern writes. His books are interesting social phenomena, some of which are necessary to the study of popular culture, but they have little or no aesthetic merit.[5]

A similar argument can be made for acquiring *some* copies of popular evangelistically Christian fiction. Some books from this genre are just as necessary to accurately reflect popular culture as any other popular culture literary format. Similar reasoning suggests that academic libraries need to have some copies available of historically important racist and anti-Semitic tracts such as *Mein Kamp* and *The Protocols of Zion*. Academic libraries are under no obligation to purchase all the books purporting to offer historical evidence that the Holocaust is a hoax, but some books in this genre do belong in our collections.

BUT DON'T WE HAVE TO DRAW THE LINE SOMEWHERE?

But where should we draw the line between a representative sample of such fringe or fugitive works and too much? That depends on an assessment of the number of users likely to want to see this material as well as on the budget. Our first responsibility is obviously to collect books of legitimate rather than illegitimate authority. Surely good sense (I hope I don't offend social scientists, but most humanists I know don't need a definition of what good sense is) is the final arbiter about how much blatantly racist or sexist or pornographic material needs to be represented in our collections in order to have a sufficient quantity of such materials for study purposes.

For some scholars and students it is essential they have actual hard copy primary texts for close study. You can't study Henry James seriously unless you have both the earliest editions of his work and the famous "New York Edition," in which James edited many of his previously published books, sometimes very extensively revising them. A library offering an old-fashioned Ph.D. in English needs a collection of manuscripts, or at least facsimiles of manuscripts, of some literary texts so that students can learn how to do close textual analysis. Although a Rare Books collection is expensive, it is not just a dispensable addition to the traditional collection. Immediate and widespread use is not the only criterion we need to apply to acquisitions of literary materials. If we were to acquire the manuscript of Garrison Keillor's novel, *Lake Woebegone Days*, it may be just as useful to some scholars as a copy of the manuscript (or facsimile) of F. Scott Fitzgerald's *The Great Gatsby*.

One of my responsibilities in building literature collections is acquiring micro format reproductions of texts that are unavailable in print or whose price in print is prohibitive. Increasingly, however, when the alternative exists, we should be obtaining electronic versions of these texts. Some potentially important fiction, for example, does not exist–at least in its first iteration–in print. Hypertext fiction, for example, either exists on CD-ROMs or on World Wide Web sites. Although the format is still so new that it is very difficult to determine which of these new works of hypertext fiction may be written well enough to be valuable to posterity, academic libraries probably need to be acquiring *some* of this fiction before it takes on the cyber equivalent of being out of print.

WHAT IS A LITERARY TEXT?

On the other hand, if we take seriously the argument raised by some postmodernist and deconstructionist literary critics, it is very short-sighted to view a literary text as a fixed object. According to many of these theorists, *any* written text–let alone one with literary staying power–is malleable. A text exists only when it is interpreted, these critics insist. Every time I read *The Adventures of Huckleberry Finn* the meaning changes a bit. My interpretation of the book the first time I read it in high school differs considerably from my understanding of it a few years later in college. Those readings, in turn, were quite unsophisticated compared to the way I read the book a number of years later when I taught it in college. Now suppose that I am the noted literary scholar Harold Bloom and assume also, that I have written notes to myself documenting each of these interpretations of Twain's novel. A deconstructionist would argue that each of these interpretations is valuable and that a collection of the works by a critic of Bloom's stature would not be complete without these manuscript notes (or facsimiles of them) as well. But why should we restrict our collections only to literary critics with established reputations? Why not also include the hitherto unrecognized insights of a Humanities Librarian?

When I was an undergraduate in the early 1960s we were cautioned to avoid the intentional fallacy. That simply meant that whatever we knew about the author's intentions in writing the literary work, we were to evaluate the book on our sense of its results, not the author's hopes for his book. But many of today's readers take an even more skeptical view of reading. They live in a far more tentative and relative world than I am comfortable with. Many of today's English majors are taught that there can be no fixed meaning to *any* text because any interpretation is always subject to re-interpretation.

SHOULD WE COLLECT HYPERTEXT FICTION?

If book selectors like me take the arguments of these critics seriously we should be collecting a lot more secondary works than most budgets would warrant. Let us consider seriously the case of hypertext fiction and poetry. Much hypertext fiction contains hot links leading readers to narrative developments that branch out from the main story line. Each time the reader chooses a forking path in the narrative she necessarily loses the thread–at least for the moment–of an alternate path. There are so many branches to choose from in some hyper-texts that the possible plot outcomes and character developments seem infinite. To further complicate matters, some hypertext fiction is collaboratively written, so that no one author is responsible for creating the text. And some of this fiction is in a constant state of flux–one hesitates to say in a state of progress–especially if the text exists online. I wonder if a hypertext that is fixed in a CD-ROM format actually qualifies as a real hypertext? However numerous the narrative trails may be, the text on CD-ROM is fixed, whereas an online version can be constantly revised. Until and unless the author or authors declare the work finished it can always change.

If the act of reading is as complex as some of the deconstructionists claim, then the "text" is always a nexus between what the author has written and what readers *think* the text means. The implications for building a literary collection of these materials in libraries are daunting. If it is true that a text can't exist without a network of interpretations, many of which, or most of which, will exist in what some still regard as the ephemeral medium of cyberspace, how does a library collect and preserve this record? Librarians surely can't, and shouldn't, buy all of the available hypertext fiction any more than they can or should buy all the fiction in print. The literature selector has an especially wearisome task now, however, because there are so many potential versions of these texts. Do various early online drafts of texts become as important as the later versions? Even if the author declares that a work is in its final form, is it really finished if it exists "only" in the online environment? If a reader can open an electronic version of a hypertext he may be able to alter that text by adding or deleting words, pictures, audio-cards, hotlinks to other texts, etc. What part of this complex bibliographic record should a library acquire? How is it to be cataloged? Can there be one legitimate authority record for such a complex and fluid text? How is it to be retrieved? Should it be linked to other texts the library owns? If so, who is qualified to choose or create those links? What's a primary and what's a secondary text in the constantly changing environment of hypertext fiction?

These questions remind me of the surrealistic library Juan Luis Borges created in his short story "The Library of Babel" ("La biblioteca de Babel"),[6] an ideal library which houses not only every book that has ever existed but all the books that can be imagined to exist, and a library in which there is a perfect catalog (Borges was himself a librarian for awhile) listing all these books. This is the ultimate dream of perfect bibliographic control. But if everything that has ever been published or could be published exists in one giant library there can be nothing new, nothing to discover or create. Borges' tale is an ironic commentary on man's hopeless dream of apprehending a perfectly reasonable design and meaning in the universe. Borges seems to anticipate the World Wide Web. But, alas, like the Library of Babel, the Web is a mirage—it only provides the illusion of completeness.

WHAT IF A LIBRARY WERE LIKE A MUSEUM?

In reality, a literary selector like me has to be content with hoping he makes some judicious selections from an increasingly bewildering array of print and electronic resources. We need some general recreational non-literary fiction in the general collection for an audience that includes many students and faculty who are not English majors. We need a thorough and comprehensive collection of canonical works for undergraduate study. We need a deeper collection of these works for the more advanced research of faculty and graduate students. But we also must be open to collecting many non-traditional and quite possibly ephemeral publication formats not hitherto acquired in academic libraries if we hope to build a dynamic collection of popular as well as classic texts. We have an obligation, I think, to build a truly representative collection not only of the established literary authors but at least some of those we think may be part of the literary canon of the future. We need to collect not only books, small magazines and journals, but also audiotapes of poets reading their work, videotapes and DVDs of important motion picture adaptations of fiction and dramatic works–and even some ephemeral material that might enhance the appreciation of literature. In some respects, I think academic libraries could take some cues about collecting from sister institutions with similar responsibilities for preserving the historical record–museums and archives. Imagine how a library collection of Emily Dickinson poetry would be enhanced if it owned one of her gloves, or how fascinating it would be to see Henry James's walking stick in a library display case! Perhaps I should be thankful I don't have the dilemma of choosing between acquiring Emily Dickinson's glove and a new edition of her works. The choices I've just described between print and electronic and canonical and non-canonical texts are agonizing enough to keep me busy for years.

REFERENCES

1. Warren St. John, "Vanity's Fare," *Lingua Franca*, 3 (September/October 1993):1, 22-25, 62.

2. Allen Ellis, ed., *Popular Culture and Libraries* (New York: The Haworth Press, Inc., 1992) Also published as volume #8 of *The Acquisitions Librarian*, 1992.

3. D. H. Lawrence, "Pornography and Obscenity" In *Sex, Literature and Censorship* (New York: Twayne Publishers, 1953).

4. David Isaacson, "Discriminating Librarians," *Library Journal*, 125 (November 15, 2000): 40B41.

5. For a different point of view, arguing that academic libraries ought to be collecting more pornography, see Juris Dilevko and Lisa Gottlieb, "Deep Classification: Pornography, Bibliographic Access, and Academic Libraries," *Library Collections, Acquisitions, and Technical Services*, 26 (Summer 2002): 113-139.

6. Jorge Luis Borges, "La Biblioteca de Babel" In *Ficciones* (Buenos Aires Emecé Editores, 1956).

Selection of Music Materials

Stephen Luttmann

SUMMARY. The conscientious selection of music materials requires an understanding of the needs of the public being served at least as much as it requires subject competence on the part of the selector. Online and print resources are available to aid in the selection of music materials in all formats, the most important of which are books, scores, audio and video recordings. The usefulness of such tools is evaluated, distinguishing, where appropriate, between tools identifying core collections and those that aid in maintaining currency. *[Article copies available for a fee from The Haworth Document Delivery Service: 1-800-HAWORTH. E-mail address: <docdelivery@haworthpress.com> Website: <http://www.HaworthPress.com> © 2004 by The Haworth Press, Inc. All rights reserved.]*

KEYWORDS. Music, selection, scores, sound recordings, video recordings, print resources, online resources

MATTERS OF PRINCIPLE

The music selector is not entirely alone in dealing with a profusion of different kinds of materials, although the challenge of dealing with those requiring

Stephen Luttmann is Music Librarian and Assistant Professor of University Libraries, Campus Box 68, University of Northern Colorado, Greeley, CO 80639-0100 (E-mail: luttmann@arts.unco.edu).

[Haworth co-indexing entry note]: "Selection of Music Materials." Luttmann, Stephen. Co-published simultaneously in *The Acquisitions Librarian* (The Haworth Information Press, an imprint of The Haworth Press, Inc.) No. 31/32, 2004, pp. 11-25; and: *Selecting Materials for Library Collections* (ed: Audrey Fenner) The Haworth Information Press, an imprint of The Haworth Press, Inc., 2004, pp. 11-25. Single or multiple copies of this article are available for a fee from The Haworth Document Delivery Service [1-800-HAWORTH, 9:00 a.m. - 5:00 p.m. (EST). E-mail address: docdelivery@haworthpress.com].

10.1300/J101v16n31_02

specialized training in order to interpret at even a rudimentary level (i.e., scores) may well be daunting to the nonspecialist selector. Obviously a trained music specialist is better capable of managing the development of a music collection of any consequence, all other factors being equal, but this is not to say that it is impossible for the nonspecialist to perform such duties with reasonable effectiveness. (No doubt the nonspecialists in music–and the specialists who are new to the mechanics of music selection–are better served by an essay such as this than are the seasoned music collection development librarians.) When considering and using various kinds of selection tools, however, all music selectors, regardless of background or training, are best served by an ability to make decisions according to established policies and meaningful principles.

It is difficult to imagine a selector operating confidently and effectively without some kind of collection development policy. While it is beyond the scope of this essay to discuss the formulation of policies in detail, certain characteristics demand consideration. It goes without saying that such a policy should mediate between firm principles and flexible application, and that it should be reevaluated periodically. Implicit in the notion of a useful policy is, above all, an understanding of the needs and desires of the institution and/or body of patrons served by the music collection. This sounds much easier than it is, especially in an age of increasingly limited budgets.

The selector for a public library may have a relatively simple time of identifying materials that will circulate (Vivaldi's *Four Seasons*, Top 40, etc.), but a more difficult time of identifying the musical interest demographics of the community in order to know whether materials likely to circulate most are being acquired. Then, too, the selector may still need to resolve the matter of whether it is the public library's duty to select exclusively according to the principle of giving 'em what they want.

The academic music selector should have less difficulty identifying the community being served–it is usually a music department or school, with curricular support paramount, and some additional consideration sometimes given to the music-related needs of other departments as well (e.g., materials on rap or country music, which tend to be of more interest in social sciences curricula than in the music schools themselves). In any case, the music selector should take care to ensure that all curricular interests are accounted for and represented. Certainly the music library that serves primarily the interests of a minority of its faculty–usually the musicologists–is in little position to complain about a lack of support from the faculty as a whole when it seeks support against budget cuts. It is understandable that an academic library should strive to acquire exemplary and usually expensive critical editions of major composers' works for study purposes. However, this should not occur to the exclusion of scores that can be used for performance (e.g., a piano score with solo part for a violin-and-piano sonata)–especially because the vast majority of worthwhile composers have not had the fortune to be sufficiently canonical or sufficiently dead to warrant a *kritische Gesamtausgabe* of their works. Nor are all aspects of music learned primarily from scores: a jazz program of any consequence must be supported by a respectable and comprehensive collection of recordings; any study of performance practice in classical music demands a collection of different performances–and different kinds of performance–of the same work. Finally, while guidelines regarding the relative size of the book, score, and recordings collections (or dollar figures spent on them) are of some usefulness, more important is the recognition that it is the scholarship that serves the music, and not vice-versa. The collection boasting more biographies of Havergal Brian than scores or recordings of his music seems to reflect misplaced priorities, or at least a lost opportunity.

GENERAL RESOURCES

Internet Tools

A number of Web sites indexing vendors, publishers, and organizations related to music are available to the selector. The most notable of these is probably "Music Selection Resources on the WWW," maintained by Anna Seaberg (King County Library System, Washington State) at http.//www.halcyon. com/aseaberg/; it also provides links to other such sites. Also invaluable is access to MLA-L, a listserv serving the Music Library Association; roughly 1,000 music librarians and other interested parties subscribe, asking and answering questions touching all areas of music librarianship, including selection and collection development. Subscription instructions are available at http://www.music.indiana.edu/tech_s/mla/mla-l.wel; archives of previous postings are available at http://listserv.indiana.edu/archives/mla-l.html.

Vendors: Approval and Notification Services

Recommending or rating individual vendors according to the quality of their service is outside the purpose of this essay, and individual vendors are discussed only in the context of the (sometimes unique) selection tools they offer. Requests for vendor recommendations, as well as responses, appear from time to time on MLA-L–another indication of that tool's value. It should also be noted at the outset that vendors with the greatest Web presence (and thus offering some of the most useful selection tools) aim for sales to the general public and as a rule do not accept purchase orders.

Approval services for books require no introduction here. Most music selectors, as members of institutions that serve a broad range of subjects, will no doubt find it easiest to use the institution's approval vendor. This is not the case for scores and recordings, but there are numerous major music vendors that provide services for these material types. Due to the highly diverse nature of much score publishing (constant reprints of public-domain materials, new works by "classical" composers that are frequently esoteric and usually expensive, and the continued deluge of choral octavos and other more popular formats), score approval profiles should be constructed with at least as much care as the book profile. The same is true with regard to CDs, because of the sheer quantity of new releases, rereleases, and (in the case of classical music) alternate performances of standard repertoire. Selectors should also err on the side of caution in establishing profiles for scores and CDs, or in deciding whether to enter into such arrangements at all, when they are less than certain that their collection is already reasonably balanced with regard to patron demand and, when applicable, curricular requirements.

Most major library vendors of books, scores, and sound recordings provide their customers with notification of new releases, usually in the form of printed slips or booklets, although online notification, .pdf lists and the like are becoming standard as well.

OCLC WorldCat

While not intended as such, the OCLC WorldCat database possesses considerable value as a selection tool. The availability of bibliographic records in the database for desired items may, depending on local procedures, assist in the entry of order records in the local ILS, and in the verification by acquisitions staff upon the items' arrival that the correct ones were supplied. In libraries where cataloging resources are limited, verification of available WorldCat copy before ordering could make all the difference between easily-processed acquisitions and the accrual of a backlog of items requiring original cataloging.

BOOKS

Because the book is a format hardly unique to music, selection of books is to a certain degree the easiest of the music selector's tasks. For notification of new publications and convenient ordering of backlisted titles, most music selectors can use the same approval and firm-order vendors as do the selectors in other disciplines; availability status can be determined by consulting Bowker's

Books in Print (available online to institutions by subscription) or the inventories of major online vendors such as Amazon (whose listings are often more reliable than those in *Books in Print*, but this will be surprising to few).

In the absence of a new-title notification service from the institution's primary vendor, the "Books Recently Published" column in *Notes*, the quarterly journal of the Music Library Association, is worth consulting. Because this column is compiled on the basis of Library of Congress cataloging, however, it is less than all-inclusive, particularly with regard to more obscure foreign titles that may be out of print by the time they are listed. The problem of ordering foreign titles is best solved by means of a good working relationship with a major music vendor that also handles books on music; firms such as Theodore Front (http://www.tfront.com) and Otto Harrassowitz (http://www.harrassowitz.com) are expert at providing approval plans, notification services, and backlisted titles.

Book reviews offer limited assistance in deciding which books to buy. While most *Choice* reviews appear before a title's initial (and often only) press run has been exhausted, the same cannot be said for reviews in many scholarly publications. Where intimate subject expertise fails to suffice, a good approval plan can reliably fill the gap, and probably more so than is the case for scores and other formats.

The major vendor of books in online format for library collections is netLibrary (http://www.netlibrary.com). netLibrary's ability to contract with major vendors for significant titles has increased somewhat since its acquisition by OCLC, but coverage of music titles is still uneven, limited (495 titles as of the end of 2002), and includes relatively few titles of appreciable reference value (only 16, all in the ML128s). The bulk of available items consists of fairly new titles (2000-02: 147 titles; 1995-1999: 218; 1990-1994: 92; <1990: 47)–a mixed blessing for academic libraries, and probably more useful for public libraries that may benefit from the large number of mass-market-oriented titles in the collection. Ultimately the decision of whether to select netLibrary titles depends on one's perception of whether patrons are likely to use online books in the first place.

SCORES

Online Listings of Available Titles

As of this writing, no comprehensive and entirely satisfactory music-in-print service exists online, although various online vendors and services are useful. Two are worthy of special mention, and are listed here in alphabetical order. The Pepper Music Network database (http://www.jwpepper.com)

offers basic and advanced search modes, the latter allowing for "exact" and "starts with" options in title word searches. Results often appear with a cover illustration, an annotation, price, and in-stock availability or estimated ship date. Results also include out-of-print/unavailable listings, but since these are indicated as such, the information does possess a certain ironic usefulness. Both are limited in classical music searches, however, by the inability to enter more than a composer's surname (or, for that matter, the names of a composer and an arranger), by a severely limited number of publishers one can limit a search by, and the use of the American distributor as publisher for works published abroad (although the annotations sometimes make up for this).

Sheetmusicplus (http://www.sheetmusicplus.com) has certain advantages over Pepper, not the least of which are somewhat better search options (keyword searching by publisher, for instance), the consistent inclusion of publisher names and edition numbers in results, and song titles in anthologies.

Of specialist interest is the "Ottoeditions" database at Otto Harrassowitz's Web site (http://www.harrassowitz.com), which is available at no charge to Harrassowitz's customers. Music listings are admirably detailed but are pretty much limited to European publications of classical music.

The venerable old Music-in-Print Series volumes published by Musicdata are being enhanced and updated by emusicquest (http://www.emusicquest.com) and sold to libraries on an annual basis via online subscription. As a snapshot of music publishing history, the database is–as were the print volumes–a valuable reference tool; as an acquisitions tool, however, many selectors may not consider it worth the $400 annual cost. The quantity of listings is impressive, and searchability is at least as good as in the online products listed above, but the listings are less a reflection of what is actually currently available. Furthermore, coverage is skewed heavily toward classical music, with a bow toward nonclassical sacred, and not all forms of classical music are yet well represented (brass music, miscellaneous chamber music).

A steadily increasing number of publishers have made their catalogs available online; their URLs are often easy to guess or root out by means of a search engine. The Music Publishers' Association of the United States also maintains an online Directory of Music Publishers (and publisher imprints) at http://www. mpa.org/agency/pal.html. Finally, the Web has aided enormously in the proliferation of self-published music, much of which no less worth acquiring for having been typeset in Finale or Sibelius and printed upon demand in the composer or arranger's spare bedroom. For these, a Web search is often the only means of finding a contact, unless a flyer has been helpfully dropped into the Suggestion Box.

Selective or Annotated Guides

No online resource approaches the all-around usefulness of the Music Library Association's *A Basic Music Library: Essential Scores and Recordings* (3rd ed., 1997), the first 12 chapters of which offer an overview of worthwhile items in every significant area of print music publication. Listed works are weighted according to an asterisk system, whereby two asterisks indicate works suitable for "public libraries that do not generally collect musical scores but wish to have on hand selected scores of often-heard works," and one asterisk indicates those which "[p]ublic libraries with a greater need for scores may prefer to acquire" (p. 4). Entries include uniform title, publisher, edition number, and price; multiple editions of the same work appear frequently. One will no doubt quibble over the inclusion of one work or the exclusion of another, but by and large the selection is sound, certainly for use as a benchmark against which one may judge one's own collection. With regard to its score listings, the greatest weakness of the *Basic Music Library* is its indexing, which doesn't always juggle successfully between title-page and uniform titles and frequently fails to cross-reference major works in collections (e.g., the Dover volume of four orchestral works by Ravel is indexed only under "Orchestra music. Selections").

Maintaining Currency

In terms of comprehensive and reasonably up-to-the-date information, nothing surpasses regular notification from a vendor. In addition to the traditional booklets and/or cards, some major vendors are providing online notification of new releases. The Music Library Association's quarterly journal, *Notes*, regularly features a listing of recent music publishers' catalogs; regular perusal of this column is essential, and not just for the listings of time-sensitive sale catalogs.

Reviews of new scores constitute a regular feature of some journals of a scholarly or specialized nature. However, as with books, it is frequently true enough that by the time a review appears, the initial (and sometimes only) press run of a score will have disappeared, that one should not rely too heavily on reviews in making one's selection decisions.

The "Music Received" and "Music Publishers' Catalogs" columns in *Notes* more than repay regular perusal, especially the latter, which includes announcements of sales catalogs and lists publishers' addresses and Web sites.

Collected Editions and Historical Sets

Curiously, the *Basic Music Library* does not list historical sets or collected editions of composers' works (roughly equivalent to the M2-M3 section in a collection arranged by LC classification), although a few of these–the complete works of Bach or Mozart, for instance–no doubt belong in any larger and yet "basic" collection that serves a classical music curriculum or large cultural center. Lists of such sets are available in any number of reference works; among vendors, Theodore Front is still committed to providing upon demand a free print catalog with current availability and prices (Catalogue 185, *Musicological Publications*, most recently updated in 2001). Otto Harrassowitz provides the same service to customers in the form of the "Ottoeditions" database referred to earlier. Additionally, prospectuses of individual available sets are available from any major vendor.

SOUND RECORDINGS

Online Listings of Available Recordings

Products analogous to Bowker's *Books in Print* do exist, but the great majority of libraries will not have direct access to them. Attempts to market to libraries an online version of the venerable (and error-ridden) *Schwann Catalog* seem to have been laid to rest once and for all with the absorption of Schwann Publications into the Alliance Entertainment Group/AEC One Stop Group. Prior to this, an online *Schwann* was being advertised to libraries at a price few could hope to afford. The same is true for Muze, a product much in use by the major retail chains; it lists the Library of Congress and the BBC among its very few non-business clients.

This is less of a disadvantage than one might suppose, as data from both companies is used by major online vendors. Vendor Web sites all have their strengths and weaknesses, and it is difficult to recommend one above all others, as the following discussion will demonstrate. In comparing them, the following considerations become relevant: (1) How meaningful is the concept of the "in print" recording? (2) How helpful is the individual vendor's search engine in accessing recordings in the database?

With regard to the first question, one should note recordings listed–even by the companies releasing them–as "in print" recordings are frequently unavailable, and sometimes unlikely to be available ever again. Remnants of an initial pressing may still be available from scattered vendors while the recording companies wait (often in vain) for demand sufficient to warrant a new pressing. There is also no doubt some truth to the assumption that recording companies have less incentive to announce deletions in a timely manner than to announce new releases. This problem is multiplied by the business practices of individual online vendors. Needless to say, not all of them seek to list every recording available through an American distributor; some drop slow-moving items from their online listings when the last copies are sold. The following comparisons among four of the leading online vendors are instructive. The British label Hyperion has recorded 19 CDs of the works of the British composer Robert Simpson. As of this writing (late December 2002), Tower (http://www.towerrecords.com) lists 6, CDConnection (http://www.cdconnection. com) 13, Barnes & Noble (http://www.bn.com) 16, and Amazon (http://www. amazon.com), which has also absorbed CDNow and Borders' online operations, all 19. However, this is only part of the story, and a different picture emerges when one wishes to know which items are actually in stock. Of Tower's 6 listings, 5 are in stock; as are 12 of the 16 Barnes & Noble listings. Amazon estimates a number of days between order placement and shipping, which ranges from "in 24 hours" for 7 listings to "8 days" for another 3, with an apparently recalcitrant final 3 listed as "special order" items, CDConnection doesn't indicate "in stock" status at all.

Each of the aforementioned online vendors offers some form of "simple" and "advanced" search option. Tower, Barnes & Noble, and Amazon offer a "simple search" that allows for the entry of multiple keywords in one search box; their "advanced" search option allows for field searching. Of these, Tower's offers the most field options (10, excluding recording format) and Amazon the least (7); both the Amazon and CDNow interfaces do an excellent job of hiding the advanced search option. CDConnection offers a fairly inconvenient choice of "simple" and "compound" searches, which amounts to the choice of entering one term on one box, or two terms, one in each of two boxes; its usefulness is further compromised by an inability to handle most first names.

Audio clips are available for many of the albums on all of the vendor Web sites (with CDconnection offering noticeably fewer than the other three). All but CDConnection offer some form of commentary on the great majority of the albums as well. Barnes & Noble reproduces commentary from the All Music Guide (see below); Tower offers snippets from leading magazines; Amazon seems to employ an in-house staff. Amazon is well known for the commentary posted by customers; Barnes & Noble offers this feature as well, although it hasn't been much used to date.

Finally, one should note that not all domestic recordings worth acquiring are distributed by major vendors, nor are all worthwhile available recordings distributed by an American distributor. In both cases, the Web is an invaluable tool. Indexes such as the one by Anna Seaberg mentioned above, or a modicum of imagination in browser searching or second-guessing URLs, will yield both useful foreign vendors and small independent labels everywhere.

Selective or Annotated Online Guides

For all kinds of music except classical, the online All Music Guide (http://www.allmusic.com) is the obvious first choice. The Web site is quite impressively constructed, with an orthographically forgiving search engine that ranks results by relevance (useful for distinguishing, say, Tom Harrell from Tom Harrell Quintet, although albums by the latter are also listed in the former's entry), biographical sketches liberally hyperlinked to any artists, albums, etc., mentioned in them, and extensive discographies. Most albums are rated on a one-to-five-star system, and the great majority of these are reviewed–intelligently–as well. Individual listings feature, among other things, release date, track listings, and (when available) even MARC formats. The commercial angle of the Web site is betrayed by hyperlinks to the Barnes & Noble Web site when albums are available for sale there. Additional (and invaluable) features include a glossary of terms, an index of styles, and a large number of "music maps" that graphically illustrate stylistic developments, personal influences, and so forth. Only the classical music section is less than satisfactory by comparison; entries under individual work titles tend to be routine, superficial program notes for a given work but do not evaluate competing recordings of it.

The Web database that most satisfactorily compensates for this is the Gramofile database of reviews from *Gramophone*, one of the leading classical music magazines, accessible at http://www.gramophone.co.uk/cdreviews.asp upon free registration. The search screen allows for field-specific searching (composer, artist, conductor, ensemble, work title, label, keyword, and a pull-down menu of genres), and the quality of the reviews is consistently high. One ought to be aware of minor technical problems, however. Limiting by "reviewed" still retrieves unreviewed listings, and the database has an annoying tendency to be unavailable in the American afternoon, a fact recognizable when a search for, say, Bizet's *Carmen* retrieves no results.

Print Resources

Unlike its predecessors, the third edition of the *Basic Music Library* includes recordings, which are ranked according to much the same asterisk system used for scores. The results in this case, however, are decidedly mixed. One may overlook, or even welcome, the fact that the sound recordings section of the book is nearly three times that of the scores section. After all, most musical traditions do not exist (certainly not as primary materials) in score format, and one would expect few academic music collections to have more recordings of Jimi Hendrix than, say, of Henry Cowell and Paul Creston combined. (The *Basic Music Library*'s preface acknowledges the former condition.) One may therefore take the asterisk ratings with a grain of salt, applicable only within the relevant genre chapter; across chapters, or within any of the miscellaneous chapters, they offer little guidance. Certainly there doesn't seem to have been any coherent effort to coordinate score and recordings collections within those genres of classical music for which such coordination is not only possible but a recognized responsibility of the collection manager as well. With regard to other styles or genres of music, the following example is striking but not atypical: On the same page (p. 389) in the "Mainstream Popular and New Age" chapter, one notes two albums (one with an asterisk) by The Flirtations, a gay a cappella quintet, and one Kenny G listing, his *Silhouette* album (no asterisk). All questions of musical value or categorization aside (are the Flirtations mainstream? is Kenny G any less a jazz artist than David Sanborn, who *is* listed in the jazz recordings chapter?), it is difficult to imagine a non-gay-specific library collection owning more CDs of the former than of the latter.

Classical music is well served by two competing British publications: *The Penguin Guide to Compact Discs* and *The Gramophone Classical Good CD Guide*. Because of the availability of the Gramofile database, one might logically prefer the Penguin publication, which contains considerably more reviews and roughly the same number of listings (the *Gramophone Guide* compensates for its smaller size by listing "additional recommendations" without review—which admittedly has its attractions for the selector pressed for time). The *Penguin Guide* also has the added virtue of being able to lie flat when opened. In addition to the reviews, both rate recordings by means of symbols. The *Penguin Guide* appears every two years in a new edition while the *Gramophone Guide* appears yearly; however, the former has much the better reputation for seriously updating its contents to include new items and delete out-of-print ones. Be aware of the obvious British bias in both works: label names and numbers sometimes vary on both sides of the Atlantic, and not all items available in Europe are distributed in the United States (the *Penguin Guide* is especially forthright about this). One shouldn't be surprised to find that both list more recordings of works by Gerald Finzi than by Gian Carlo Menotti, Alan Hovhaness, or even Philip Glass.

Finally, for those preferring to work with print indexes, the *All Music Guide* exists as a hefty, handy volume accompanied by a number of specialized spin-off volumes—those for jazz and country music are especially fine. Selectors supporting broad or ambitious world music collections should also consider the two-volume *World Music*, part of the Rough Guides series, which is outstanding not only for the depth and breadth of its coverage, but also in its nonjudgmental differentiations along the spectrum from ethnomusicological field recordings to modern, culturally heterogenous "world beat" styles. Additional *Gramophone* products worth mentioning include "good CD guides" to musicals and film music.

Maintaining Currency

Comprehensive listings of new releases are best and most reliably supplied by vendors. With regard to classical music, vendor lists can and should be supplemented by the listings in the two premier English-language record review magazines, *International Record Review* and *Gramophone*. Both are British publications; the latter well established and the former, founded in 2000, meriting much wider currency than it receives at present. In recent years *Gramophone* has tended toward a larger number of shorter reviews while *International Record Review* strives toward depth and breadth; if the time-pressed selector prefers the former, patrons will be pleasantly surprised by the latter. Two other publications occupy the next rank: *Fanfare*, for the sheer quantity of its (usually intelligent) reviews, and *BBC Music Magazine*, which perfected the quick and dirty (by British standards) review on the other side of the Atlantic. The *American Record Guide* also enlists the services of a number of fine critics, but its strange editorial practices and its current editor's curious (when not alarming) rants–not always on musical matters–have made it a target of much justified criticism.

Regular perusal of the periodical literature in other genres and styles yields worthwhile reviews as well. It is hard to imagine maintaining a popular music collection without a current and well-thumbed subscription to Billboard; jazz is particularly well covered by such titles as *Down Beat* and *Jazz Times*; country music has *Country Music*, and so forth.

VIDEOS

For the next few years at least, the selector will need to collect actively in both VHS and DVD formats. As any visit to the local Blockbuster will demonstrate, DVD is now the medium of choice in the home video entertainment market, and whenever a particular content is available in both formats, the DVD will as a rule be preferable (as well as more durable and more often than not less expensive)–especially if only one copy of the content can be purchased. However, not all patrons have yet made the switch to (or addition of) a DVD player, so selectors who decide to purchase DVDs whenever possible should at least be sure that the institution has players available for on-site viewing. Furthermore, not all subject areas within the broad category of music-related video recordings are yet well represented on DVD. These are, as one might expect, precisely those one is least likely to find in a Blockbuster. Educational videos in particular remain stubbornly available in VHS format only.

Most video recordings of any broad appeal, unless vendored exclusively by their publishers, are available from the great majority of CD vendors, whether library specialists or large commercial enterprises such as Barnes & Noble or Amazon. To these one should also add Facets Video (http://www.facets.org), whose advantages include broad and intelligently annotated catalogs (both on-line and in print), as well as a rental library of titles often otherwise unavailable. Educational videos, including many not available from generalist vendors, are the specialty of the print and online catalogs of Films for the Humanities and Sciences (http://www.films.com) and Insight Media (http://www. insight-media.com).

Web sites and publications primarily concerned with critiquing video recordings rather than selling them are not yet common or well developed. Coverage in the All Movie Guide (http://www.allmovie.com, a partner product to the All Music Guide) is still sketchy—music videos and operas are listed fairly exhaustively, but in the great majority of cases without commentary. For opera, the best all-around works are in paper format: *The Metropolitan Opera Guide to Opera on Video*, and the opera-on-video section of *The Penguin Guide to Compact Disks*. (Note when using the latter that one should never order according to the British catalog numbers because of the incompatibility of VHS and DVD formats on both sides of the Atlantic.)

Of the various periodicals that specialize in reviewing classical CDs, only two of the British publications, *Gramophone* and *International Record Review*, regularly include a small section of video reviews of operas and concerts. Video reviews also appear sporadically in other specialist journals (e.g., in areas such as ethnomusicology and music education), but in no case with the depth and breadth of coverage that would identify any of them as a primary source.

PERIODICALS

The nature of periodical subscription obviates the need for comprehensive decision-making in most cases. Unless a collection is being built from scratch, selection work will involve adjustments to a preexisting subscription profile (usually maintained with the same jobber used by the institution's other subject selectors)—and more often than not these days, sadly enough, this will involve cuts mandated by shrinking budgets. Obviously any profile changes are much more a matter of negotiation with potentially affected parties (the musicology faculty, for instance) than is, say, the acceptance or rejection of an approval book. A rejected approval book can more often and more easily be purchased after the complaints start washing in than a canceled serial subscription can be reinstated with all of the missing back issues.

The selector charged with beginning a subscription profile from scratch can spend many edifying hours poring over *Ulrich's*, requesting sample copies from publishers, and studying the copies that are actually provided for their appropriateness. Much simpler, and much more sensible, would be to identify institutions similar to one's own, and analyze their subscription profiles with the advice of the selectors at those institutions.

OUT-OF-PRINT ITEMS

Only the largest and wealthiest libraries, or those supporting specialized archives, are likely to need the regular services of an antiquarian dealer or make much use of auction catalogs. The Internet has increased access to rare items to a great degree. Abebooks (http://www.abebooks.com) is the obvious first choice among networks of antiquarian booksellers, as it facilitates direct contact between buyers and sellers (some of whom may well take purchase orders). The Bibliofind network provided much the same service, although since its absorption by Amazon the number of genuinely rare offerings has declined sharply, and direct contact with vendors is not exactly encouraged (an e-mail address is usually available after clicking a few links). The service offered by Alibris (http://www.alibris.com) is similar in breadth and content. Ebay (http://www.ebay.com) certainly requires no introduction, except perhaps as a site where even materials of interest to graduate-level academic music collections are regularly available.

Among music-specific antiquarian dealers, the most prominent is J & J Lubrano (http://bookmarque.net/Lubrano/), which also buys and sells scores. Major vendors in out-of-print/rare/used recordings advertise regularly in the record review periodicals listed above; of these, the Princeton Record Exchange (http://www.prex.com) is probably the most notable. For those selectors with the time, patience, or staff to make such an effort worthwhile, the Berkshire Record Outlet (http://www.berkshirerecordoutlet.com) sells thousands of overstocks and cutouts (CDs, but also some LPs, cassettes, and books) at prices normally ranging from $2.99-$8.99 per disc and thus offers an opportunity to acquire a large number of sometimes first-rate recordings at low cost. On a smaller scale, Daedalus Books (http://www.daedalus-books.com) has listings of overstock recordings and books on music that are worth regular browsing.

RESOURCE LIST

American Record Guide. ISSN 0003-0716. 4412 Braddock Street, Cincinnati, OH 45204. $42/per year (6 issues).

BBC Music Magazine. ISSN 0966-7180. North American subscriptions: P.O. Box 57243, Boulder, CO 80322-7243. $79.95/year (12 issues plus supplements). Web site: http://www.bbcmusicmagazine.com.

Bogdanov, V., Woodstra, C., & Erlewine, S. T. (Eds.). (2001). *All music guide: The definitive guide to popular music.* Ann Arbor: All Media Guide. 1491 p. ISBN 0-87930-627-0. $34.95.

Broughton, S., Ellingham, M., & Trilklo, R. (Eds.). (1999) *World music: Vol. 1. Africa, Europe and the Middle East; vol. 2. Latin & North America, Caribbean, India, Asia and Pacific.* London: Rough Guides. 762, 673 p. ISBN 1-85828-635-2 (vol. 1), 1-85828-636-0 (vol. 2). $53.90 (set).

Erlewine, M., Bogdanov, V., Woodstra, C., & Erlewine, S. T. (Eds.). (1997). *All music guide to country: The experts' guide to the best recordings in country music.* San Francisco: Miller Freeman. 611 p. ISBN 0-87930-475-8. $22.95.

Fanfare: The Magazine for Serious Record Collectors. ISSN 0148-9364. P.O. Box 17, Tenafly, NJ 07670. $39/year (6 issues). Web site: http://www.fanfaremag.com.

Gramophone: The Classical Music Magazine. ISSN 0017-310X. North American subscriptions: Haymarket Publications Ltd, c/o Smartmail, 140 58th Street, Suite 2b, Brooklyn, NY 11220-2561. $110.40/year (13 issues). Web site: http://www.gramophone.co.uk.

Gruber, P. (Ed.). (1997). *The Metropolitan Opera Guide to Opera on Video.* New York: Metropolitan Opera Guild and W. W. Norton. 483 p. ISBN 0-393-04536-6. $35.

International Record Review. ISSN 1468 5027. 1 Haven Green, London W5 2UU, Great Britain. $90/year (12 issues). Web site: http://www.recordreview.co.uk.

Jolley, J. (Ed.). (2002). *Gramophone classical good CD guide 2003.* Harrow, Middlesex: Gramophone. 1376 p. ISBN 0860249026. $27.95

March, I., Greenfield, E., & Layton, R. (2001). *The Penguin guide to compact discs* (2002 ed.). London: Penguin. 1566 p. ISBN 0-140-51497-X. $25.

Music Library Association. (1997). *A basic music library: Essential scores and recordings* (3rd ed.). Chicago: American Library Association. 665 p. ISBN 0-8389-3461-7. $95.

Musicology Department, Broude Brothers Limited. (2001). *Musicological publications: A reference catalogue 2001.* Williamstown, MA: Broude Brothers. 87 p. Free.

Notes: Quarterly Journal of the Music Library Association. ISSN 0027-4380. 8551 Research Way, Suite 180, Middleton, WI 53562. $90/year (4 issues).

Walker, M. (Ed.). (1998). *Gramophone film music good CD guide.* Harrrow, Middlesex: Gramophone. 260 p. ISBN 1-902274-00-8. $16.95.

Walker, M. (Ed.). (1998). *Gramophone musicals good CD guide.* Harrow, Middlesex: Gramophone. 263 p. ISBN 1-902274-01-6. $16.95.

Selecting and Acquiring Art Materials in the Academic Library: Meeting the Needs of the Studio Artist

Elizabeth A. Lorenzen

SUMMARY. As technology is shaping today's art world, parallel changes are happening in the ways art book collections are identified and acquired. The purpose of this article is to identify the changes transpiring in the worlds of the artist and library acquisitions, and to evaluate the ways in which the changes effected by technological applications in the arts may affect the way that librarians acquire monographic art collections. As artists are constantly finding new ways to challenge definitions of art, so must acquisitions librarians respond to the challenges of the art book market in new and creative ways. *[Article copies available for a fee from The Haworth Document Delivery Service: 1-800-HAWORTH. E-mail address: <docdelivery@haworthpress.com> Website: <http://www.HaworthPress.com> © 2004 by The Haworth Press, Inc. All rights reserved.]*

KEYWORDS. Artists, libraries, fine art, fine artists, acquisitions, academic libraries, art libraries, art books, vendor relations, publishing, acquisitions surveys, acquisitions budgets

Elizabeth A. Lorenzen is Acquisitions Librarian, Cunningham Memorial Library, Indiana State University, Terre Haute, IN 47809. She is also the art subject specialist, and is an artist, having received a BFA in Painting from the Herron School of Art, IUPUI, Indianapolis, IN (E-mail: liblore@isugw.indstate.edu).

[Haworth co-indexing entry note]: "Selecting and Acquiring Art Materials in the Academic Library: Meeting the Needs of the Studio Artist." Lorenzen, Elizabeth A. Co-published simultaneously in *The Acquisitions Librarian* (The Haworth Information Press, an imprint of The Haworth Press, Inc.) No. 31/32, 2004, pp. 27-39; and: *Selecting Materials for Library Collections* (ed: Audrey Fenner) The Haworth Information Press, an imprint of The Haworth Press, Inc., 2004, pp. 27-39. Single or multiple copies of this article are available for a fee from The Haworth Document Delivery Service [1-800-HAWORTH, 9:00 a.m. - 5:00 p.m. (EST). E-mail address: docdelivery@haworthpress.com].

http://www.haworthpress.com/store/product.asp?sku=J101
© 2004 by The Haworth Press, Inc. All rights reserved.
10.1300/J101v16n31_03

INTRODUCTION

To get started, let's take a look at the following scenario: It's a few years into the future, but not too far, because really it could be happening now, with all the technology that's available in the marketplace today. It's late at night and things aren't going so well in the studio . . .

A painter, working in her remote art studio located in the wilds of North Dakota, is suddenly faced with a block and needs to find an image that is key to her current project. It's an image of a horse she found in a book about Chagall that was particularly inspiring, and she needs to look at it once more. Being a distance education graduate student at an East Coast art school, she has access to an immense image database, which houses millions of indexed images that are free to view and download. Whipping out her trusty flip phone, she gets access to the Internet and visits her school's virtual library in order to access the database. After moving around in that database for a few minutes and finding the image, she re-members that the particular painting that she is interested in analyzing was discussed in a survey course she took through the Web a few semes-ters ago. She checks out the electronic book that was a companion to the course, views its images, and reads the accompanying analysis. After looking at the horse imagery in these sources, she becomes even more in-terested in Chagall's animal imagery and how it might relate to her work, so she wants to see more. She decides to visit the web sites of two muse-ums that curated some Chagall exhibits a few years ago, to view their collections online. She also wants to look at the electronic versions of their exhibition catalogs in order to gather more information about the images in which she is interested. In addition, she visits the website of a university in the Midwest that has a collection of Chagalls that it has dig-itized and made available through the university's website. What made finding all of these images so easy, of course, was that they were all con-nected within her school library's online catalog. Looking at all of these images is an addiction, really; before she knows it, several hours have passed and her inspiration has been fueled. Now she is ready to finish tackling the series of paintings that has to be completed in time for an up-coming virtual gallery exhibit. She just found out about it on an online bulletin board. She recently joined this artist's discussion group, and has conversations regularly with her online colleagues about her work and best ways to promote herself. She then checks her scheduler, which re-minded her of the videoconference that was called for tomorrow after-noon by the gallery director. This director wants to meet with all of exhibition participants and iron out some logistical details involving the upcoming exhibit. She'd better get some sleep if she wants to be coher-ent. But wait, she is out of cobalt violet oil paint and a few other vital supplies. She quickly visits her favorite online art supply store and orders the necessary materials, asking for the shipping to be rushed. Whew! She might just get done in time after all . . .

Is this scenario a snapshot of the future or a picture of the present day? Even though I am both an artist and an information professional, and in my own opinion, fairly comfortable with technology, until recently I might not have found this description to be anything but ambitious futurism. But, now, I'm not so sure. Even though there is quite a body of literature that suggests that fine artists don't particularly like technology or even doing research, there is also more current literature that suggests that the student of today did not come to technology the same way as the previous generation did. He/she was actually born right in the midst of it, and is completely at home in the environment which it creates. This makes for a much different art student, a more technologically aware art student (Becker, 1996). The purpose of this "snapshot" was to give a glimpse of what information needs might be both possible and probable for today's studio artist, and to also illustrate the parallel developments in art and technology that make access to information for artists any time and any place a total and complete reality

What does this mean for those of us who must identify and acquire the materials that will meet the broad needs of this unique group? While artists are still making art using traditional formats, they are also exploring ways to do so in cyberspace. At the same time, while librarians still need to provide traditional sources of information such as books, they may need to identify the types of needed information sources that will parallel the development of new art forms (Tang, 1993). In other words, the development of virtual libraries will parallel the influence of technology on the art world of the future.

It is obvious that acquiring collections that meet the broad and diverse needs of today's art student is a challenging proposition. Technology is changing the landscape of the art world, with traditional practice running parallel with new art forms whose development has been shaped by the advances of technology. In tandem, the Internet is changing the way acquisitions librarians do business with publishers and vendors. Following is an overview of the current climate of both the art and publishing worlds, along with some discussion about art book collections in academic libraries, and how current practices are taking place through the introduction of a survey. It will also be demonstrated that although many aspects of art book collections may be unique and special, a large number of them are acquired in very traditional, mainstream ways. Finally, some examples will be given of how cyberspace is helping all types of art and acquisitions librarians to collect a variety of art books from many different sources and in many different formats. Let's first, though, talk about the information needs of today's art student.

INFORMATION NEEDS OF THE ART STUDENT

The information needs of the artist are by their very nature broad and cross disciplinary. This makes the collection development process a challenge that is rife with endless possibility. There are several studies in the literature that gather information on the information seeking behavior of artists, and they are largely anecdotal in nature. This is probably because of the nature of artistic research. Cobbledick (1996) mildly criticizes this methodology in her particular article, but the fact of the matter is that all of the studies seem to come to the same conclusion.

Artistic inspiration can literally come from any source; there are some artists that couldn't even begin to explain what to put in or take out of a library, since any image could be potentially helpful (Phillips, 1986). Artists have a great need for images, and it really doesn't matter to them what source from which they come. It is this attitude that illustrates the sort of mystery that can come into play when it comes to creative process, and might explain why an artist's research methods might seem rather spontaneous and haphazard, although they may not be that way at all in the mind of the artist!

The process of finding information sources in itself is creative and can have distinct meaning in and of itself to an artist (Frank, 1999). Artists love to browse through many different resources on a range of topics. For example, the painter up in North Dakota might want to look at a variety of resources in order to fuel her need for imagery related to horses. Besides looking at work by other artists, or visiting museum websites, she could also be looking at things as desperate in relatedness as calendars, books on horse care, veterinary manuals, websites devoted to the horse, and farm equipment catalogs, to name a few. They could all be part of the process of seeing how the images that end up being used will emerge from the artist's mind. Many artists will admit to you that chance and accident play a significant role in the their information seeking processes (Stam, 1995). They need to be able to get at any information that could be a source of inspiration to them, and are compulsive browsers, looking at everything from books on materials and techniques to current trends and information on individual artists (Pacey, 1982). Artists aren't sticking to any one artistic form, either–the medium may not be as significant as the idea that is being conveyed, and whatever format will transmit the idea that is being presented the best, that is what will be used. Even the notion of being sole creator is gradually changing. Technology is creating an environment that makes it easy to collaborate with other artists in the making of artistic works, without ever even meeting face to face (Becker, 1996).

Artists don't just need information that could be of help to them in their art-making processes; they also need to have a level of technical knowledge that allows them to function as entrepreneurs and business owners so that they can effectively promote themselves as professional artists. Not only do they need traditional types of resources, like gallery directories, exhibition catalogs, or other basic reference items, but they need to keep up on the latest materials and techniques, which could mean anything from a paintbrush to cyberspace. They need to be aware of the trends surrounding the use of the Internet to facilitate the creation and promotion of art: collaborative art making online, exchanging ideas with other artists through the use of online discussion groups and websites, interacting with online galleries, actually exhibiting art online–these are just some of the trends that students might need to be aware of. As support for the arts in this country continues to dwindle, artists are needing to find other creative ways beyond the traditional gallery/client relationship in order to market themselves (Becker, 1996). Other examples of new technologies that are being used by artists to create new forms of art are artist's online networks, satellite transmissions, telefascimile projects, interactive video and computer works, even art created in virtual reality. These new technologies give artists the opportunity to participate in the art process on a global, not just local, level, and to share easily their own ideas and artwork with others, regardless of cultural background (Tang, 1993). It will continue to be a unique challenge for librarians to keep up with these trends in order to be able to provide access to these unique types of resources. It also remains to be seen how the artistic community as a whole will gradually respond to the resources that are now available to them because of the technological advances that have been made over the last few years (Cobbledick, 1996). It is for this reason that there will always be parallel developments in the arts, across a myriad of different media, levels of collaboration, and subject matter, both traditional and futuristic. The same could also be said for the art publishing market.

CURRENT TRENDS IN ART BOOK PUBLISHING

Every year the Bowker Annual publishes information regarding trends in the book market, and gathers its information in a variety of ways. Yankee Book Peddler, Blackwell's, Baker and Taylor, and *Choice* all supply information on cost increases or decreases observed over the years in the books that they have supplied to their constituents. Information also is garnered from Bowkers' own *Books in Print*. In addition, research is also contributed to *The Bowker Annual* by the ALA ALCTS Library Materials Price Index Committee. Their preliminary figures for the year 2001 hint at an effect that September 11 may have had on the book market. There was overall a slight decrease in the number of books being produced, driving book prices up again, after an opposing trend which began earlier in the 1990s.

What the statistics have to say about art book publication over these last few years is similar to the statistics for other areas of the humanities. According to information on books that appeared in *Books in Print*, art book prices were dropping quite dramatically between 1999 and 2000, with an average price in 1999 of $59.31 U.S. and of $50.31 U.S. in 2000, reflecting a difference of 15%. This was a change from the '80s, when prices were steadily rising. However, preliminary figures from 2001 say that prices rose again slightly to $53.29 U.S. per book at 6%. Book production dropped 9.1% in 2001 also, according to the preliminary figures.

The statistics vary slightly in the figures for *U.S. College Books*, which are comprised of books reviewed by *Choice*. Between 1999 and 2000 book prices dropped 12%, going from $53.21 U.S. to $46.12 U.S. per book. Costs did rise in 2001, though, with a rise of 8% for a price of $49.90 U.S. per book. Finally, according to statistics garnered for academic books supplied by vendors Baker and Taylor, Yankee Book Peddler, and Blackwell's, average book prices held steady between 1998 and 1999, but dropped 8% between 1999 and 2000, from $46.21 U.S. to $45.84 U.S.

What conclusions can be drawn from this information on art book pricing trends? That maybe the art book market in the U.S. was affected by the events of September 11 when the overall economy experienced depression, resulting in fewer books being produced, driving the prices up? That the academic market did not experience as much fluctuation in the past few years, but has been affected anyway to say the least? That overall through the '90s book prices dropped instead of rose, with more books available to purchase at cheaper prices? It will be interesting to see final figures for 2001 to see if the statistics bear these suppositions out.

What the numbers do reveal is that the art book market is still vital and that books in print format are still a strong choice for building art collections in libraries. The academic art book market has also maintained a steady stream of production over the years and is still producing as many books as ever for use by the art student, scholar, and art professional alike. Art, as well as other areas in the humanities, still depends on the book as its main means of communication. Next, let's look at funding trends in academic libraries and see how it might affect collection development in the area of art.

ACADEMIC LIBRARY FUNDING AND NEW FORMATS

Collecting library materials in the humanities is becoming more difficult, as there are more relevant books, journals, databases and other sources of digital information from which to choose than ever before. Unfortunately, library budgets have not kept up the pace with the increases in the volume of information available and the result is that the choices involved in what to collect are becoming more difficult than ever before (Dillon, 1997).

According to a recent academic library acquisitions survey from *Library Journal*, there is a gradual shift taking place with regard to the purchasing of monographs versus print journals and digital resources. The shift to digital formats is having a profound effect on what subject areas libraries are purchasing (Albanese, 2001). Spending on digital resources is expected to continue to rise sharply over the next few years, with a focus on aggregator databases and e-journals. The perception is that these types of resources are what the students want to access, so print budgets are being slashed in favor of purchasing electronic resources, which are deemed to be more cost effective. They also provide easy access to information for the distance education students. The survey also points out, though, that circulation of arts print materials continue to be in the "top ten," in libraries, even though overall circulation is down in academic libraries and the number of hits in the databases continues to rise.

What does this mean for budgeting for art book collections? It could mean that funding for this area of the collection in academic libraries could become quite a bit more problematic. For example, while art librarians are trying to figure out how to pay for access to the many art databases and digital image databases that are becoming available, there are still types of art information that are only available in print. If academic libraries continue to devote more and more of their budgets to the purchase of information in digital formats, it could become very difficult to get funding for the print resources that are needed by art students. Another problem to point out is the issue of image quality in the aggregator databases. Although there are many art periodicals available within these resources, the image quality is not always as good as the print and in some cases duplication may be desirable. But, the budget may not allow it in some cases and then some tough choices have to be made.

Other formats having an affect on budgets are video, DVD, and the ebook. Faculty are integrating the use of media into their course syllabi, and are requesting these items more frequently. Academic libraries are also beginning to devote portions of their budgets to the purchase of electronic books, but at this time it is not a viable format for art books. This is yet another example of a new format that is drawing buying power away from the more traditional print formats.

ACQUISITIONS TOOLS FOR ART BOOK SELECTION: A SURVEY

As was mentioned in the previous section, it is getting more and more difficult for librarians to appropriately identify what they want to select for purchase for their art materials collections, just because of the sheer volume of items in different formats that have become available. So what selection tools are art librarians using in order to keep a handle on what selections to make? A survey was taken in order to get information from librarians out in the field and find out what the most commonly used tools were to make their selections. Following are the answers, some of which are pretty predictable, and some which may be surprising.

THE ART LIBRARIES SOCIETY OF NORTH AMERICA

The Art Libraries Society of North America (ARLIS/NA) is an organization dedicated to the support of art librarians in a variety of institutional settings, whether they are academic, museum, public, private, or non-profit. Their online discussion group, ARLIS-L, was used to get a pool of respondents for the survey. The respondents represented several different areas, with the four-year academic institution, art school, museum library, and public library being among them. The respondents also came with varying levels of responsibility, being directors, acquisitions librarians, art librarians who were not directors, and librarians with selection responsibility in the arts.

Besides being a resource for the survey itself, ARLIS-L is also a resource for selectors. There is discussion about resources, and publishers, particularly small press, are members, and send announcements about new titles and services. Artists who make books also make announcements of availability of new offerings. Members also make announcements regarding older titles being withdrawn that might be of use to another library.

ARLIS/NA's web site is also a valuable resource, serving as an archive for its publication entitled *Art Documentation*, which is a great source of articles, bibliographies, and reviews. ARLIS/NA also has other publications available for purchase which cover a variety of topics related to art librarianship. Several survey respondents reported their regular use of *Art Documentation* as a source of reviews.

REVIEW SOURCES

Review sources were listed by respondents as one of the most important resources for identifying titles. *Choice* was listed as the second most common source of any kind used in the entire survey. Other review sources that were cited included *Library Journal* (the second most popular review source), *Booklist, Publishers Weekly*, and *Books in Print with Reviews.* A couple of respondents didn't want to rely on just review sources from the library science field, but also looked at reviews in subject specific periodicals such as *Art in America, The Art Book,* and *Art Forum,* for example. An issue involved in waiting to look at a review before making a decision on a purchase is that there is a higher likelihood that the item will be more difficult to acquire, especially if there was a short run printed and it is no longer available. That is most likely the reason why most survey respondents relied on notification from vendors as their number one identification tool for art titles.

VENDOR DATABASES, PRINT NOTIFICATIONS, AND APPROVAL PLANS

Many survey respondents take advantage of slip notification plans that are offered by vendors, although only a few took advantage of the actual approval plan system. The pattern of usage of approval plans seemed to coincide with the size of the institution in this survey; the larger the institution, the greater likelihood that approval plans would be used. Approval plans for specific formats such as exhibition catalogs are available through vendors, and are utilized by every type of library represented in the survey. This could be a very helpful service to any library that is committed to collecting exhibition catalogs, as there will be a greater chance of actually getting the catalog before the item goes out of print. Jobbers such as Worldwide who are directly connected to the suppliers of the catalogs can increase these chances (Houghton, 1984).

Still others went one step further and made their selections electronically through the vendor's online database. A selector can select the online "slip," and the collection development or acquisitions person can look at their selections before sending them electronically. Then, the information can be entered into the library's online system by loading an electronic file holding the order information supplied by the vendor. The order in which these steps happen depends on the library's individual system and established workflow.

Some survey participants also use the vendor's database as an initial verification tool at the beginning of the selection process, in much the same way as one would use *Books in Print*. Some vendors also incorporate *Choice's Outstanding Books* titles into their online databases, and they can be specifically searched with this designation, by the year that they were selected.

There is an advantage in consolidating purchasing activities with a specific vendor in order to utilize some of the aforementioned services. Shortened turnaround time, the power to negotiate larger discounts, and the ability of the vendor to supply management reports are just a few of the benefits, helping the acquisitions librarian to greatly streamline processes and procedures.

PUBLISHER CATALOGS

Publisher catalogs were tied with *Choice* for second place in the list of important tools for selectors to use in the process of acquiring art books for their collections. Online as well as print versions were consulted equally. Some selectors consulted the catalogs of a core list of publishers that they identified as being the most important producers of titles for their collections. Using the Web to quickly find out about forthcoming titles from publishers made the selection process even more timely. Blanket orders of all the titles produced by an individual publisher is another way to insure easy acquisition of specific offerings. Incorporating core lists of publishers into an approval plan gives the added benefit of a negotiated volume discount on those titles.

THE INTERNET AS AN ACQUISITIONS TOOL

Almost everyone participating in the survey agreed that the Internet has revolutionized the acquisitions process, especially in the area of identifying sources for rare and out of print items. *AbeBooks* and *Bookfinder* were the two most popular resources listed for identifying rare and out of print titles for purchase. Several librarians in the survey also mentioned the use of *Amazon.com* as a verification tool in place of *Books in Print* and also as a source for reviews. Communications with publishers and jobbers alike through web sites and via email makes the follow-up process much more efficient and timely.

AcqWeb, a site designed and maintained by acquisitions librarians, is an invaluable one-stop resource which indexes publisher links by geographic location and subject area, indexes links to jobbers both in this country and abroad, and acts as a resource for professional development for the acquisitions and collection development specialist.

CONCLUSION

To conclude, let's look at the following scenario. It's a few years into the future, but not too far, because really it could be happening now, with all the technology that's available in the marketplace today . . .

> The art library of the future is working hard and well at identifying the resources that are necessary in order to support its programs and services. There are many strong collections of art materials all over the country that are well funded and strong. Even though government support for the arts faded long ago, art librarians have had the foresight to help their surrounding communities get private support for their arts endeavors through worldwide connections on the Web. Art librarians are also learning to more efficiently handle their acquisitions processes and proce-

dures regarding mainstream items. They are utilizing resources available through the Internet, and specialized services provided by the vendors and publishers alike, in order to make the acquiring of art materials an easier and more timely experience. They can also get additional assistance from their vendors in the way of online management reports that help them in their collection development efforts. Maximizing the use of their online library information systems will also help them to more easily identify areas of the collection that need to be strengthened so that they can maximize the purchasing power of their budgets. All of the systems to which they have access interface with each other in seamless communication, so that selection, ordering, receiving, and payment processes are all totally compatible. With the day to day operations of their libraries running so much more efficiently, the art librarian will have more time to explore acquisitions possibilities that are more unusual, ephemeral, and out of the mainstream. Online formats will be of great support to the many artists who cannot physically visit their libraries. Students will have access to literally millions of images, ideas, and resources that will help them to maximize their creative abilities.

Presently academic institutions are working to make distance education programs viable. How art programs will become involved in this remains to be seen, but art librarians will be in at the ground floor in the development of distance education programs for artists, because they will have already studied the trends in the publishing, education and business markets and seen the changes coming. The online environment, with its technically savvy art student, is here to stay.

Art libraries will need to continue to develop better ways to point artists to relevant Web information, showing them types of information they didn't even know they needed and showing them how to effectively use it. Art librarians will teach art students to have the heart of an entrepreneur through the types of research skills that they demonstrate to them, and the types of resources which they have acquired. Art librarians will help artists be able to make their art accessible in the global marketplace, even though they are limited in their ability to travel and physically be exposed to the big art centers of the world. This is the art librarian of the 21st century.

REFERENCES

Albanese, A. R. (2001). Moving from books to bytes. *Library Journal*, 126(14), 52-54. Retrieved on October 28, 2002, from Proquest Direct database.

Becker, C. (1996). A new generation of artists and art schools. *The Chronicle of Higher Education*, 43(11), B8. Retrieved on September 22, 2000 from Proquest Direct Database.

Bogart, D., (Ed.). (2002). *The Bowker annual: Library and book trade almanac.* Medford, NJ: Information Today.

Cobbledick, S. (1996). The information seeking behavior of artists: Exploratory interviews. *Library Quarterly,* 66(4), 343-372.

Dillon, D. (1997). The changing role of humanities collection development. *The Acquisitions Librarian,* 17/18, 5-15.

Frank, P. (1999). Student artists in the library: An investigation of how they use general academic libraries for their creative needs. *Journal of Academic Librarianship,* 25(6), 445-455.

Houghton, B. (1984). Acquisition of exhibition catalogs. *Art Libraries Journal,* 9, 67-78.

Pacey, P. (1982). How art students use libraries–if they do. *Art Libraries Journal,* 7(1), 33-38.

Phillips, T. (1986). Artists on libraries 1. *Art Libraries Journal,* 11(3), 9-10.

Stam, D. (1995). Artists and art libraries. *Art Libraries Journal,* 20(2), 21-24.

Tong, D. (1993). New art technologies: Tools for a global culture. *Art Documentation,* 12(3), 115-117.

ADDITIONAL READINGS

Becker, C. (1999). The art of crossing the street. *Art Journal,* 58(1). Retrieved on September 23, 2000 from Proquest Direct database.

Dole, W.V. (1983). Austerity and the arts: Collection development in the 1980's. *Drexel Library Quarterly,* 19(3), 28-37.

Heller, A., & Lorenzen, E. (1999). Online ordering: Making its mark. *Library Journal,* 124(14). Retrieved on October 28, 2002 from Proquest Direct database.

Layne, S.S. (1994). Artists, art historians, and visual art information. *The Reference Librarian,* 47, 23-36.

McClung, P. (Ed.). (1985). *Selection of library materials in the humanities, social sciences, and sciences.* Chicago: American Library Association.

Miller, H. (1992). *Managing acquisitions and vendor relations: A how to do it manual.* New York: Neal-Schuman.

Ojala, M. (1993, Fall). Core competencies for special libraries of the future. *Special Libraries,* 84, 230-233.

Olin, F. (Ed.). (1983). The state of art librarianship. *Drexel Library Quarterly,* 19(3).

Owens, I. (Ed.). (1997). *Acquisitions and collection development in the humanities.* New York: The Haworth Press, Inc.

Pacey, P. (Ed.). (1985). *A reader in art librarianship.* New York: K.G. Saur.

Schmidt, K. (Ed.). (1999). *Understanding the business of acquisitions* (2nd ed.). Chicago: American Library Association.

Trepanier, P. (1986). Artists on Libraries 2. *Art libraries journal* 11(3),11-12.

Whiteside, A.B., Born, P., & Bregman, A.A. (2000). *Collection development policies for libraries and visual collections in the arts* (Occasional papers, 12). Tucson, AZ: Art Libraries Society of North America.

Couch, N. & Allen, N. (Eds.). (1993). *The humanities and the library* (2nd ed.). Chicago: American Library Association.

INTERNET ADDRESSES CITED IN THIS ARTICLE

AbeBooks http://www.abebooks.com/

Acqweb http://acqweb.library.vanderbilt.edu/

Alibris http://www.alibris.com/

Amazon.com http://www.amazon.com/

Arlis/NA http://www.arlisna.org/

Art Libraries Society Discussion List http://www.arlisna.org/arlisl.html

ARLIS/NA Publications http://www.arlisna.org/publications.html

Bookfinder http://www.bookfinder.com/

Native American Resources:
A Model for Collection Development

Rhonda Harris Taylor
Lotsee Patterson

SUMMARY. This construct for collection development as it relates to Native American resources utilizes Thomas Mann's *Library Research Methods* (1993) concepts of the Traditional Model, the Actual-Practice Model, and the Principle of Least Effort to organize recommendations for both strategies and resources. The three-pronged hierarchical approach to selection/acquisition is illustrated with examples of print, non print, and Internet collection development resources useful for a variety of library settings. *[Article copies available for a fee from The Haworth Document Delivery Service: 1-800-HAWORTH. E-mail address: <docdelivery@haworth press.com> Website: <http://www.HaworthPress.com> © 2004 by The Haworth Press, Inc. All rights reserved.]*

KEYWORDS. Native American resources, American Indian resources, acquisitions, collection development, selection

Rhonda Harris Taylor is Associate Professor, School of Library and Information Studies, University of Oklahoma, 401 West Brooks, Room 120, Norman, OK 73019-6032 (E-mail: rtaylor@ou.edu). Lotsee Patterson is Professor, School of Library and Information Studies, University of Oklahoma, 401 West Brooks, Room 120, Norman, OK 73019-6032 (E-mail: lpatterson@ou.edu).

[Haworth co-indexing entry note]: "Native American Resources: A Model for Collection Development." Taylor, Rhonda Harris, and Lotsee Patterson. Co-published simultaneously in *The Acquisitions Librarian* (The Haworth Information Press, an imprint of The Haworth Press, Inc.) No. 31/32, 2004, pp. 41-54; and: *Selecting Materials for Library Collections* (ed: Audrey Fenner) The Haworth Information Press, an imprint of The Haworth Press, Inc., 2004, pp. 41-54. Single or multiple copies of this article are available for a fee from The Haworth Document Delivery Service [1-800-HAWORTH, 9:00 a.m. - 5:00 p.m. (EST). E-mail address: docdelivery@haworthpress.com].

10.1300/J101v16n31_04

INTRODUCTION

The authors acknowledge Mann's (1993) *Library Research Models* as the inspiration for the conceptual models used for categorizing selection/acquisition sources in this article. Mann's concept of the Traditional Model, the Actual-Practice Model, and the Principle of Least Effort serve as the construct on which we built our approaches to the acquisition of American Indian materials.

BACKGROUND

In approaching the task of selecting appropriate resources that are focused on topics about Native Americans and/or that represent Native American perspectives, basic principles for collection development will facilitate the process. However, there are also strategies that are particularly useful for these types of resources.

Basic selection techniques that remain valid are literally "textbook." Evans' (1995, pp. 97-120) review of the literature of the selection review process culminates in a list of ten suggestions for selectors: (1) remembering that selection is only part of the collection development process; (2) understanding the basics of the production of information resources; (3) becoming familiar with the editors and producers of information resources; (4) being familiar with the offerings of the publishers of the best material; (5) reading reviews from many sources; (6) being familiar with trade and national bibliographies; (7) knowing the library's community; (8) understanding "book selection, reviewing, and acquisition activities"; (9) making independent judgments about titles and comparing them to reviews; and (10) being "interested in what is going on in the world, and read, read, read!" (pp. 120-121).

It is critical for the selection process that each library which is building a Native American collection have a collection development policy that is formally adopted and that is followed by selectors. This document, unique to the institution, should specifically address selection/acquisition of Native American resources. To meet local needs, the institution might want to limit the scope of Native American materials acquisition to specific tribes, topics, levels of interest, or time periods.

The ten selection guidelines offered by Evans (1995), and the importance of the adoption and implementation of a collection development policy, are interwoven with our vision of a hierarchical model for collection development in the arena of Native American resources.

Our model groups selection resources into three levels: (1) The Traditional Model, (2) The Actual-Practice Model, and (3) The Principle of Least Effort.

We recommend the use of all three levels when identifying appropriate resources centering on Native American people and issues.

The Traditional Model

The most common approach for acquisition of materials is to use standard library reviewing journals, such as *Library Journal* or *Booklist*, for selection of current materials, retrospective selection tools such as H. W. Wilson's serial publication, *Public Library Catalog* (Yaakov, 1999), or Libraries Unlimited's monograph, *American Indian Studies: A Bibliographic Guide* (White, 1995), or Kuipers' *American Indian Reference and Resource Books for Children and Young Adults* (1995), to fill in gaps in the collection, and national and trade bibliography tools, such as ALA's *Guide to Reference Books* (Balay, 1996), the *American Reference Books Annual* (Hysell, 2002), and Bowker's annual *Books in Print* (2002), to search for additional resources available through normal routes in collection development. This approach, however, has its limitations since a large volume of materials on the topic of American Indians is produced by non-mainstream publishers and may not be found in standard selection tools.

What the resources in the traditional approach share in common is that they are widely available, are intended to be used for selection processes, and have the advantage of being viewed as credible by the profession. Producers of these resources are, in essence, credentialed. Familiarity with these tools, including their reliability, the subject knowledge of their selectors/reviewers/compilers, and the tool's past record for dependability or biases is the key to successful selection of both newly published materials and those used for retrospective collection building.

On the negative side, these resources cannot be presumed to always be credible or reliable. Reviewers in current reviewing sources often lack expertise or extensive knowledge on the topic of American Indians. Such tools tend to cover only mainstream publishers, often not picking up small press or entrepreneurial publishers/producers. Of course, these selection sources are able to cover only a small percentage of each year's publications/productions.

The standard reviewing and other professional resources in librarianship do provide useful lists of recommended sources, and those standard tools do from time to time focus on American Indian titles and feature bibliographic essays. For example, *Booklist*, *Emergency Librarian*, and *Library Journal*, among others, have recently included listings of recommended American Indian titles and bibliographic essays focused on the topic of Native American resources (Burch, 2002; Helmer, 2000; Higgs, 1998; Seaman, 2000; Young, 2002). A decade ago *Choice* published a special compilation of titles on the subject of Native American Studies (*Choice*, 1992). A more recent list on that same topic is exemplified by White's (1995) monograph, *American Indian Studies: A Bibliographic Guide*. Even more recently, a bibliographic essay in *Choice* covered "American Indian Studies: Notable Publications, 1990-2001" (Gagnon, 2002).

Several monographic bibliographies have addressed the topic of American Indian literature, including Ruoff's (1990) *American Indian Literatures: An Introduction, Bibliographic Review, and Selected Bibliography*. Scarecrow Press has a *Native American Bibliography Series* that includes *The Native American in Long Fiction: An Annotated Bibliography* (Beam & Branstad, 1996), covering the 1880s to the 1990s, and *A Biobibliography of Native American Writers, 1772-1924: A Supplement* (Littlefield & Parins, 1985), which supplements *A Bibliography of Native American Writers, 1772-1924* (Littlefield & Parins, 1981). The recent proliferation of the published works of Native writers, coupled with wider appreciation of the works, has resulted in publication of bibliographic resources such as "Native American Literature: Expanding the Canon" (Kratzert & Richey, 1998). Reference resources, such as Garland Publishing's *Handbook of Native American Literature* (Wiget, 1996), formerly the *Dictionary of Native American Literature* (Wiget, 1994) and which is a guide to oral and written literature of Native Americans, are useful to collection developers for the bibliographical references and for the background information about Native literature.

There are a number of mainstream press monographic bibliographies that cover very specific topics, such as White's (2000) *Peyotism and the Native American Church: An Annotated Bibliography* and his *The Native American Sun Dance Religion and Ceremony: An Annotated Bibliography* (1998). There are also monographic bibliographies that offer broad coverage, such as *Native Americans: An Annotated Bibliography* (Hoxie & Markowitz, 1991).

In the periodical literature, there are good bibliographic essays that have covered topical areas focused on American Indians, such as Roy's (1997) "Dream Catchers, Love Medicine, and Fancy Dancing: Selecting Native American Studies Material in the Humanities" and Lawrence's (1992) "Native American Art and Culture: Documentary Resources." For a general overview of collection development in this area, there is Davis' (1992) article, "Developing a Native American Collection."

Collection developers will also find lists of recommended titles about or by Native Americans in bibliographies that address multiculturalism in general. These types of bibliographies are particularly useful for children's materials. Three examples are *This Land is Our Land: A Guide to Multicultural Literature for Children and Young Adults* (Helbig & Perkins, 1994), *Culturally Diverse Library Collections for Children* (Totten & Brown, 1994), and *Culturally Diverse Library Collections for Youth* (Totten, Garner, & Brown,

1996). More focused monographic resources for developing children's and young adult collections include *Through Indian Eyes: The Native Experience in Books for Children* (Slapin & Seale, 1998), useful for its perspective on commonly found children's books that portray Native Americans and for its list of criteria, with illustrative examples, for evaluating such materials. Another example is *Native Americans Today: Resources and Activities for Educators, Grades 4-8* (Hirschfelder & Beamer, 2000), which collection developers will appreciate for its resource lists.

A specialized periodical utilized by teachers and librarians interested in multiculturalism, *MultiCultural Review*, has provided reviews of Native film (McDonald, 2000; McDonald, 2001; McDonald, 2002) and bibliographic essays of print resources about Native Americans (Atleo et al., 1999; Slapin, 2000).

Encyclopedias, dictionaries, and handbooks are sources for bibliographies that are useful for collection development. For instance, the *Reference Encyclopedia of the American Indian* (Klein, 2003) provides lists of books, films, videos, recordings, prints, photographs, maps, Web sites, and periodicals; however, a listing should not be construed as a recommendation, and librarians are cautioned to be judicious when selecting from such tools.

Museums, which collectively control huge holdings of Native American resources, also publish bibliographies relevant for Native American collection development. For instance, the Library of Congress has published an annotated and illustrated guide to its resources, *Many Nations: A Library of Congress Resource Guide for the Study of Indian and Alaska Native Peoples of the United States* (Frazier & The Publishing Office, 1996). *Many Nations* is useful not only as an acquisition for potential researchers, but is an excellent reminder for the collection developer of the diversity of resources pertinent for the study of Native Americans, ranging from maps to motion pictures to music to photographs to manuscripts. Museums have provided some resources online, such as the Smithsonian Institution's listings of resources, including Web sites, of "Native American History and Culture" (http://www.si.edu/resource/faq/nmai/start.htm). When the Smithsonian's new National Museum of the American Indian (http://www.nmai.si.edu/index.asp) opens in the fall of 2004, it is expected to be a welcome source of up-to-date, online bibliographies.

A major source of excellent monographs by and about American Indians are university presses. And, while publishers' catalogs as selection "tools" lack the vetting offered by review sources, they can represent a reliable source of types of titles when the publisher has built a reputation in an area. For instance, the presses at the Universities of Oklahoma (http://www.oupress.com/index.asp), New Mexico (http://www.unmpress.com/unmpress.html), Nebraska (http://www.nebraskapress.unl.edu/), and Arizona (http://www.uapress.

arizona.edu/) are well-known for their extensive listing of titles about and by Native Americans. They also often retain titles in their inventories for a longer period of time than do many commercial publishers.

Besides the standard review journals normally utilized by librarians, other credible sources of reviews, although not often readily available to many librarians, are periodicals directed at Native readers. Two examples that cover education/career information for Native Americans are *TCJ: Tribal College Journal of American Indian Higher Education* (http://www.tribalcollegejournal. org) and *Winds of Change* (http://bioc09.uthscsa.edu/winds/). Both have book reviews and post their tables of contents (and some full-text excerpts from issues) on the Web. The first title will be of particular interest to collection development specialists because of its regular feature entitled "Resource Guide." These annotated bibliographic essays have included such subjects as "Resources for Native Education Leaders" (Begaye, 2002) and "Resource Guide for Indigenous Communities Building a College" (Allen & Allen, 2001). Periodicals for Native readerships are useful for their highlighting of resources and also for their provision of the context of issues, perspectives, and profiles of individuals and events so necessary for the effective collection development specialist. Increasingly such periodicals have a presence on the Web, and many are now covered in specialized databases such as *Ethnic NewsWatch* (http://www.umi.com/products/pt-product-ethnic-newswatch.shtml).

Collection development librarians in various types of library settings, not just those serving Native American studies programs, will find that the well-known interdisciplinary, juried journals in Native American Studies, such as *Wicazo Sa Review*, from the University of Minnesota Press, and *American Indian Quarterly*, from the University of Nebraska Press, are important sources of both book/media reviews and annotated bibliographic essays. For instance, *American Indian Quarterly* has published "An Annotated Chiricahua Apache Bibliography–Selected Books" (Stockel, 2001) and *Wicazo Sa Review* has published an "Annotated Bibliography of the Basic Literature Needed for an Understanding of Tribal Governance" (Wilkinson & Ulrich, 2002). *Wicazo Sa Review* has produced thematic issues on such topics as Native American health, film and video, and tribal sovereignty and governance. Also, the tables of contents of this periodical, back to the Fall of 1992, are available on the Web at http://www.upress.umn.edu/journals/wsr.

In addition to journals, collection developers will find many citations of interest in more popularly-read specialized periodicals, such as *Native Peoples* (http://www.nativepeoples.com/), which began as a magazine for the membership of the Heard Museum in Phoenix, Arizona. It focuses on the art and lifeways of Native peoples of the Americas, and its affiliates include a number of museums and libraries. Issues contain book, audio, and video reviews. Articles, with a focus on contemporary artists, musicians, events, and exhibits, often include Web citations and other resource and contact listings.

The Traditional Model, using standard selection tools, offers the advantage of reliability. It is also a time-tested model for retrospective collection building. However, there is always the question of timeliness with print resources, including the added issue of out-of-print or unavailable titles. With the Internet offering easier, broadly-based access to vendors for out-of-print titles, the problem has been eased somewhat.

No one resource can be comprehensive, and even the collective body of these resources would not purport to fulfill that role. For access to many resources relevant for Native American collection development, the connectivity of the Internet is a very useful complement to familiar tools.

The Actual-Practice Model

This approach might be labeled the short-cut way, because with multiple resources accessible though the Internet, librarians have integrated these quickly obtainable sources of information into library practice.

This approach focuses on Internet resources that can be utilized for selection activities, although that is not necessarily the intent of the creators, and that because of their electronic nature are not yet, in most cases, as stable as the familiar print-based resources found in the traditional model. Some of their disadvantages include the fact that they can literally disappear from one day to the next, that there is often no standard that can be used for applying our normal criteria for judging material, such as accuracy or authoritativeness, and that their agendas can vary widely. Identifying the source of the information found is not always an easy task, and without that knowledge a librarian has no simple way to validate the information contained on a site. However, there are outstanding resources for collection development on the Web.

Two credible and stable portals collocating links to Native American resources on the Web have been Mitten's *Native American Sites* (http://www.nativeculture.com/lisamitten/indians.html) and Strom's *Index of Native American Resources on the Internet* (http://www.hanksville.org/Naresources). Both sites are well-organized and have categorized the resources offered, but differ in their orientation. The purpose of Mitten's site is "to facilitate communication among Native peoples and between Indians and non-Indians by providing access to home pages of Native American Nations and organizations, and to other sites that provide solid information about American Indians" (2002). Strom's goal is "to provide information resources to the Native American community and only secondarily to the general community. The information is organized, insofar as possible, to make it useful to the Native American community and the education community" (1994-2002). Both of these sites offer the advantage of selecting and organizing Web sites from the available multitude, ranging widely in quality and reliability, that are accessible to potential users. And, there are many quality Web sites that would be useful to the acquisitions librarian. For instance, the Internet Public Library's *Native American Authors* database is useful for its collocation of those authors, information about them, and listings of their works (http://www.ipl.org/div/natam/). Also important to remember is that Web sites that are well-established in particular areas of information, such as Howells' *Cyndi's List of Genealogy Sites on the Internet* (http://www.cyndislist.com), will often provide access to a subset of resources focused on Native Americans (http://www.cyndislist.com/native.htm).

For a wider coverage of Internet resources centered on Native Americans and related topics, see Taylor's (2002) article, "Focusing on Native Americans: Basic Web Resources Pathfinder."

However, the discovery of some Internet sites is literally accidental in nature, which leaves one to wonder how to approach locating available resources in a more predictable manner, as is done when using the search skills normally applied to our use of indexes. Where are the reliable access tools for the Internet sources? Also, the very nature of the Internet changes this actual-practice model into one of reassessment of ownership as the primary goal of acquisition practices. The increasing availability of free online, full-text materials certainly improves access to primary sources for users. This access is especially important to users of American Indian materials as museums, libraries, archives, and other entities, including professional associations, mount their specialized collections in digital form onto Web sites. However, librarians will need to facilitate not only linking patrons with such resources but also to facilitate the navigation of these sites: oftentimes the sites are not well-known, and even for those sites that are familiar, frequently the wealth of resources is buried in several levels of links. For example, the University System of Georgia Board of Regents has the *GALILEO* site (http://www.galileo.peachnet.edu), which mounts documents and images related to Native Americans of the Southeastern United States, including archival sources related to the Indian Removals of the 1830s. The sequence of links to access the appropriate search engine is first the URL for *GALILEO*, next a link titled "Digital Library of Georgia," and then down a list of links to "Southeastern Native American Documents, 1730-1842." Another example of a unique and information-dense resource is the University of Arkansas *American Native Press Archives* (http://www.anpa.ualr.edu/), which is dedicated to "collecting and archiving the products of the Native press and materials related to Native press history, collecting and documenting the works of Native writers, and constructing bibliographic guides to Native writing and publishing" (n.d.). Many of the actual resources are available online through the Web site.

The Principle of Least Effort

A grassroots networking approach reflects the principle of least effort and is not unlike that strategy employed by laypeople when they want information. Librarians will contact individuals or institutional/organizational sources known to them in order to obtain quick responses to information needs. This strategy usually requires the least effort and is often an effective method for locating a specific item for collection development. This approach may include posting a question to a distribution list, sending an e-mail message to someone whose Web site is familiar to the librarian, or calling a colleague. Case (2002) discusses the origins of this Principle, credited to George Zipf, and the evidence which supports it, in *Looking for Information: A Survey of Research on Information Seeking, Needs, and Behavior.*

The advantage to this approach is the ability to identify outstanding resources, often unique, that might not appear in mainstream sources, reviewing tools, or bibliographies. It also may mean sacrificing standard selection criteria such as preferred style, aesthetic qualities, and physical characteristics in exchange for authoritativeness, accuracy, and relevance since the item may be in paperback form, published by a small, little-known publisher with limited marketing, and not carried by any major vendor.

These small publishers and producers of primarily Native American materials will likely not be found exhibiting at library conferences or advertising in library journals. They may, however, be found exhibiting at specialized conferences such as the National Indian Education Association's (NIEA) annual conference (http://www.niea.org/). The titles of small publishers/presses may also be picked up by less well-known distributors. Collection development librarians need to actively seek out the distributors who carry primarily Indian-authored or focused titles. Such distributors include Clear Light Books in Santa Fe, New Mexico (http://www.clearlightbooks.com), Oyate in Berkeley, California (http://www.oyate.org), The Greenfield Review Press in Greenfield Center, New York (http://www.greenfieldreview.org) and Written Heritage (http://www.writtenheritage.com) in Folsom, Louisiana. The latter distributor has a number of excellent, hard to find videos made by independent producers, many of whom are Native. Examples of video titles include *Brain Tanning Bison Robes the Native American Way* (Belitz, 2001), which depicts the age-old technique demonstrated by two Canadian First Nations People, and *Into the Circle: An Introduction to Native American Powwows* (Swearingen & Rhoades, 1992), filmed in Oklahoma and featuring local dancers. The producers of these videos chose lesser-known distributors in order to keep the cost of the videos affordable (in the $20 range). These distributors also serve as reminders that resources by and about Native Americans include not only print, but also video, digital, and other formats, and are not focused completely on historical events, but include contemporary culture and issues. For instance, Cherokee Publications in Cherokee, North Carolina (http://www.CherokeePub. com) offers an assortment of materials, including books, video and audio tapes, kits, and maps, and includes some unusual, hard-to-find resources, such as census records and other genealogy resources sought by those individuals tracing Indian ancestry. This distributor markets the most recent iterations of two genealogical resources compiled by Blankenship, *Cherokee Roots* in two volumes (1992) and *Dawes Roll 'Plus' of Cherokee Nation '1898'* (1994), containing over 36,000 names of members of the Cherokee Nation. Also available are Cherokee language materials/instructional guides and audio tapes of Cherokee language and music.

One advantage of the Principle of Least Effort is actively establishing a presence in people networks that can continue to provide guidance in resource selection. This approach is also an excellent way to identify media products that are produced by small or independent groups, or even individuals, and to support those production efforts with purchases. However, selectors will find that credibility can vary from outstanding to almost impossible to identify. Locating or identifying these resources can be problematic, but these resources can also provide coverage and perspectives that are difficult to find in mainstream production.

ACTION PLAN: RECOMMENDATIONS

In the best of all collection development worlds, identifying and obtaining resources for Native American collection development would require only one approach. However, effective collection building requires the use of all three models discussed here. It is also critical that collection development librarians be attuned not only to the changing environment of acquisition and other information tools, but also to the contemporary nature of Native Americans as both the focus of information resources and as the producers of information resources. Native Americans do eloquently articulate their own stories, and they are very much a viable presence in the 21st century. Effective acquisition/selection in this specialized arena requires being informed about resources and also being willing to continue learning about the complex political, historical, and cultural realities, current and historical, of the many diverse peoples called Native Americans. Is it time for the development of a national or trade bibliography devoted to the topic of American Indians?

REFERENCES

Allen, M., & Allen, T. (2001, Spring). Resource guide for indigenous communities building a college. *TCJ: Tribal College Journal of American Indian Higher Education, 12*. Retrieved December 13, 2002, from http://www.tribalcollegejournal.org/.

American Indian Quarterly. (n.d.). Retrieved December 13, 2002, from http://www.unp.unl.edu/aiq.html.

Atleo, M., Caldwell, N., Landis, B., Mendoza, J., Miranda, D., & Reese, D. et al. (1999, September). *My heart is on the ground* and the Indian boarding school experience. *MultiCultural Review, 8*, 41-46.

Balay, R. (Ed.). (1996). *Guide to reference books*. Chicago: American Library Association.

Beam, J., & Branstad B. (1996). *The Native American in long fiction: An annotated bibliography*. Lanham, MD: Scarecrow Press.

Begaye, T. (2002, Summer). Resource guide: Resources for Native education leaders. *TJC: Tribal College Journal of American Indian Higher Education, 13*. Retrieved December 13, 2002, from http://www.tribalcollegejournal.org/.

Belitz, L. (Videographer & Commentator). (2001). *Brain tanning bison robes the Native American way* [Motion picture]. Hot Springs, SD: Belitz.

Blankenship, B. (Ed.). (1992). *Cherokee Roots. Volume 1: Members of the Cherokee tribe residing east of the Mississippi River during the period 1817-1924* (2nd ed.). Cherokee, NC: B. Blankenship.

Blankenship, B. (Ed.). (1992). *Cherokee Roots. Volume 2: A listing of the members of the Cherokee tribe residing west of the Mississippi River during the period 1851-1909* (2nd ed.). Cherokee, NC: B. Blankenship.

Blankenship, B. (Ed.). (1994). *Dawes Roll 'plus' of Cherokee Nation '1898'* (2nd ed.). Cherokee, NC: Cherokee Roots Publication.

Books in print 2002-2003. (2002). New Providence, NJ: Bowker.

Burch, J. R. (2002, September 1). From time immemorial. *Library Journal, 127*, 59-63.

Case, D. O. (2002). *Looking for information: A survey of research on information seeking, needs, and behavior*. Amsterdam: Academic Press.

Cherokee Publications. (n.d). Retrieved December 13, 2002, from http://www.cherokeepub.com/.

Choice Editorial Staff (Ed.). (1992). *Native American studies*. Middletown, CT: Choice.

Clear Light Books, Inc. (2000-2002). Retrieved December 13, 2002, from http://www.clearlightbooks.com.

Davis, M. B. (1992, December). Developing a Native American collection. *Wilson Library Bulletin, 67*, 33-37.

Ethnic NewsWatch. (2002). Retrieved December 13, 2002, from http://www.umi.com/products/pt-product-ethnic-newswatch.shtml.

Evans, G. E. (1995). *Developing library and information center collections* (3rd ed.). Englewood, CO: Libraries Unlimited.

Frazier, P., & The Publishing Office (Eds.). (1996). *Many nations: A Library of Congress resource guide for the study of Indian and Alaska Native peoples of the United States*. Washington: Library of Congress.

Gagnon, G. (2002, September). American Indian studies: Notable publications, 1990-2001. *Choice, 40,* 47-57.

Greenfield Review Press. (n.d.). Retrieved December 13, 2002, from http://www. greenfieldreview.org.

Helbig, A., & Perkins, A. (1994). *This land is our land: A guide to multicultural literature for children and young adults.* Westport, CT: Greenwood Press.

Helmer, D. (2000, January 1/15). Native American reference sources. *Booklist, 96,* 956+.

Higgs, J. (1998, March-April). All my relations. *Emergency Librarian, 25,* 47-49.

Hirschfelder, A., & Beamer, Y. (2000). *Native Americans today: Resources and activities for educators, grades 4-8.* Englewood, CO: Teacher Ideas Press.

Howells, C. (1996-2002). *Cyndi's list of genealogy sites on the Internet.* Retrieved December 13, 2002, from http://www.cyndislist.com.

Howells, C. (1996-2002). *Cyndi's list of genealogy sites on the Internet: Native American.* Retrieved December 13, 2002, from http://www.cyndislist.com/native.htm.

Hoxie, F. E., & Markowitz, H. (1991). *Native Americans: An annotated bibliography.* Pasadena, CA: Salem Press.

Hysell, S. G. (Ed.). (2002). *American reference books annual.* Greenwood Village, CO: Libraries Unlimited.

The Internet Public Library. *Native American authors.* (2002, June 12). Retrieved December 13, 2002, from http://www.ipl.org/div/natam/.

Klein, B. (2003). *Reference encyclopedia of the American Indian* (10th ed.). Nyack, NY: Todd Publications.

Kratzert, M. Y., & Richey, D. (1998). Native American literature: Expanding the canon. *Collection Building, 17,* 4-15.

Kuipers, B. J. (1995). *American Indian reference and resource books for children and young adults* (2nd ed.). Englewood, CO: Libraries Unlimited.

Lawrence, D. (1992, December). Native American art and culture: Documentary resources. *Wilson Library Bulletin, 67,* 40-42.

Littlefield, D. F., & Parins, J. W. (1981). *A bibliography of Native American writers, 1772-1924.* Metuchen, NJ: Scarecrow Press.

Littlefield, D. F., & Parins, J. W. (1985). *A biobibliography of Native American writers, 1772-1924: A supplement.* Metuchen, NJ: Scarecrow Press.

Mann, T. (1993). *Library research models: A guide to classification, cataloging, and computers.* New York: Oxford University Press.

McDonald, C. (2000, December). The Native Forum at the 2000 Sundance Film Festival. *MultiCultural Review, 9,* 42-47.

McDonald, C. (2001, December). The Native Forum at the 2001 Sundance Film Festival: Redefining indigenous film. *MultiCultural Review, 10,* 50-53, 59-60.

McDonald, C. (2002, December). The Native Forum at the 2002 Sundance Film Festival. *MultiCultural Review, 11,* 44-46.

Mitten, L. *Native American sites.* (2002, September 29). Retrieved October 2, 2002, from http://www.nativeculture.com/lisamitten/indians.html.

National Indian Education Association. (2002, December 7). Retrieved December 13, 2002, from http://www.niea.org/.

Native Peoples. (n.d.) Retrieved December 13, 2002, from http://www.nativepeoples.com/.

Oyate. (n.d.). Retrieved December 13, 2002, from http://www.oyate.org.

Roy, L. (1997). Dream catchers, love medicine, and fancy dancing: Selecting Native American studies material in the humanities. In Owens, I. (Ed.), *Acquisitions and collection development in the humanities* (pp. 141-57). New York: The Haworth Press, Inc.

Ruoff, A. L. B. (1990). *American Indian literatures: An introduction, bibliographic review, and selected bibliography*. New York: Modern Language Association of America.

Seaman, D. (2000, December 15). Read-alikes: Contemporary Native American fiction. *Booklist, 97*, 787.

Slapin, B. (2000, March). Photo essays of American Indian children. *MultiCultural Review, 9*, 28-40.

Slapin, B., & Seale, D. (Eds.). (1998). *Through Indian eyes: The native experience in books for children*. Los Angeles, CA: American Indian Studies Center.

Smithsonian Institution. (n.d.). Native American history and culture. Retrieved December 13, 2002, from http://www.si.edu/resource/faq/nmai/start.htm.

Smithsonian Institution. National Museum of the American Indian. (2002). Retrieved December 13, 2002, from http://www.nmai.si.edu/index.asp.

Stockel, H. H. (2001, Winter). An annotated Chiricahua Apache bibliography–Selected Books. *American Indian Quarterly, 25*, 153-176.

Strom, K.M. (1994-2002). *Index of Native American resources on the Internet*. Retrieved October 2, 2002, from http://www.hanksville.org/Naresources.

Swearingen, S., & Rhoades, S. (Producers). (1992). *Into the circle: An introduction to Native American powwows* [Motion picture]. Tulsa, OK: Full Circle Communications.

Taylor, R. H. (2002). Focusing on Native Americans: Basic web resources pathfinder. *Collection Building, 21*, 60-70.

TCJ: Tribal College Journal of American Indian Higher Education. (2001-2002). Retrieved December 13, 2002, from http://www.tribalcollegejournal.org.

Totten, H. L., & Brown, R. W. (1994). *Culturally diverse library collections for children*. New York: Neal-Schuman.

Totten, H. L., Garner, C. & Brown, R. W. (1996). *Culturally diverse library collections for youth*. New York: Neal-Schuman.

University of Arizona Press. (n.d.). Retrieved December 13, 2002, from http://www.uapress.arizona.edu/.

University of Arkansas at Little Rock, American Native Press Archives. (2002, Dec. 10). *Sequoyah Research Center, American Native Press Archives*. Retrieved December 13, 2002, from http://www.anpa.ualr.edu.

University of Nebraska Press. (2001). Retrieved December 13, 2002, from http://www.nebraskapress.unl.edu.

University of New Mexico Press. (n.d.). Retrieved December 13, 2002 from http://www.unmpress.com/unmpress.html.

University of Oklahoma Press. (n.d.). Retrieved December 13, 2002, from http://www.oupress.com.

University System of Georgia Board of Regents. (2002). *GALILEO*. Retrieved December 12, 2002, from http://www.galileo.peachnet.edu.

White, P.M. (1995). *American Indian studies: A bibliographic guide*. Englewood, CO: Libraries Unlimited.

White, P. M. (1998). *The Native American Sun Dance religion and ceremony: An annotated bibliography.* Westport, CT: Greenwood Press.

White, P. M. (2000). *Peyotism and the Native American Church: An annotated bibliography.* Westport, CT: Greenwood Press.

Wicazo Sa Review. (n.d.). Retrieved December 13, 2002, from http://www.upress. umn.edu/journals/wsr.

Wiget, A. (1994). *Dictionary of Native American literature.* New York: Garland.

Wiget, A. (1996). *Handbook of Native American literature.* New York: Garland.

Wilkinson, C. F., & Ulrich, A. N. (2002, Spring). Annotated bibliography of the basic literature needed for an understanding of tribal governance. *Wicazo Sa Review, 17,* 7-12.

Winds of Change. (1999). Retrieved December 13, 2002, from http://bioc09.uthscsa. edu/winds/.

Written Heritage. (2001, 2002). Retrieved December 13, 2002, from http://www.written heritage.com.

Yaakov, J. (Ed.). (1999). *Public library catalog: Guide to reference books and adult nonfiction* (11th ed). New York: H.W. Wilson.

Young, J. (2002, September 1). Native voices: Old and new. *Library Journal, 127,* 244.

Selecting and Acquiring Library Materials for Chinese Studies in Academic Libraries

Karen T. Wei

SUMMARY. Focusing on academic libraries in North America, this article describes the selection and acquisition of library materials for Chinese Studies from the People's Republic of China, Hong Kong, and Taiwan. It provides an historical overview of the Chinese book publishing and exporting practice, identifies and evaluates current online and printed resources for selection and methods of acquisition, and discusses the problems commonly faced by academic libraries. It also addresses the current state of book publishing and book exporting operations as they respond to China's new status as a member of the World Trade Organization and what this means to libraries in North America. *[Article copies available for a fee from The Haworth Document Delivery Service: 1-800-HAWORTH. E-mail address: <docdelivery@haworthpress.com> Website: <http://www.HaworthPress.com> © 2004 by The Haworth Press, Inc. All rights reserved.]*

KEYWORDS. Academic libraries, acquisitions, selections, China, Chinese materials, WTO

Karen T. Wei is Professor of Library Administration; Head, Asian Library; and Coordinator, Area Studies Division, University of Illinois at Urbana-Champaign, 325 Main Library, 1408 West Gregory Drive, Urbana, IL 61801 (E-mail: k-wei@uiuc.edu).

[Haworth co-indexing entry note]: "Selecting and Acquiring Library Materials for Chinese Studies in Academic Libraries." Wei. Karen T. Co-published simultaneously in *The Acquisitions Librarian* (The Haworth Information Press, an imprint of The Haworth Press, Inc.) No. 31/32, 2004, pp. 55-65; and: *Selecting Materials for Library Collections* (ed: Audrey Fenner) The Haworth Information Press, an imprint of The Haworth Press, Inc., 2004, pp. 55-65. Single or multiple copies of this article are available for a fee from The Haworth Document Delivery Service [1-800-HAWORTH, 9:00 a.m. - 5:00 p.m. (EST). E-mail address: docdelivery@haworthpress.com].

INTRODUCTION

China, including Hong Kong and Taiwan, has long been recognized as a major publishing country in the world. The 2000 edition of the *Zhong hua ren min gong he guo nian jian* [People's Republic of China Yearbook 2001] reports an annual output of 143,376 titles, including 84,235 new titles and 59,141 reprinted titles on demand in all subjects in 2000. China also published 8,725 serial titles, including 1,408 yearbooks in the same year.[1] Additionally, Taiwan produced 34,533 titles in 2000.[2] The sheer number would make it difficult for any academic library in North America to comprehensively collect the books and serials published in China. On the other hand, Western interest in China, which dates back several centuries, and the rise of area studies programs since World War II, have directed library resources to the procurement of Chinese materials in the last few decades. From the initial focus on collecting materials in Chinese language and culture to the new areas on information relating to Chinese agriculture, business, law, and social conditions, academic libraries have made a great effort to allocate their limited resources to meet the increasing demands in teaching and research needs of their faculty and students.

Focusing on academic libraries in North America, this article describes the selection and acquisition of library materials for Chinese Studies from the People's Republic of China (PRC), Hong Kong, and Taiwan. It provides an overview of Chinese book exporting practice, identifies and evaluates current online and printed resources for selection and methods of acquisition, and discusses the problems commonly encountered by academic libraries. Finally, it addresses the current state of book publishing and book exporting operations as they respond to China's new status as a member of the World Trade Organization and what this means to the libraries in North America.

CHINESE BOOK EXPORTING PRACTICE

Prior to President Nixon's historic visit to China in 1972 and the subsequent normalization between the two countries in 1978, China was tightly controlled by the Chinese Communist Party and effectively closed to the outside world. While books continued to be published and the number of volumes continued to rise during the period, the number of titles allowed for exportation was extremely limited and the costs were much higher than their domestic prices. The circumstances created a unique challenge for academic librarians in North America in making their selections and acquisitions of Chinese materials, as a large number of books were not slated for direct exportation. It was necessary for selectors to find a way to acquire books intended for "internal use" and books that were not listed in exporting sources. In addition, bibliographic control was also seriously lacking during these years.

Except for an elite few who had special "guanxi" or connections, most librarians turned to vendors in Hong Kong to acquire Chinese publications prior to the normalization of relations between the two countries, paying much higher prices. The percentage of books that was available in the Hong Kong market was about 11% of the total Chinese output in 1979.[3] As a result, many academic libraries acquired more Chinese books that were published in Hong Kong and Taiwan, as they were more readily available than from the PRC. A 1983 article by William Wong on acquiring library materials from the PRC provides an excellent overview of the Chinese publishing industry, its features, and the problems facing acquisitions librarians in the 1970s.[4]

Since the early 1980s, direct contact and purchase from Chinese sources became possible, although some libraries continued to rely on vendors in Hong Kong because of their efficient and speedy service. More, however, began to explore doing business directly with the PRC. Once the book market was open to foreigners, China permitted only three state-run agencies for book exportation: China International Books Trading Corporation (CIBTC), China National Publishing Industry Trading Corporation (CNPITC), and China National Publications Import & Export Corporation (CNPIEC). The so-called "big three" have since dominated the overseas book market for most of the last two decades.

In the early 1990s, the "big three" formed a Book Exporting Committee, stipulating the price structure for all exports as follows: for books priced under RMBY50, overseas customers would be charged at 2.5 times the domestic price; RMBY50-100, 2.25 times; RMBY100-1,000, 2 times; RMBY1,000-10,000, 1.3 times; and lastly, for large sets priced at RMBY10,000 and above, it would be possible to negotiate. This practice was in effect for much of the last decade. However, the price structure has recently been adjusted as China quickly learned the workings of the free market and capitalist economy. Furthermore, China had also begun to prepare for joining the World Trade Organization prior to the turn of the 21st century, opening more private or semi-private businesses in response to the market needs of the world.

At present, the climate is relatively favorable for the overseas libraries to purchase directly from China, as more and more companies, state-run, collectively owned, or privately owned, are allowed exporting. Prices have become more competitive although charges for foreigners are still higher than the domestic price, albeit not double or more. Discounts for expensive items or large sets are often obtainable. New vendors who are eager to establish relationships with overseas customers are also likely to entertain other reasonable terms.

SOURCES FOR SELECTION

Unlike American sources, there are no standard Chinese selection tools such as *Choice, American Reference Books Annual, Library Journal*, or the *Journal of Asian Studies* to facilitate the selection of Chinese materials. Selectors often rely on dealers' catalogs (some of which have brief annotations), linguistic expertise and subject knowledge of individuals, book reviews in selected journals or newspapers (most of which are not indexed), and publishers' advertisements. Occasionally, personal relations with dealers will bring information on items that are not intended for wide circulation. The following are selected sources for acquiring Chinese materials from China, Hong Kong, and Taiwan.

1. *Zhongguo tu shu zai ban bian mu kuai bao* [Weekly Bulletin of China's CIP]–Published weekly on Fridays by the PRC's Information Center of the General Administration of Press & Publication since late 1998, this is at present the most comprehensive and authoritative selection tool for Chinese publications. It features nearly 2,000 new book publication announcements each week collected from publishers all over China, providing the most recent, timely, and complete publication information. Entries are arranged by broad subjects; titles within each subject contain standard cataloging in publication data, including ISBN number, subjects, and price. Some of the entries are also annotated. The disadvantage of this tool is that selectors will not know the exact publication dates of particular books and could easily encumber their collection funds but not receive the books for some time. It would be advisable always to monitor pre-publication orders carefully so that the budget will not be overly committed, or to use this bulletin and work with vendors when placing orders. In addition to the printed version, the Weekly Bulletin is also available in CD-ROM format, and on a monthly basis as CIP Machine Readable Catalog at the annual subscription rate of RMBY3,880 or US$470. The domestic price for the printed version is RMBY364 a year, postage included.

2. *She ko xin shu mu* [New Catalog for the Humanities and Social Sciences]–This is probably one of the most popular selection tools for Chinese materials published by the Xinhua shu mu bao she, Beijing. It is published three times a month on books in the humanities and social sciences, with standard bibliographic information, ISBN, academic level, price, and annotations. Entries are arranged by subjects. Most of the titles are pre-publication announcements with anticipated dates of publication. The orders will be filled only when the books are actually published. As with the first source listed above, funds may be encumbered and orders not received due to publications being delayed or, if the publishers receive too few pre-publication orders, even being cancelled.

The same precaution given above should apply. On the other hand, it is necessary to place orders immediately after their announcement to ensure receipt of books on high demand, as some publishers produce books based on the number of pre-publication orders received. This catalog is available free of charge from the vendors.

3. *Zhong wen he xin qi kan yao mu zong lan* [A Guide to the Core Journals of China]–Based on bibliometric studies of more than 10,000 PRC journals and published by the Peking University Press, this is the best and most authoritative source for serials selection. It contains 75 ranked listings of core journals covering all fields of study. Each identified core journal includes a standard bibliographic description, a synopsis, and URL address if available. Various dealers also provide their own annual catalog of Chinese newspapers and periodicals for their overseas customers. No annotations are provided in the dealers' catalogs, however.

4. *Quan guo zong shu mu* [National Bibliography]–Published by Zhong hua shu ju annually, this source is authoritative and comprehensive. However, it is often several years behind and hence, not effective for the selection of current publications. It is a valuable resource, however, for retrospective collection development if the items listed are still available.

5. Dealers' catalogs–Dealers' catalogs are heavily used by selectors in their daily work, in particular the catalogs for books in stock. More information about dealers' catalogs is described below under Vendors.

6. Electronic resources and other non-print materials–From the earlier CD-ROM products to the web-based databases, China has steadily overcome obstacles in developing and producing non-roman electronic resources to meet the needs of its domestic users and the overseas market. In order to attract and service North American users, China realizes that an authorized agent in the U.S. would facilitate the promotion of its products and deal with complicated licensing issues, purchases by consortia, and services. One such agent is East View Publications of Minneapolis, which is authorized to market the China Academic Journal Database in the U.S. Chinese vendors normally handle other forms of non-print materials as they do printed materials.

VENDORS

1. People's Republic of China–Most Chinese vendors such as the aforementioned CIBTC, CNPITC, and CNPIEC have issued monthly or bi-monthly catalogs, which are sent to their overseas customers in print and/or online on a regular basis. These catalogs are generally divided into three types: catalogs for books in stock (xian huo), catalogs for new books (xin shu), and special catalogs. Selection and acquisition from the in stock catalogs, which contain basic bibliographic information and

pricing with no annotations, would most likely ensure receipt of books ordered in a relatively reasonable amount of time. Ordering from catalogs of new books, which usually have more information on the titles and include annotations, depends on the books actually being available. It may take a longer time to receive the items ordered. The special catalog is normally subject or format based, and is issued irregularly. Printed catalogs typically contain more information than their online counterparts. Excellent services, speedy delivery of books, and competitive prices often determine with whom the library will do business.

Aside from the "big three," numerous vendors are eager to do business with U.S. libraries. Chinese bibliographers routinely receive catalogs or announcements from such vendors as the Chinese Corporation for Promotion of Humanities, Chinese Academy of Social Sciences (Beijing), China Educational Publications Import & Export Corporation (Beijing), and Shanghai Book Traders (Shanghai), or from regional companies such as Jiangsu New Trade Import & Export Corporation (Nanjing), and Sichuan Publishing Industry Trade Corporation (Chengdu).

2. Hong Kong–Hong Kong publishers and vendors played important roles prior to the opening of the PRC in offering overseas libraries selected titles from China. Even after direct purchase became available in the late 1970s, some overseas libraries continued to rely on Hong Kong publishers for the acquisition of Chinese materials. Hong Kong vendors supply books from China, Hong Kong, and Taiwan; some view this as a one-stop shop for Chinese materials, particularly for libraries with small Chinese collections and limited funds for new acquisitions. A survey of Chinese vendors conducted in 2001 also indicated a higher degree of satisfaction with vendors in Hong Kong, citing their good communication skills, accurate and efficient services, good selections, and faster delivery of orders placed.[5] Among the popular vendors used in the U.S. are: Chinese University Press, Chiao Liu, Commercial Press, Far East, Hsing Kuang, Joint, Man's, and Universal. However, for medium and large Chinese collections it would be wise to purchase directly from PRC sources, as they offer wider coverage and more titles for selection.

3. Taiwan–Vendors in Taiwan normally sell books published locally although occasionally titles published in the PRC and Hong Kong also appear in their catalogs. Like their counterparts in China and Hong Kong, vendors in Taiwan also supply their catalogs in print and/or online to their regular overseas customers. Online purchase has become popular as it shortens the times between ordering and receiving. In general, vendors in Taiwan do not charge more than the published prices; oftentimes discounts are offered. Among the vendors used by U.S. libraries are: Cheng Wen, China Post, Lexis, Linking, San Min, Shin Wen Feng, Student, and Sun Crown. Nonetheless, reliable vendors in Taiwan that are willing to handle serial subscriptions are yet to be found.

4. U.S.–During the last decade, many companies in the U.S. also began importing books from China, Hong Kong, and Taiwan and selling them to academic and public libraries across the country. These companies also supply their own catalogs, printed or online, to libraries upon request. These catalogs normally contain very basic information with no annotations. Book prices are noticeably higher but services are generally good, as communications are much easier in the States. Problems arise, however, when the items ordered are not in stock and the vendors have to order them from their original sources in China, Hong Kong, or Taiwan. These U.S. establishments include China Books and Periodicals, China Classics, China Publications Services, Evergreen, Paragon, Service Center for Chinese Publications, and Tsai Fong.

METHODS OF ACQUISITIONS

Firm orders are a preferred method of acquisitions of Chinese materials by almost all academic libraries in North America. Blanket orders are currently used by only three or four libraries and in conjunction with the firm orders method. Exchanges are popular but problems of not receiving and not being able to claim are of major concern. Unlike the past practice where many exchange partners in China or Taiwan unconditionally sent materials to U.S. academic libraries, it is now a common practice for exchange partners to demand balanced exchanges as budget constraints become more apparent everywhere. One other aspect of acquiring Chinese materials that has been very important to selectors, and one should not ignore its effectiveness, is the acquisitions trip to China. One can select books first hand on the spot, which differs greatly from selecting from a catalog, especially an unannotated one. One can also build personal relations with vendors that prove to be extremely valuable in the procurement of Chinese materials.

PROBLEMS IN ACQUIRING CHINESE MATERIALS

In March 2001, a report on the performance of Chinese vendors was delivered at the Committee on Chinese Materials, Council on East Asian Libraries (CEAL) annual meeting in Chicago. This report identified several problems in selecting and acquiring Chinese materials from China, Hong Kong, and Taiwan. It is ironic that some of the known problems mentioned in the Wong article in 1983 persist. Following are some of the more prominent shortcomings:

1. Bibliographic control–This has remained a continuing challenge for Chinese bibliographers in the U.S. China's national bibliography, *Quan guo zong shu mu*, has been behind, making it less effective as a selection tool for current publications and frustrating many librarians. However, because of its comprehensiveness, it would serve well as a means for retrospective acquisition of materials.
2. Accuracy of dealers' catalogs–Providing standardized catalog entries and accurate information are extremely important to selectors. Some dealers' catalogs are inconsistent. For example, some entries are entered as series titles followed by individual titles while others are entered directly under the individual titles, creating confusion and possibly duplicate orders.
3. Communication and customer service–Overall, the communications between North American selectors and Chinese dealers have improved significantly over the years. From Internet access to dealers' catalogs to placing orders online, communications are more direct and speedy. However, selectors have complained about some dealers' slowness in response to their claims, inquiries, rush orders, or filling orders. Further improvement in these areas is critical, or selectors may find other more responsive and reliable dealers.
4. Standing orders–Standing orders are difficult for libraries to monitor. Unfortunately, Chinese vendors do not handle standing orders very well. As such, some titles may be incomplete until users or bibliographers discover missing volumes by chance. Building a system to help selectors maintain standing orders should top all dealers' priorities in the future.
5. Low percentage of fulfillment rate–This has been identified as one of the problems in the survey of Chinese vendors mentioned earlier, as most vendors keep only a limited inventory. Even titles listed in their catalogs as in stock often are not in stock. Consequently, it takes much longer time to fill orders. Selectors also find it more difficult to buy older books from all vendors.

WTO AND CHINA'S PUBLISHING GROUPS

Since December 2001, both China and Taiwan have become members of the World Trade Organization (WTO). Its impact on the Chinese publishing industry and its effects on the overseas book market are yet to be determined. It is clear, however, that China's accession to the WTO will have positive impacts on its economy and its overseas market in the long run. In fact, China has been preparing for over a decade prior to its official membership in the WTO.[6]

In late 1988, the first publishing group in China, the Regional Literary Publishing and Distribution Group, was created. It consisted of eleven literary publishing houses and by 1989 had expanded to include fifteen publishing houses.

In mid-1989, Eastern Provincial Xinhua Bookstore Distribution Group was established in six eastern provinces and one major city. The publishers in these two groups are generally widespread geographically and are endorsed by the publishers, not the government.

Between 1991 and 1995, more regulated publishing groups were formed under the guidance of the local government to systematically organize large-scale conglomerates. Among the major groups established during this period are: Shangdong Publishing Group, Sichuan Publishing Group, and Jiangxi Publishing Group.

Since 1996 more publishing groups have been formed and supported by the Chinese Central Government. Included in this group are: Shanghai Centennial Publishing Group, Guangdong Provincial Publishing Group, Liaoning Publishing Group, China Science Publishing Group, and Beijing Publishing House Group. The latest addition is the China Publishing Group, a large-scale national publishing institution, launched at a time when China had been accepted as a member of the WTO, in order to accelerate the development of the publishing industry. The group consists of nine large publishing houses and three publications wholesalers,[7] including CNPITC and CNPIEC discussed in this article.

Although it is not yet clear how these large-scale publishing groups will impact the overseas book market, it is worth noticing that they will likely monopolize the publishing industry and book market, very much as large organizations do in the U.S. However, it is unlikely that there will be dramatic changes in the immediate future for overseas customers such as academic libraries in North America. In the meantime, the establishment of large-scale publishing groups probably means that with more consolidated capital and resources, overseas customers will likely enjoy receiving orders more quickly and with higher fulfillment rates. Whether the prices will become even more competitive as a result remains to be seen.

CONCLUSION

Accessing and acquiring Chinese materials have improved slowly but steadily over the last two decades. In recent years, the advancement of technology has brought Chinese vendors and North American customers closer together in dealing with problems that may have arisen during the selection and acquisition process. Through e-mail and Internet access the timing for communication, ordering materials, and solving problems has been reduced considerably. The changing landscape of the Chinese publishing and exporting industry in response to its accession to the WTO should also bring improved services to overseas customers. At present, direct contact and purchase from China, Hong Kong, and Taiwan should prove to be beneficial to selectors in academic libraries in North America.

REFERENCES

1. *Zhong hua ren min gong he guo nian jian* [People's Republic of China Yearbook]. (2001). (p. 913). Beijing: Zhong hua ren min gong he guo nian jian she.
2. *Zhong hua min guo tong ji nian jian* [Statistical Yearbook of the Republic of China]. (2001). (p. 98). Taibei: Xing zheng yuan zhu ji chu.
3. Wong, W. S. (1983). Acquiring library materials from the People's Republic of China. *Library Acquisitions: Practice & Theory*, 7, 47-57.
4. Ibid.
5. Wei, K. T. (2001, March). *Chinese vendors: A preliminary survey of their services to East Asian libraries in North America*. A paper presented at the annual meeting of the Committee on Chinese Materials, Council of East Asian Libraries, Association for Asian Studies annual meeting, Chicago, IL.
6. Yu, M. (Ed.). (2001). *Chu ban ji tuan yan jiu* (pp. 6-28). Beijing: Zhongguo shu ji chu ban she.
7. The nine publishing houses are: the People's Publishing House, the People's Literature Publishing House, the Commercial Press, Zhonghua Book Company, Encyclopedia of China Publishing House, China Fine Arts Publishing Group, People's Music Publishing House, SDX Joint Publishing Company, and China Translation and Publishing Corporation. The three publications wholesalers are: Xinhua Bookstore Head Office, China National Publishing Industry Trading Corporation (CNPITC) and China National Publications Import & Export (Group) Corporation (CNPIEC).

BIBLIOGRAPHY

Bishop, E, Chan, Y. S. & Miller, W. G. (1982). Recent Australian Experience with China and Southeast Asia. *Library Acquisitions: Practice & Theory*, 6, 149-160.
Chan, C. R. (1990). U.S. Acquisitions of Chinese-Language Materials. *Journal of Library and Information Science*, 16, 43-47.
Dai, L. J., Zhang, Q. S., & Cai, J. H. (Eds.). (2000). *Zhong wen he xin qi kan yao mu zong lan* [A Guide to the Core Journals of China]. (3rd ed.). Beijing: Peking University Press.
Hahn, T. H. (1997). A Short Note on Current Chinese Online Bookdealers. *Journal of East Asian Libraries*, 113, 26-32.
Kilton, T. D. (1999). Selecting and Acquiring Materials from Abroad. In K. A. Schmidt (Ed.), *Understanding the Business of Library Acquisitions* (pp. 100-142). (2nd ed.). Chicago: American Library Association.
Li, H. C. (1995). The Will to Serve: Chinese Booksellers in Hong Kong. *Committee on East Asian Libraries Bulletin*, 106, 39-44.
Lo, K. (1990). East Asia. In C. Johns (Ed.), *Selection of Library Materials for Area Studies. Part I. Asia, Iberia, the Caribbean, and Latin America, Eastern Europe and the Soviet Union, and the South Pacific* (pp. 10-35). Chicago: American Library Association.
Tao, H., Zuang, Z. & Cole, C. (1989). How to Acquire Chinese Materials from the People's Republic of China: An Easy Way to Solve the Mystery. *Library Acquisitions: Practice & Theory*, 13, 11-31.

Wong, W. S. (1983). Acquiring Library Materials from the People's Republic of China. *Library Acquisitions: Practice & Theory*, 7, 47-57.

Zhong hua min guo chu ban nian jian [Publications Yearbook of the Republic of China]. (2000). Taibei: Xing zheng yuan xin wen ju.

Zhong hua min guo tong ji nian jian [Statistical Yearbook of the Republic of China]. (2001). Taibei: Xing zheng yuan zhu ji chu.

Zhong hua ren min gong he guo nian jian [People's Republic of China Yearbook]. (2001). Beijing: Zhong hua ren min gong he guo nian jian she.

Zhongguo chu ban nian jian [China Publications Yearbook]. (1999). Beijing: Zhongguo chu ban nian jian she.

Zhou, P. (1996). Acquisitions of Hard-to-Find Backfiles of Chinese Periodicals from the People's Republic of China. *Library Resources & Technical Services*, 40, 62-65.

Yu, M. (Ed.). (2001). *Chu ban ji tuan yan jiu* [Study of the Publishing Groups]. Beijing: Zhongguo shu ji chu ban she.

Yu, M. (Ed.). (2001). *Jia ru WTO yu Zhongguo chu ban ye fa zhan* [Joining WTO and the Development of Chinese Publishing Industry]. Beijing: Zhongguo shu ji chu ban she.

Routes to Roots:
Acquiring Genealogical
and Local History Materials
in a Large Canadian Public Library

Arthur G. W. McClelland

SUMMARY. Using the London Room of the London Public Library in London, Ontario, Canada, as an example, this article will examine the nature of local collections, the sources and methods of acquiring genealogical and local history materials and the constraints related to such

Arthur G. W. McClelland is London Room Librarian, London Public Library, 251 Dundas Street, London, Ontario, Canada N6A 6H9 (E-mail: arthur.mcclelland@lpl london.on.ca).

Arthur G. W. McClelland is a fifth-generation Canadian whose roots have been traced back to Market Hill, Northern Ireland and Glasgow, Scotland. Mr. McClelland, who holds an Honours B.A. in Classical Civilization and Linguistics, received his Masters in Library Science from the University of Western Ontario in London, Ontario in 1984 and has been a librarian at the London Public Library since 1988. He cultivated his interest in local history while attending high school in Norwich, Ontario, which was settled in 1810 by Quakers from Dutchess County, New York. Mr. McClelland has been the London Room librarian since 1998 and is currently researching the history of Norwich Township churches which he hopes to publish in 2010 for Norwich's bicentennial.

[Haworth co-indexing entry note]: "Routes to Roots: Acquiring Genealogical and Local History Materials in a Large Canadian Public Library." McClelland, Arthur G. W. Co-published simultaneously in *The Acquisitions Librarian* (The Haworth Information Press, an imprint of The Haworth Press, Inc.) No. 31/32, 2004, pp. 67-76; and: *Selecting Materials for Library Collections* (ed: Audrey Fenner) The Haworth Information Press, an imprint of The Haworth Press, Inc., 2004, pp. 67-76. Single or multiple copies of this article are available for a fee from The Haworth Document Delivery Service [1-800-HAWORTH, 9:00 a.m. - 5:00 p.m. (EST). E-mail address: docdelivery@haworthpress.com].

10.1300/J101v16n31_06

acquisitions. This article will also present a brief history of the London Room and show how acquisition practices have changed over the passage of time. *[Article copies available for a fee from The Haworth Document Delivery Service: 1-800-HAWORTH. E-mail address: <docdelivery@haworthpress.com> Website: <http://www.HaworthPress.com> © 2004 by The Haworth Press, Inc. All rights reserved.]*

KEYWORDS. Genealogy, local history, London Public Library, London Room

INTRODUCTION

I'd like to begin with a quotation which has been in the past and sometimes still is representative of some people's views on genealogy and local history:

> I did not realize that the old grave that stood among the brambles at the foot of our farm was history. (excerpted from "The Place of History in Canadian Education," a paper given by Canadian humourist, Stephen R. Leacock (1869-1944) at the 1925 annual meeting of the Canadian Historical Association)

This quotation also highlights one of the other issues respecting local collections–that of public education. The librarian is constantly trying to convince private individuals that their local materials are worth preserving for future generations.

HISTORICAL BACKGROUND TO THE LONDON ROOM

Fred Landon (1880-1969), chief librarian of London Public Library (1916-1923) and the first full-time librarian at the University of Western Ontario (1923-1950), was one of the first librarians in Canada to suggest that public institutions such as libraries play an active role in acquiring and preserving local materials. In a 1917 *Ontario Library Review* article, Mr. Landon advocated the preservation of local records in libraries. Following his advice, the London Public Library began to collect historical material about London and Londoners. This Londoniana collection was eventually housed in a room next to the bindery in the basement under the front steps of the Central Library.

During the 1940s and 1950s, Miss Eleanor Shaw, head of the Reference Room, chose the books of London authors for the out-of-print Canadiana collection housed in the Humanities Department on the first floor of the west wing of the Central Library. The original concept for a London Room came from former Chief Librarian Charles Deane Kent (1961-1973) whose interest in developing an easily accessible local history collection began about 1965 when plans for an addition to the Central Library were being investigated. Mr. Kent instructed Miss Elizabeth Spicer, who later became the first London Room librarian, to undertake a detailed survey of local history materials so as "to build the best collection in the world on London, Ontario." In 1967 the London authors collection and the Londoniana collection formed the nucleus of the London Room which was officially opened on July 31st at 1:00 p.m. in a room next to the Humanities Department. It was furnished by the Rotary Club to mark the 50th anniversary (1915-1965) of its existence in London. Following the departure of the Art Gallery in 1980, the second floor was renovated enabling library services to move into the space, including expanded facilities for the London Room. The former London Room on the first floor was converted into a staff workroom. On August 25th, 2002, the London Room was open for the public at its new quarters on the third floor of the new Central Library at 251 Dundas Street, London, Ontario. The London Public Library now has 15 branches serving a large urban area with a population of almost 400,000 inhabitants.

HISTORICAL BACKGROUND TO LOCAL HISTORY ACQUISITIONS

Since Canada was one of the last Western countries to establish a national library in 1953, it was left up to large libraries such as London Public Library to acquire Canadian materials and make them readily available to the public. Consequently in its early period of local material acquisitions, the London Public Library acquired many items of a broader scope–provincial and national. As well, during this early period, there was a scarcity of local publications until the 1960s when, in anticipation of celebrating Canada's centennial as a nation in 1967, many localities began to publish their own histories.

The number of local histories being published has accelerated exponentially, especially in the last decade due to the increased number of municipal amalgamations. For example, in Middlesex County of which London is the seat, three townships to the north of London–Delaware, Lobo and London– were amalgamated on January 1st, 1998 to form the new municipality of Middlesex Centre. In order to preserve its history, London Township published two volumes in 2001 entitled, *London Township A Rich Heritage, 1796-1997* and *London Township: Families Past and Present*. This two-volume history is now representative of the type of local history being published. Recognizing the increased interest in genealogy, local communities are now publishing their histories in which half of the book usually contains the history of township families. This has not always been the case.

HISTORICAL BACKGROUND TO GENEALOGICAL ACQUISITIONS

Even twenty years ago, most libraries viewed genealogists as outside their realms of interest. They were, at best, people with narrow interests whom libraries served only as a fringe of society; some librarians regarded genealogists as cranks. There are still those who do. However, genealogy is now one of the most popular hobbies in North America and every public library will now feel some obligation to provide services to genealogists. Some will have money to dedicate considerable sections of their space for family history research; small ones will be confined to a shelf of reference materials. (*Routes to Roots: A Collection of 'Tracing your Roots' Columns from the Kitchener-Waterloo Record, 1993-1997* by Ryan Taylor. 1997. p. 7)

One may ask why genealogy is now so popular? I believe the popularity can be attributed to a number of factors. With increasing globalization and the breakdown of the nuclear family, many baby boomers are seeking a sense of community and stability in their present situation by exploring their past. The Internet has fueled this interest in genealogy by making readily available an immense amount of genealogical information. "With only minimal coaching, people are flocking to Web sites such as the Mormons' new www.Familysearch. org or www.RootsWeb.com to transport themselves back in time. Genealogy has become second to pornography as the most popular use of the World Wide Web, with two million sites and counting. When the Church of Jesus Christ of Latter-Day Saints, the Mormons, set up their free Internet site in May, it received a staggering 30 million electronic hits its first day of operation" (*Maclean's*, September 20, 1999, pp. 42-43). Many genealogists visit the public library in the area where their ancestors lived, hoping to increase their knowledge about their family by conducting research in the library's local history area. By its very definition, local history often includes genealogy since the history of a particular family usually includes the role that family played in the community in which they lived.

LONDON ROOM COLLECTION PROFILE

What types of materials are found in a local collection? The London Room is a research facility for genealogy and local history, housing a wealth of primary and secondary source materials on a specific geographic area to which I have given the acronym, LEMON, as an mnemonic. LEMON stands for the city of London and the counties of Elgin, Middlesex, Oxford and Norfolk which were originally an administrative area known as the London District. The London Room collection has a primary emphasis on the city of London and a secondary emphasis on the county of Middlesex. The primary materials include audio cassettes, charts, compact discs, diaries, documents and papers of local organizations, films, journals, land records, letters, manuscripts, maps, municipal documents, photographs, prints, realia, scrapbooks on famous local people such as Sir Frederick Banting (London surgeon who conceived the idea of using insulin to battle diabetes), Sir Adam Beck (former mayor of London and first chairman of the Ontario Hydro-Electric Power Commission, 1906-1925) and the Donnellys (Irish family involved in long-standing feud and whose six members were brutally murdered by a vigilante group on February 4, 1880), sound recordings, videos and vital statistics; secondary sources include atlases, biographies, books, cemetery records, census records, city directories, ephemera, genealogies, magazines, newspapers on microfilm, novels, pamphlets, programmes, reports, school yearbooks, surveys, telephone directories and vertical files of newspaper clippings. The London Room also has some very specialized collections such as the A-series (fiction written by local authors and non-fiction–not about the LEMON area but written by local authors), the P-series (books with a local imprint) and the Seaborn Collection compiled by Dr. Edwin Seaborn (1872-1951) and consisting of 56 volumes which include clippings, diaries, histories and reminiscences, mostly of a medical nature. Most public libraries will acquire local materials on the geographic area they serve. These materials will usually include the local newspaper, scrapbooks of local events, histories of the community and its organizations, works by local authors.

METHODS OF ACQUIRING LOCAL MATERIALS

How does one acquire materials for a local collection? One must keep in mind the users of their collections when acquiring local materials. Of the users of the London Room, 90% are genealogists and high school students working on local history assignments; 10% are architects, lawyers, local historians, researchers, etc. Previously 90% of the collection was local history and 10% was genealogical but this is rapidly changing because of the explosive increase of the interest in genealogy. By their very nature, published local materials are usually advertised locally through book fairs such as Norfolklore held every September in Simcoe, Ontario and through community magazines and newspapers (such as the *East Side Story* and the *North London Beacon*) and genealogical newsletters such as *London Leaf* to a very specific audience and have a small print run. Consequently most of these titles do not appear in the well-known resources such as *Booklist, Choice, Library Journal* and *Publishers' Weekly*, although a few local titles appear under the headings of Genealogy and History (Canada) in the *Forthcoming Books* supplement to the Canadian publishing industry's journal, *Quill and Quire*. Some local materials are also advertised in special Canadiana catalogues such as those published by the Alexander Gallery, Ask Alice Books and Bookfinder as well as used and rare bookstores such as Attic Books in London. Some specialized bibliographies have been published which will list various local resources–e.g., *Selected Genealogical and Historical Resources for London and Middlesex County* by Alastair Neely, former genealogy librarian at the Central Library and now head of the Westmount Branch of the London Public Library. I would also recommend the following two published works for local resources:

Genealogy–*Genealogy in Ontario: Searching the Records* by Brenda Dougall Merriman.

> This book approaches genealogy from a layman's point of view and is excellent in telling the reader what records are available and where to find them.

Local history–*Local Histories of Ontario Municipalities: A Bibliography* by Barbara B. Aitken.

> This title has been published in three installments–1951-1977; 1977-1987; 1987-1997 and continues a preceding title, *Canadian Local Histories to 1950: A Bibliography*. Vol. III–*Ontario and the Canadian North* by William F. E. Morley.

All these volumes give complete bibliographic details about the local histories as well as library locations where the titles can be found.

ACCESS TO AND STORAGE OF LOCAL MATERIALS

One must also keep in mind the extent to which you will allow public access to materials as this has an impact on how you store local materials. In the London Room, use of the local archival material is as unrestricted as physical condition will allow: some materials are fragile or unique; others are irreplaceable and rare and could be destroyed by excessive handling. Digitization would be an excellent means of providing access to these fragile materials. The Federal Government of Canada has a number of digitizing initiatives including the National Library of Canada's Inventory of Digital Initiatives–www.nlc-bnc.ca/initiatives/erella.htm (e.g., Toronto Public Library's work on digitizing its city directories). These resources require special care, processing and conservation and are therefore stored in a secure climate-controlled area to limit unnecessary handling. The London Room collection does not circulate and access is limited to library staff only. Materials are retrieved by staff upon request for use within the London Room. One must also build into one's acquisition budget the repair and replacement of both books and microfilm.

RELATIONSHIPS TO COMMUNITY GROUPS

It also has been extremely important to cultivate relationships with local organizations such as London and Middlesex County Branch of the Ontario Genealogical Society, London and Middlesex Historical Society and the London Region Branch of the Architectural Conservancy of Ontario. It is often through these relationships that one learns of the availability of local materials. The librarian in charge of local collections cultivates such relationships by advertising the events of the organization in the library, attending the meetings of the organization, giving library tours to the members of the organizations, offering to be a speaker at their meetings or volunteering at their community functions such as genealogy fairs and heritage days. Some of these community groups are quite active in preserving local records through publishing their research. Often, because of the good relationships maintained between these groups and the library, copies of their published works are donated to the local collection at the public library. For example, the London Region Branch of the Architectural Conservancy of Ontario publishes a tour booklet for their Geranium Walk (through architecturally significant buildings) held the first Sunday in June and they donate two copies to the London Room. The London and Middlesex Historical Society annually publishes a historical calendar of events from 100 years ago and the London Room receives two free copies. In fact, donations are extremely important to local collections since they constitute a significant avenue by which valuable material is obtained.

Most communities have genealogical, heritage and historical organizations in which the librarian can become involved and this involvement often results in reciprocal benefits for both parties–the organization becomes more aware of what the library has to offer and the librarian can offer his or her expertise to the organization.

The most active group is the Ontario Genealogical Society (OGS) whose members volunteer their time to transcribe the inscriptions from gravestones and then compile personal name indexes to the cemeteries. The London Room has these cemetery indexes for the eight counties surrounding London–Elgin, Huron, Kent, Lambton, Middlesex, Norfolk, Oxford and Perth. These same volunteers have also compiled personal name indexes to the nominal censuses taken by the government every ten years from 1851 onwards. Because of privacy legislation, the nominal census is released years after it has been taken and consequently only the censuses from 1851 to 1901 have been released. The OGS volunteers have also indexed the births, marriages and deaths from many local newspapers. Most branches of the Ontario Genealogical Society have websites on which they advertise their publications, usually highlighting the newer ones. Checking these websites is an efficient way of discovering what has been published.

It is also very important to develop and maintain healthy relationships with various departments of the local municipal government, especially the engineering and planning departments since they generate many local reports and studies. Often these draft reports and studies require public input and thus are deposited in the London Room for public examination. When the final reports and studies are released, the London Room usually receives a copy. Municipal records also include land registry records. Recently the Ontario Government microfilmed all their land registry records and as a cost-cutting measure, decided not to retain these older land records, some dating back to the 1860s. The local land registry offices, where these records had been stored, are administered by the provincial government. They were asked to find new homes for the records, preferably in the local community. Consequently, the London Room was approached by the Middlesex County Land Registry and asked if the land records could be transferred to the London Room. This transfer will occur in the Spring of 2003.

PRESERVATION OF LOCAL MATERIALS

Part of the cost of acquiring local materials involves rebinding or re-formatting high-demand materials in order to preserve them by reducing the handling of the originals. Thus the London Room has on microfilm the London city directories from 1856 to 1980; the *London Advertiser* from 1864-1936; the *London Free Press* from 1849 to the present; the London telephone books from 1883 to 1980 and most of the scrapbooks of newspaper clippings. This microfilming also has other budgetary implications–i.e., it needs special storage cabinets and special machines for reading/printing as well as a dimly-lit area for viewing. Because of heavy usage the London Room also rebinds many genealogical items such as census indexes, marriage register indexes and newspaper indexes. Other local materials such as maps and photographs also require special storage cabinets, folders and sleeves. London Room staff have encapsulated certain popular maps and photographs in acid-free plastic to facilitate their handling. Other materials such as beta videos, reel-to-reel films and slides require special equipment to view the material.

In its archival collection, the London Room also retains the records of the London Mechanics' Institute, the predecessor to the London Public Library from 1841 to 1895 as well as records for the public library from 1895 to the present. These records include annual reports, board minutes and committee and financial records.

INDEXES TO LOCAL MATERIALS

To improve public access to non-indexed materials, London Room staff have compiled indexes such as Analytics to Books, Buildings and Places and Landmarks Index, Business Clippings Index, Photograph Index, Scrapbooks Index and Where to Look File. At present these indexes are maintained on cards housed in a card catalogue from the 1940 Central Library. These indexes especially the Buildings, Places and Landmarks Index, would be an ideal candidate for a digitalization project and mounting on the library's website. A great example of such a project is the Architectural Index for Ontario (Archindont) which can be found on the Toronto Public Library's website at http://indexes.tpl.toronto.on.ca/archindont/index.asp

The following materials are not acquired by the London Room: artifacts, children's works, municipal by-laws, original copies of newspapers (exceptions are made for special editions), framed photographs, school textbooks and wall maps. Very little de-acquisitioning occurs with local materials. Any weeded genealogical materials are offered to the London and Middlesex County branch of the Ontario Genealogical Society and weeded local historical materials are either offered to other archives or to Attic Books for credit.

CONCLUSION

Although this article has concentrated on local materials in a large library, many of the practices and procedures are applicable to any public library. Local materials are the most valuable part of a library's collection because they are so rare, unique and often irreplaceable. Acquiring local materials will attract visitors to your library, whether they be genealogists intent on finding the missing link in their family tree or the student who has to complete a project on some well-known local figure. Most local collections are dependent on donations as a means of increasing their holdings. Thus, networking with community groups, genealogists and local historians and researchers is crucial and must be continuous since history is always happening. The Canadian humorist, Don Harron, through his character, Charlie Farquharson, has said, "Histry is somethin' you can't never finish, so you might jist as well git it started at the beginnin' " (*Charlie Farquharson's Histry of Canada* by Don Harron. 1972, p. 3). The most permanent legacy of a local collection is the preservation of the unique materials related to a local community for future generations.

Building a Dental Sciences Collection in a General Academic Library

Eva Stowers
Gillian Galbraith

SUMMARY. This article discusses the web and print resources used in selecting material for a dental sciences collection in an academic library at a public university without a medical library. The process of creating a collection quickly and with limited resources is described, from the initial collection assessment to the decision-making processes involved in actual selection. *[Article copies available for a fee from The Haworth Document Delivery Service: 1-800-HAWORTH. E-mail address: <docdelivery@haworthpress.com> Website: <http://www.HaworthPress.com> © 2004 by The Haworth Press, Inc. All rights reserved.]*

KEYWORDS. Collection development, dental science, academic libraries

BACKGROUND

The University of Nevada, Las Vegas (UNLV) was founded in 1957 as a regional division of the University of Nevada (Reno). It gained autonomy in

Eva Stowers is Health Sciences Subject Librarian, Lied Library, University of Nevada, Las Vegas, 4505 Maryland Parkway, Las Vegas, NV 89154-7014 (E-mail: estowers@ccmail.nevada.edu). Gillian Galbraith is Chair of Integrated Biosciences, School of Dentistry, University of Nevada, Las Vegas, 4505 Maryland Parkway, Las Vegas, NV 89154-3055.

[Haworth co-indexing entry note]: "Building a Dental Sciences Collection in a General Academic Library." Stowers, Eva, and Gillian Galbraith. Co-published simultaneously in *The Acquisitions Librarian* (The Haworth Information Press, an imprint of The Haworth Press, Inc.) No. 31/32, 2004, pp. 77-88; and: *Selecting Materials for Library Collections* (ed: Audrey Fenner) The Haworth Information Press, an imprint of The Haworth Press, Inc., 2004, pp. 77-88. Single or multiple copies of this article are available for a fee from The Haworth Document Delivery Service [1-800-HAWORTH, 9:00 a.m. - 5:00 p.m. (EST). E-mail address: docdelivery@haworthpress.com].

10.1300/J101v16n31_07

1968 and in the succeeding 34 years has grown at a phenomenal rate, as has the population of the Las Vegas valley. UNLV's Fall 2002 FTE enrollment was 17,777. The University offers 92 undergraduate degrees and 94 graduate degrees (including 24 at the doctoral level). In 1998 it opened its first professional school, the Boyd School of Law.

UNLV was for many years primarily an undergraduate institution. It recently attained the "Doctoral/Research University–Intensive" status as defined by the Carnegie Foundation for the Advancement of Teaching (Carnegie Foundation, 2000). The University's master plan includes an emphasis on research in the biomedical sciences. In conjunction with that plan eleven research "macrothemes" have been identified. Number nine is "Biomedical and Health Sciences/Biotechnology" as defined below:

> Biomedical and Health Sciences/Biotechnology provides a broad array of research and creative activity into understanding the causes, treatments, and cures of human diseases as well as development of strategies promoting and maintaining human health. Examples of current research and creative activity include mechanisms underlying the development and treatment of cancer; applications of biotechnology to forensic science; innovations in prosthesis design, forensic dentistry, and mobile testing of student oral health; environmental toxicology and health; and environmental health promotion. (University of Nevada, Las Vegas, 2002)

In 1998 the Board of Regents voted to ask the Nevada State Legislature to set aside $12 million to build a dental school at UNLV (Patton, 1998). The legislature did approve the dental school in the final days of the 1999 legislative session, but did not fund the school at the requested amount. The only funding the University Libraries received in support of the dental school was a one-time allocation from the Provost in the amount of $100,000. This funding was received in 2000, and was designated for the purchase of materials in dentistry and pharmacy. Preliminary planning for the dental school began at the library level in 1998 and went into an intense mode in 2000. The first class of 76 dental students matriculated in the fall of 2002.

The University Libraries include Lied Library (the main library) and three branches (Architecture, Curriculum Materials, and Music). The University Libraries own 916,838 books and subscribe to 5,825 print journals (plus 1,351 in online-only packages from publishers such as Blackwell Science, Kluwer, Lippincott, Williams & Wilkins, and Wiley). The Boyd School of Law also has a library, which is not part of the University Libraries' administrative structure.

PROBLEM

The only medical school in Nevada is located at the University of Nevada in Reno (UNR), 341 miles away. The nearest dental school is at the University of Southern California, 231 miles away. UNLV does not have a medical library and had, in fact, made a conscious decision long ago not to collect in the area of medicine. The only health material that had traditionally been collected supported the nursing science and allied health programs. Medical books that were in the collection were largely outdated. Medical journals were limited to a few core titles such as *JAMA* and *The New England Journal of Medicine*.

It was decided that the dental science collection would be incorporated within a general academic library unfamiliar with the special needs of dental students and faculty. There are no plans for a physical branch library, although a task force is investigating the creation of a "virtual branch library."

Traditionally, dental schools are located within health science complexes and have access to their resources. However, the UNLV School of Dentistry, in a departure from this norm, is located for its first two years on the university campus. In 2004 it will relocate to a building near a large hospital, University Medical Center (UMC), which is affiliated with the Medical School at UNR. Library resources at UMC are limited, and do not include dental science resources. The Savitt Medical Library at UNR, which provides support to UNR's medical students doing their residencies in Las Vegas, is not in a position to provide the same services to the students of UNLV.

Compounding these problems is the fact that the University Libraries have been operating under a static budget for the prior seven years. Worse yet, this budget faces major cuts in FY 2002/2003. This situation, combined with serials inflation, had reached a crisis point where the UNLV Libraries had to decide whether to stop purchasing books or reduce its subscriptions. This is a familiar problem in most academic libraries. So, in 1999 and again in 2000 the UNLV Libraries implemented major journal "assessment" projects. Those led to cancellations that had an especially heavy impact on the science departments both because their high-priced and high-inflation journals were targeted and their faculty are heavily reliant on current journal literature for their research needs.

BUILDING A DENTAL COLLECTION

As the library liaison to the dental school, I began by reviewing existing resources to see what the University Libraries already owned in dentistry and relevant medical subject areas. The review was fairly easy to do because there were so few books or journals in those areas in the University Libraries collection. In order to obtain the required data I executed a management report on our Innovative Interfaces Innopac system. In 1998 the library owned only fifty-seven books and media resource items in the Library of Congress call number area for dentistry (RK). Most of those were seriously outdated. Interestingly, the titles that circulated the most frequently were in the Curriculum Materials Library and covered such topics as preparing children for their first visit to the dentist. There are now 380 books and media, a six-fold increase, but still a small number. Library monograph collections in the call number areas QP (Physiology), QR (Microbiology), R (Medicine, General), RA (Public Health), and RC (Internal Medicine) were fair in number but, as predicted, largely outdated. We showed serious deficiencies in the call number areas QM (Human Anatomy), RB (Pathology), and RD (Surgery).

The University Libraries owned no journals in the dental sciences in 1998. By the time the first dental students matriculated in 2002 the library had access to eight online dental journals, seven of which were published by Blackwell Science. The library had managed to increase greatly the number of medical and health science journals available to students and faculty by purchasing (generally in partnership with various consortia) access to a number of publisher packages. This increased access from 351 titles in the call number R (excluding RK) to 693 (again, excluding the dental titles) for a growth of 97.5%. All of the growth came from the online-only packages of: Annual Reviews (4), BioOne (1), Blackwell (133), IEEE (4), Kluwer (90), Lippincott Williams and Wilkins (124), MCB (6), Project Muse (6), and Wiley (74). The total number of health sciences titles in those packages was 442; however, an intervening print journal cancellation project reduced the net gain to 342.

These journals, though useful, were not selected in terms of need for the collection. It remained to select materials based on the specific curricular and research needs of UNLV's dental students and faculty.

COLLECTION DEVELOPMENT PLANNING

In the normal course of events a subject librarian in an academic library works closely with the academic faculty to select library materials in their discipline. In our case we were hampered by the fact that most of the dental school faculty did not arrive on campus until two months before classes began in Fall 2002. Understandably, when they did arrive, libraries were not their top priority.

Faced with building a collection from scratch we did consider purchasing an opening day collection. As we began planning for our new dental school, the dental school at Northwestern University was closing and we speculated about the possibility of purchasing their collection. For a variety of reasons, that turned out not to be an option. We were offered the opportunity to pick up backsets of some journals, but decided that we would not do so because they were in the most cases broken runs of journals to which we would probably not be initially subscribing. What follows are ideas for building a dental science collection quickly and with limited resources.

In the initial stages of planning, it is crucial to review the proposed curriculum. This provides an idea of the program's focus. The curriculum will certainly be available somewhere as a planning document. In our case it was available on the school's web site at least a year before classes began.

Most accrediting agencies address the issue of library resources, some in more detail than others. It is important to review those standards so that the library will be prepared for the accreditation team's site visit. The accrediting agency for dental schools is the Commission on Dental Accreditation of the American Dental Association. According to Standard 2-1: "Residents must be given assignments which require critical review of relevant scientific literature." Standard 4-1, in the section on educational support services, goes on to say: "The sponsoring institution must provide adequate and appropriately maintained facilities and learning resources to support the goals and objectives of the program." In the "intent" paragraph of Standard 4-1 a mention is made that "library resources that include dental resources should be available" (Commission on Dental Accreditation, c2001). These are not, obviously, useful as selection tools but are vital in demonstrating the need to secure funding to support the program. It should be noted that when we began planning there was a somewhat stronger standard in place that addressed libraries in more detail:

> Library: Institution library resources should include a diversified collection of current dental, medical and other pertinent reference books and audiovisual resources. Appropriate current and back issues of major dental and other scientific periodicals and appropriate indexes should be available for students and faculty reference. If these resources are not available within the institution, ready access to these resources must be available to the students. (Commission on Dental Accreditation, 2000)

The particular mission of the school is important to understand. Nevada has a very low dentist per capita ratio and the lack of adequate dental care for its citizens was a motivating force for the Legislature to approve the school. For this reason, the UNLV School of Dentistry has a special focus on public health, and especially on rural health. Although the majority of Nevada's population lives in Las Vegas or Reno, there are many isolated rural towns that are in especial need of readily accessible healthcare.

One of the most difficult aspects of the collection planning was the interdisciplinary nature of dental science. I would recommend reviewing David Tarlow's *Dental Aptitude Test Practice Examinations* (Tarlow, 1999) as well as the school's proposed curriculum in order to learn what other medical and related resources need to be collected to support the program.

PLAN FOR THE FUTURE!

The dental school will be at the remote campus in two years, therefore on-line access to journals will be critical. In addition, during their training students will be located throughout the state in rural areas to serve residents of very small communities. At that time they will have limited access to libraries and will need to rely primarily on their laptop computers for access to medical resources. The UNLV School of Dentistry is very much an online-culture. All of the students were issued a laptop computer during orientation week. Their textbooks are all contained on one DVD created by Vital Source Technologies (http://www.vitalbook.com) of Raleigh, N.C., under contract with the dental school. A copy of the DVD is not in the University Libraries for contractual reasons, but the Libraries worked closely with the School of Dentistry in an effort to ensure that the dental school students would be able to use their own DVD on specified library PCs if necessary. This involved Systems working with Vital Source Technologies to work out technical issues.

The students and faculty use WebCT (http://www.webct.com) extensively. This software is a course management system that is widely used by professors at UNLV to enhance their classes. For the distance education students it is their primary means of interacting with their instructors and their fellow students.

In the following sections I will examine the tools that are available to select library materials for the dental science collection.

JOURNALS

Academic faculty in the biomedical sciences are much more reliant on journals than books. However, because it would require a major commitment of limited funds, we opted to delay ordering new journals for the School of Dentistry until the faculty arrived to assist in making the selections. As noted earlier, most did not arrive until a month or two before classes began. That gave us about two months to set up subscriptions. The University Libraries are moving in the direction of ordering journals in online rather than print format whenever possible. The faculty of the School of Dentistry, coincidentally, also preferred online over print.

Normally, new subscriptions were ordered in October to begin in January of the following year. In this case we attempted to order them in July and have online access by the beginning of classes at the end of August. In order to get immediate online access we had to, in most cases, pay for two years (2001 and 2002). In a couple of cases the print arrived before online access was established. Only a few titles were online only, most publishers requiring a print subscription in order to get online access. Most were from small publishers. Some did not offer IP recognition, so we made an exception to our regular practice and went ahead with password authentication. This is not an optimal arrangement from our point of view, but we felt it was necessary.

IDENTIFYING APPROPRIATE JOURNALS

There are many sources for identifying available dental journals. A valuable resource is your journal subscription agent. The University Libraries use two subscription agents: Ebsco and Otto Harrassowitz. Ebsco's database of journal titles provided useful information on titles, including price, frequency, and online availability. Harrassowitz, based in Germany, is especially useful in obtaining European material.

A list of the journals received by the library of the American Dental Association is available at http://www.ada.org/prof/prac/issues/library/titles.html. The ADA's library is one of the largest dental science collections in the world, subscribing to over 800 journals.

A list of dental journal backsets in microform is available at the UMI web site, http://www.umi.com/. If you click on "SIM–Serials in Microform" you will be taken to their catalog. At the catalog you can select by subject of publication (dentistry). On November 7, 2002 this pulled up 117 titles. Information on format and price is available in the catalog.

The web sites of other dental schools, such as the University of Southern California (USC) and Louisiana State University (LSU) are very useful, not only in collection development but also in getting ideas for services that should be provided. The Jennifer Ann Wilson Dental Library at USC (http://www.usc.edu/hsc/dental/library/) lists all of its journals, both online and print. The online list includes all online health sciences journals available at USC, but the print list, which includes holdings and older titles, lists only dental library journals. The web site of the School of Dentistry Library at LSU (http://www.lsusd.lsuhsc.edu/Libr/) lists its current serials. Both of these schools also post lists of recently added monographs.

These sites are very useful in discovering what journal titles are available. Unfortunately, with limited financial resources available it is necessary to be very careful about which titles one selects for subscription. The following three sources are especially useful in this effort.

The database *Journal Citation Reports* from the Institute for Scientific Information provides a table of dental journals ranked by impact factor. The impact factor is "a measure of the frequency with which the 'average article' in a journal has been cited in a particular year or period" (Garfield, 1994). It is important to note, however, that a journal's impact factor can and does change from year to year. In addition, various studies have pointed out flaws. Still, it is a very good guide to the quality of a journal. Further, many schools do rely on citation analysis in promotion and tenure decisions, and as the faculty start to publish they are probably going to look closely at highly-ranked journals.

Subscribing to a journal that is not indexed in *PubMed* or *Science Citation Index* would be of limited value since students depend on these sources when doing literature reviews. A list of the titles indexed in *PubMed* is available in print in *Index Medicus* and also online. The 2001 edition of *Index Medicus* listed fifty-five titles in the dental sciences. Twenty-seven (49%) of those titles were also listed in *Journal Citation Reports*.

Excellent print resources for journal information include *Ulrich's International Periodicals Directory* (also available online) and *Serials Directory*.

BOOKS

A search of OCLC's WorldCat retrieves most books published in the English language. It is searchable by keyword as well as by Library of Congress subject heading. Results can also be limited to publication year in order to retrieve the items most likely to be still in print. Each bibliographic record also lists the number of libraries that hold the item, which can reflect the popularity of the item.

The University Libraries cancelled its subscription to *Books in Print* several years ago, except for a subscription in the Materials Ordering and Receiving Section. This was done partly for budget reasons, but also because we had observed that, for student needs, the online bookstore Amazon.com (http://www.amazon.com) was serving well. This was a useful tool for identifying dental science books, but its unsophisticated search engine did make it difficult to glean the academic titles from the consumer health titles. Amazon.com is good however, at indicating if a title is still available, or not yet released. It was also quite useful in identifying major publishers of dental titles, such as Quintessence.

Quintessence Publishing is a major publisher of books, journals, and multimedia in dentistry. Their catalog is online at http://www.quintpub.com/. The company Majors publishes medical books, including dentistry, and also offers an approval plan. Their catalog can be searched at www.majors.com, and they link to the Brandon-Hill lists of "Books for small medical libraries" which is a useful tool. The Brandon-Hill lists are also regularly published in the *Bulletin of the Medical Library Association.*

Another source of information about monographs that we used at UNLV was the database of YBP, a vendor that we rely on for our approval plan. We also modified our approval profile with YBP at this time so that we would be notified of new books in dentistry. At present we have no plans to start receiving dental books on the approval plan. This decision was driven primarily by budget concerns, but also a relative lack of interest in monographs on the part of the dental school faculty.

One should not underestimate the usefulness of professional associations and listservs in building a collection. For example, the Dental Section of the Medical Library Association http://www.db.uth.tmc.edu/mla/ has posted a "reading list" that consists of the titles that appeared in "A basic list of recommended books and journals for support of clinical dentistry in a nondental library" (Johnson, 1997). The site also contains a link to subscription information for their listserv, DentaLib (http://www.db.uth.tmc.edu/mla/dentalib.htm).

A valuable, although dated, selection tool is *Books for College Libraries: A Core Collection of 50,000 Titles.* 3rd ed. (Association of College and Research Libraries, 1988). There are few dental titles listed, but it is a good guide to the types of materials you need to purchase in related clinical areas. Although many of the titles are out of print, some have more current editions.

Because we had to expend our $100,000 allocation before the end of the fiscal year in which it was budgeted, we had to purchase books before the arrival of faculty. As stated earlier we prefer to do selection with faculty input. It is early to determine what kind of circulation the books we did order will receive, and it is not possible to determine if usage is by dental students or others. In conversations with the faculty, it does seem that we should have purchased more in the area of reference materials than in circulating items. But even more valuable would have been the opportunity to purchase journals instead of being restricted to book purchases. Experience shows that one-time allocations are not the best use of funds; rather, emphasis needs to be placed on increasing the base budget, so that journals can be added and supported.

GOVERNMENT PUBLICATIONS

A source of information that should not be overlooked is the U.S. government. In particular, the National Institute of Dental and Craniofacial Research (http://www.nidr.nih.gov/) issues reports that can enhance the collection. The *Guide to U.S. Government Publications* (Hedblad, 2003) is useful in deciding which federal documents in the health sciences to start collecting.

DOCUMENT DELIVERY

With the limited resources available at our library one must have to accept document delivery services as a part of collection development. At our library, indeed, the Document Delivery Services Department (DDS) is part of the Knowledge Access Management/Collection Development Management division. Faculty are provided with access to an unmediated document delivery service, Infotrieve, which is coordinated by two subject librarians. In addition, an agreement was made with the Savitt Medical Library at the University of Nevada in Reno to be a Loansome Doc supplier for the School of Dentistry. This arrangement is between the Savitt Library and the School of Dentistry. At present, due to staffing issues, UNLV is not a Loansome Doc supplier. This will undoubtedly change in the future, since even before the dental school opened, 75% of document delivery requests made by faculty were from medical journals. DDS continues to order non-PubMed material and does not charge for its services.

RESULTS

The faculty of the Dental School requested the following journals:

American Journal of Epidemiology
Archives of Oral Biology‡
Caries Research‡
Forensic Odontology
*Health Services Management Research**
*Health Services Research**
*JAMA**
Journal of Aging and Health
Journal of Dental Research‡
Journal of Epidemiology and Community Health
Journal of Periodontology‡
Journal of Prosthetic Dentistry‡
Journal of Public Health Dentistry‡
Journal of Public Health Management and Practice
*Journal of Rural Health**

Journal of the American Dental Association‡
Journal of the American Geriatrics Society*
Journals of Gerontology*
New England Journal of Medicine*
Operative Dentistry
Oral Surgery, Oral Medicine, Oral Pathology, Oral Radiology and
    Endodontics‡
Quality of Life Research*

*Already owned
‡ Listed in *Journal Citations Report* category for dentistry.

The Libraries subscribed to eight (36%) of these titles already. The titles we owned would not have been considered "dental" but were purchased with other programs in mind. Eight (36%) of the requested titles (not the same eight) were on the list of the top fifty dental journals in ISI's *Journal Citation Reports* (2001 edition). That left six titles (27% of the request) that the library would not have even considered for purchase had it not been for faculty input. In addition, because of budget constraints, the Libraries would have probably only purchased the top ten of the ISI list, which would have included three instead of eight titles.

CONCLUSION

The importance of close collaboration among the various departments in the library and the faculty of the dental school cannot be emphasized enough. In our case, various departments within the library had to make exceptions to general procedures in order to make sure that library support for the dental school was in place when classes started. There are a large number of resources to help identify materials for purchase, but the input of the end-users of this material is crucial. We were initially hampered by the inability to work closely with dental school faculty, but have benefited greatly from their input since.

REFERENCES

Association of College and Research Libraries. (1988). *Books for college libraries: A core collection of 50,000 titles.* (3rd ed.). Chicago: American Library Association.
The Carnegie classification of institutions of higher education. (2000). Retrieved November 25, 2002, from the Carnegie Foundation for the Advancement of Teaching Web site: http://www.carnegiefoundation.org/Classification/index.htm. As defined

by the Carnegie Foundation, "These institutions typically offer a wide range of baccalaureate programs, and they are committed to graduate education through the doctorate. During the period studied, they awarded at least ten doctoral degrees per year across three or more disciplines, or at least 20 doctoral degrees per year overall."

Commission on Dental Accreditation. (2000). *Standards for advanced education programs in general dentistry and general practice residency.* Chicago: Author.

Commission on Dental Accreditation. (2001). *Accreditation standards for advanced education programs in general dentistry.* Retrieved November 25, 2002, from American Dental Association Web site: http://www.ada.org/prof/ed/accred/stand/aegd.pdf.

Garfield, Eugene. (1994, June 20). *Current contents.* Retrieved December 2, 2002, from Institute for Scientific Information, Journal Citation Reports Web site: http://www.isinet.com.

Hedbad, Alan. (2003). *Guide to U.S. government publications.* McLean, Va.: Documents Index.

Johnson, R. (1997). A basic list of recommended books and journals for support of clinical dentistry in a nondental library. *Bulletin of the Medical Library Association,* 85, 233-28.

Patton, Natalie. (1998, July 6). Dental school plan gnaws at critics. *Las Vegas Review-Journal.* Retrieved November 25, 2002, from http://www.lvrj.com.

Tarlow, David. (1999). *DAT-Dental aptitude test: practice examination (nos. 1-4).* St. Louis, MO: Datar Publishing.

Ulrich's international periodicals directory. (2000). New York: R. R. Bowker.

Research Macrothemes. (2002). Retrieved November 25, 2002, from University of Las Vegas, Nevada Web site: http://www.unlv.edu/pubs/planning/macrothemes.html.

Nursing:
Tools for the Selection
of Library Resources

Janet W. Owens

SUMMARY. The selection of resources for nursing is influenced by the type of nurse client and the institutional setting. Clients include students, professionals and educators. They may use academic and public libraries or resource centers in patient care settings such as hospitals. Nursing collections support four purposes: education, research, clinical care, and accreditation. Current resources predominate. A variety of formats are selected, some unique to nursing. While none of the nursing selection tools adequately addresses every purpose and meets the needs of all client types and institutions, the Brandon/Hill lists have broadest applicability. These and other selection tools are evaluated. *[Article copies available for a fee from The Haworth Document Delivery Service: 1-800-HAWORTH. E-mail address: <docdelivery@haworthpress.com> Website: <http://www.HaworthPress.com> © 2004 by The Haworth Press, Inc. All rights reserved.]*

KEYWORDS. Nursing, libraries, selection, education, research, clinical care, accreditation, Brandon/Hill

Janet W. Owens is Health Sciences Librarian and Assistant Professor, University Libraries, University of Northern Colorado, James A. Michener Library, Campus Box 48, Greeley, CO 80639-0091 (E-mail: janet.owens@unco.edu).

[Haworth co-indexing entry note]: "Nursing: Tools for the Selection of Library Resources." Owens, Janet W. Co-published simultaneously in *The Acquisitions Librarian* (The Haworth Information Press, an imprint of The Haworth Press, Inc.) No. 31/32, 2004, pp. 89-99; and: *Selecting Materials for Library Collections* (ed: Audrey Fenner) The Haworth Information Press, an imprint of The Haworth Press, Inc., 2004, pp. 89-99. Single or multiple copies of this article are available for a fee from The Haworth Document Delivery Service [1-800-HAWORTH, 9:00 a.m. - 5:00 p.m. (EST). E-mail address: docdelivery@haworthpress.com].

10.1300/J101v16n31_08

INTRODUCTION

The selection of library resources for nursing is driven to a large degree by the type of nurse clients being served and by the institutional settings in which they operate. The clients could be licensed practical nurses, student nurses in an associate or baccalaureate degree or diploma program, professional registered nurses, or nursing professors involved in teaching and research. The most common institutional settings that provide libraries or resource centers used by nurses are hospitals, large private practice groups, public health agencies, and academic institutions, from community colleges through universities granting doctoral degrees. Additionally, most public libraries want to serve the needs of nurses in their communities. Some institutions will serve several nurse types: a health sciences university with a teaching hospital, for example, would include professional nurses, nursing students, and nursing professors. On the other hand, a small rural public library with no nursing school in the area could serve only professional nurses, perhaps many of them in the role of primary care providers and without access to a hospital library. The public library for them could be a vital resource.

Client types and institutional settings should be viewed within the context of the four purposes of a nursing collection, which are clinical care, research, education, and accreditation (Eldredge, 1997). Educational and research purposes are more important in academic institutions, while libraries in hospitals and other patient care settings emphasize resources to support clinical care decision making. There is of course some overlap in purposes, since student nurses must complete clinical rotations, and professional nurses need to meet requirements for continuing education. Both hospitals and academic institutions must meet accreditation standards, although the accrediting agencies are different. Moreover, collections serving nursing students and professors need to include supporting literature in the social, behavioral, and life sciences (Eldredge, 1997), which results for many selectors in a collaborative relationship with librarians responsible for subjects in these sciences. Budgets for nursing resources will also vary depending on the type and size of the parent institution; accordingly, greater selectivity in relation to purpose, client, and institution may be necessary for some libraries.

Selectors should also be aware of the diversity in nursing literature formats. In addition to resources that are common to most collections, such as monographs, textbooks, reference books, journals, audiovisuals, software, and perhaps newsletters and pamphlets, nurses need some unique resources, and these include position papers, practice guidelines, practice acts, and standards of practice (Pravikoff, 1997). Web sites are another format that libraries are selecting, in the sense that providing a link is selection; good tools are especially needed to identify web sites that provide authoritative health information nurses can trust. Libraries in clinical settings might consider making web documents available in printed form if copyright permits; many nurses in hospitals cannot access the Internet in patient care settings. Also, cataloging the selected web sites would increase the chances that nurses would find and use them.

Most nursing collections emphasize current resources. Even in large academic institutions, where resources may be available to support research into nursing history, the current budget will largely be expended on the most recently published materials. Some well-endowed libraries have budgets or gift lines to build retrospective collections. Accordingly, the selection tools listed here will be divided into two sections, one dealing with current and the other with retrospective selection.

Although none of the selection tools is adequate to address every purpose of a nursing collection and meet the needs of all clients and institution types, the Brandon/Hill lists have the broadest applicability and are therefore listed first. The order of subsequent entries should not be interpreted as lending priority to one tool over another; rather, clustering of some entries aids in understanding those tools.

SELECTION TOOLS FOR CURRENT RESOURCES

Brandon/Hill Lists

Anyone responsible for selecting nursing library resources should be familiar with the Brandon/Hill lists, which include the "Selected List of Nursing Books and Journals" (B/H Nursing), "Selected List of Books and Journals for the Small Medical Library" (B/H Medical), and "Selected List of Books and Journals in Allied Health" (B/H Allied). The original Brandon/Hill list was developed in 1965 by Alfred N. Brandon, former Director of Welch Medical Library of the Johns Hopkins School of Medicine. In contrast to its early select audience of librarians in small hospitals (Hill, 2001), the Brandon/Hill lists are used today even by large academic health sciences libraries (Murphy & Buchinger, 1996 as cited in Eldredge, 1997).

The first B/H Medical lists included nursing publications (Brandon, 1965); however, since nursing schools had begun to move out of hospitals and into academic institutions, where librarians had little experience selecting nursing resources, by 1979 B/H Nursing was developed as a separate biennial publication (Hill, 2001). Now in its 12th version, including 370 books in 55 broad categories and 86 journals, B/H Nursing is published in the journal *Nursing Outlook*, traditionally in the January/February issue, and online at http://www.Brandon-Hill.

org. The current authors of B/H Nursing, Dorothy Hill and Henry Stickell, are medical librarians at the Mount Sinai School of Medicine in New York. They choose publications for the list that "accurately represent the contemporary concepts, theories, and trends of nursing and set forth sound clinical methodologies." Nurses and librarians provide input, and nurse textbook evaluation research informs selection to produce the final list (Hill, 2002). Since nurses of all types require supporting literature in medicine and allied health, selectors cannot rely exclusively on B/H Nursing for collection development in this field, but must also consult the other Brandon/Hill lists. Hill (2002) is forthright in stating that B/H Nursing "would not adequately support most nursing programs." Responsibility for selection in nursing, medicine and allied health may be in the hands of one person or several, depending on the institution.

B/H Allied has traditionally been published biennially in the April issue of *Bulletin of the Medical Library Association*, which changed title in 2002 to *Journal of the Medical Library Association*. In the future it will be an online only publication (Gustave L. and Janet W. Levy Library, 2002). B/H Medical is available at http://www.brandon-hill.org. Between biennial publications, all the Brandon/Hill lists are updated quarterly by *A Major Report*, published by Majors Scientific Books, and available online at http://www.majors.com/libraries/majrep.htm. Brandon/Hill lists focus on relatively current publications. Price, date, and publisher information are provided, and titles considered "minimal core" acquisitions are indicated. Another useful feature is a table showing average price increases for Brandon/Hill listed journals and books since the inception of the list. The limitations of Brandon/Hill include the fact that the lists cover only print formats, mostly of U.S. origin, and exclude reference works. They also have minor errors, although a disclaimer indicates the information "is accurate at the time of manuscript submission" (Hill, 2002).

"Book of the Year Awards"

Each January the *American Journal of Nursing* (AJN) publishes its "Book of the Year Awards," listing the best nursing books chosen by its panel of judges. The books are listed in about fifteen categories including but not limited to such nursing specialties as critical care, community health, advanced practice, and medical-surgical. An electronic media category covers CD-ROMs. Titles, authors, publishers, and brief annotations are provided, but no ISBNs or pricing (AJN, 2002). In addition to the annual list, the monthly AJN includes a section called "Nursing Resources" in which reviews of new books appear. For the forty-five books on the 2002 AJN annual list, there was only slight overlap with 2002 B/H Nursing, so it is a useful supplement, though limited by size and scope.

Doody's Review Service *(Doody's)*

Doody Publishing has been reviewing books relevant to the health sciences, including nursing, for the past decade. Most of the nursing book reviews in Doody's are provided by the members of Sigma Theta Tau International (STTI), a nursing scholar honor society. In previous incarnations, Doody's was comprised of print journals that focused on nursing and allied health or medicine; today all the reviews are accessed through *Doody's Review Service* at http://www.doodys.com, which requires an annual subscription. Doody's can also be accessed on a trial basis by registering through the STTI web site at http://www.nursingsociety.org/ and clicking on "My Info Search." STTI members access Doody's at no charge. Doody's claims to review about 2,800 titles of books and software from 300 health sciences publishers each year (Doody Publishing, n.d.). Nursing reviews fit into the broad categories of administration, clinical specialties, fundamentals, and research and theory, each with more specific subcategories. In addition to applying a standardized rating scale for sixteen features, such as "pedagogical value of illustrations" and "helpfulness of index," reviewers provide a 250-word narrative description and overall assessment of the resource. The authority of the STTI reviewers is one of Doody's strengths, as is the size of the database, although not all the books in Doody's are reviewed. The major weakness is that it requires a paid subscription.

Essential Nursing References (ENR)

To call this tool "essential" is no exaggeration. Anyone building a reference collection for nursing should review ENR. Even those with existing nursing reference collections would benefit by comparing their resources to this list. Produced by the Interagency Council on Information Resources for Nursing, ENR is in its 22nd edition as of 2002. It is published biennially in the official journal of the National League for Nursing, *Nursing Education Perspectives*, and online at http://www.nln.org/nlnjournal/nursingreferences.htm. Some of the resource types covered by ENR include indexes and abstracts, both online and print, archival materials, grants, reviews, statistics, style manuals, web sites (several with material safety data sheets available), bibliographies, booklists, dictionaries, and directories. Canadian resources have their own section. The topics of bioethics, drugs, toxicology, environmental and occupational health, and the history of nursing are given detailed treatment. Many of the resources covered by ENR are selection tools in themselves. ENR is free when accessed on the web.

Resources for Nursing Research: An Annotated Bibliography

As the title implies, this bibliography (Clamp, 1999) covers literature of interest to those involved in nursing research. The authors are a nurse researcher and librarian based in the UK, and many of the citations are British or American. The latest edition covers electronic media as well as print and includes 2,760 entries. The book is divided into topics such as research design, data collection, and measurement. Within each topic, references are arranged alphabetically, not by format, so selectors must browse through all entries, many of which are journal articles.

Associations

There are 23,000 nonprofit associations in the United States, and annually they spend 8.5 billion dollars on education for their membership and the public (*Encyclopedia of Associations*, 2002). Book publishing is one component of that educational enterprise. The major nursing associations with publication programs are the American Nurses Association (ANA) and the National League for Nursing (NLN). The ANA publishing program, focusing on the needs of the professional nurse, includes electronic media, books, and standards. ANA's online bookstore can be accessed at http://nursingworld.org/anp/phome.cfm. The catalog supports both a browsing (alphabetic or category) and searching (word or phrase) feature. Orders can be placed online or by toll-free number. Signup is available for e-mail alerts advising of new publications, sales, and discounts.

NLN has had an extensive publishing program since the 1950s. NLN's role and publishing focus more on nursing education than does ANA. As of this writing, the NLN publishing program is in transition (National League for Nursing, n.d.). Although NLN plans to continue publishing, selectors should check the NLN web site at http://www.nln.org/ for more current information. ANA and NLN publications are also indexed in CINAHL, described later in this article, although there may be a time lag before they appear in that database.

Going beyond ANA and NLN, selectors with larger budgets or more specialized needs may also want to review a list provided by Eldredge (1996) of nearly 300 associations that publish materials of interest to the health sciences including many nursing associations. Most associations have a web site, and those that publish usually provide a link to their publications. Alternatively, the *Encyclopedia of Associations* provides contact information. Corollary associations with publishing programs of interest to nursing selectors are the

American Medical Association, the American Hospital Association, the Joint Commission on Accreditation of Health Care Organizations, the American Association of Colleges of Nursing, and any association that publishes materials dealing with a specialty practiced by the nurse client, such as the American Academy of Pediatrics or the American Association of Diabetes Educators.

Some state nursing associations publish as well and could be a more convenient source for the various rules issued by state boards of nursing or other regulatory agencies. They may also repackage the "Nurse Practice Acts," which are the enabling laws defining the scope of nursing practice within the state.

The disadvantage of using association publishers is that, for some types of associations, the procedures for ordering are not as streamlined as most library acquisitions departments would prefer (Eldredge, 1997). Some discounts, moreover, are available only to members of the association.

Medical and Health Care Books and Serials in Print *(MBIP)*

In the 2002 edition, this two-volume Bowker annual includes 95,000 books and 3,000 U.S. and foreign serials related to the health sciences, including nursing. The audience for most of the titles is the health care professional or college student. MBIP is useful for checking the print status and publishers of titles identified using other selection tools, although libraries with comprehensive collections might check the nursing titles against their holdings. Subscribers to the online version of the Bowker's *Books in Print* product are getting access to MBIP online as part of that subscription. MBIP is a convenient source, but not critical for smaller libraries not specializing in the health sciences.

Cumulative Index to Nursing & Allied Health *(CINAHL)*

CINAHL is one of the major tools for accessing the literature of nursing. Although most CINAHL subscribers use the database to search the journal literature of nursing and allied health, other formats of interest to selectors are indexed, including books, theses, audiovisuals, web sites, software, practice acts, pamphlets, practice guidelines, proceedings, and standards. The database includes about 775,000 total records going back to 1984 and uses its own thesaurus, *CINAHL Subject Heading List*. CINAHL is available in print, on CD-ROM, and online on a subscription basis. Information can be found at http://www.cinahl.com/prodsvcs/prodsvcs.htm. CINAHL's strength lies in its very specific focus and use of a controlled vocabulary relevant to nursing. Its disadvantages include the subscription cost, the time lag before citations appear in the database, and the need usually to check titles in another source to determine availability.

NLM LOCATORplus

LOCATORplus (LP) is the National Library of Medicine's (NLM) catalog of books, audiovisuals, journals and reports. NLM currently has six million items. For librarians new to the health sciences, LP is not MEDLINE. The latter is NLM's database of journal literature. Only the bibliographic information for journals will be found in LP, not journal articles. LP can be accessed at http://locatorplus.gov/. Nursing is well represented, though not the star as in CINAHL, and medicine is predominant. LP's usefulness lies in identifying materials that have been acquired by the world's largest medical library. Though LP is updated daily, new titles will probably show up in other selection tools before appearing in LP. And of course, LP has no evaluations. Once titles are identified they will need to be checked elsewhere to determine availability. LP uses Medical Subject Headings (MeSH), so for precise searching, users might want to consult MeSH, available online at http://www.nlm.nih.gov/mesh/meshhome.html. More so than with some databases, LP requires reading the tutorials or help screens to formulate good searches using truncation, Boolean operators, and limits. A useful limit in the catalog is "Item Type," which would allow searching for audiovisuals. LOCATORplus incorporated NLM's AVLINE, formerly a separate catalog for audiovisuals.

Library Journal *(LJ) and* Choice

With all the specialized selection tools for nursing, what is the place of traditional reviewing sources like LJ and *Choice*? If the library in which a selector is working is already receiving *Choice* and LJ for other reasons, selectors for nursing would probably find it worthwhile to look over the listings. Occasionally there are some good nursing publications not picked up by the nursing selection tools described here. However, most of the reviews in LJ under the heading of "Health and Medicine" are actually for consumer health publications. While nurses may read these books and recommend them to patients, they cannot take the place of books written specifically for a nurse audience by authors with credentials in the field. The November supplemental issue of LJ that covers reference books is better in terms of identifying clinical level publications of use to nurses. This issue separates the consumer health titles from the medical titles. With its audience of academic libraries, *Choice* does a marginally better job identifying titles of use to nurses than the regular LJ issues. Although many of the "Health Sciences" publications from *Choice* fall into the category of "general medical interest," a few good nursing texts are evaluated.

RETROSPECTIVE SELECTION TOOLS

Some of the current selection tools identified in the previous section can also be used for retrospective collection development. LP, CINAHL, ENR and Brandon/Hill, for example, go back nearly twenty years or more. The resources listed below cannot be used for the selection of current materials. Moreover, some of the materials identified may be difficult to acquire or exist only in special collections and archives. Out of print book dealers may need to be consulted. Some rare medical [and nursing] books could take up to twenty years to find (Overmeier, 1985 as cited in Richards & Eakin, 1997).

Nursing Studies Index, 1900-1959 *(NSI)*

NSI is a four-volume set published between 1963 and 1972 by the Yale University School of Nursing. As its subtitle explains, it is an "annotated guide to reported studies, research methods, and historical and biographical materials in periodicals, books, and pamphlets published in English" from 1900-1959. There are subject and author indexes.

International Nursing Index *(INI)*

INI was published between 1966 and 2000 as an index to journal literature. Each volume also had a section listing new books published by selected organizations, including national nursing associations of various countries, and a section listing nursing books received by the *American Journal of Nursing* Company that year. There are no annotations.

Bibliography of Nursing Literature, 1859-1960, 1961-1970, 1971-1975, 1976-1980

This four-volume bibliography covers materials located in the Royal College of Nursing Library, London, representing the first hundred years of nursing.

Nursing: A Historical Bibliography

This bibliography (Bullough, 1981) is arranged by broad subjects such as "Biographies and Autobiographies," "Nursing Specialties," and "Histories of Nursing." There are some unique sections as well, such as "Nurses and Nursing in Literature," which includes novels and plays. An author index is provided. The entries are not annotated.

CONCLUSION

Most of the selection tools identified here have a well established tradition of identifying and evaluating nursing resources, and health sciences librarians have come to rely on them. However, two publishing trends make access to them both easier and at the same time less stable than in the past. First, the merging of publishers and vendors often means changes in their publications. Second, more and more publications are discontinued in print and transformed into online services with web addresses that change frequently. That was the case for two of the entries in this list, one of which has announced a change from print to online as this is being written (B/H Allied), and the other which has terminated its relationship with a publishing partner and not yet found a new one at the time of writing (NLN). A good web search engine in the hands of an experienced searcher will usually relocate selection tools, both print and online, that seem to have disappeared.

REFERENCES

Book of the year awards. (2002). *American Journal of Nursing, 102(1),* 52-57.

Brandon, A. N. (1965). Selected list of books and journals for the small medical library. *Bulletin of the Medical Library Association, 53(3),* 329-364.

Brandon, A. N., & Hill, D. R. (1979). Selected list of nursing books and journals. *Nursing Outlook, 27(10),* 672-680.

Bullough, B., Bullough, V. L., & Elcano, B. (1981). *Nursing: A historical bibliography.* New York: Garland Publishing.

Clamp, C. G. L., & Gough, S. (1999). *Resources for nursing research: An annotated bibliography* (3rd ed.). Thousand Oaks, CA: Sage Publications.

Doody Publishing. (n.d.). *Doody's Review Service presents Doody's Electronic Journal for the busy medical librarian.* Retrieved December 8, 2002, from http://www.doody.com/Rev400WebScripts/AboutDEJ.asp?ShoppingCartID=0DEJUAP1016-120802-140348-0.

Eldredge, J. D. (1996). Associations that produce significant publications for the health sciences: Results from tracking a phantom literature. *Bulletin of the Medical Library Association, 84(4),* 572-579.

Eldredge, J. D. (1997). Collection development and evaluation. In D. L. Moore (Ed.), *Guide for the development and management of nursing libraries and information resources* (pp. 137-179). New York: National League for Nursing Press.

Gustave L. and Janet W. Levy Library. (December 12, 2002). *Announcement.* Retrieved December 14, 2002, from http://www.brandon-hill.org.

Hill, D. R., & Stickell, H. N. (2002). Brandon/Hill selected list of print nursing books and journals. *Nursing Outlook, 50(3),* 100-113.

Hill, D. R., & Stickell, H. N. (2001). *A history of the Brandon/Hill selected lists.* Retrieved November 1, 2002, from Mount Sinai School of Medicine, The Gustave L. and Janet W. Levy Library Web site: http://www.brandon-hill.com/history.shtml#4.

Hunt, K. N. (Ed.). (2002). *Encyclopedia of associations* (38th ed. Vols. 1-3). Farmington Hills, MI: The Gale Group.

Murphy, S. C., & Buchinger, K. (1996). Academic health sciences librarians' use of the Brandon-Hill selected list in book selection activities: Results of a preliminary descriptive study. *Bulletin of the Medical Library Association, 84(3)*, 427-431.

National League for Nursing. (n.d.). *News about N.L.N. Press.* Retrieved December 7, 2002, from http://www.nln.org/pressreleases/publishingpartner.htm.

Overmeier, J. (1985, May). *Rare books and special collections.* Paper presented at the meeting of the Medical Library Association Postconference on Collection Development in Health Sciences Libraries, New York, NY.

Pravikoff, D. S., & Hawkes, W. G. (1997). *Introduction: Information resources and services for nursing.* In D. L. Moore (Ed.), *Guide for the development and management of nursing libraries and information resources* (pp. 1-25), New York: National League for Nursing Press.

Richards, D. T., & Eakin, D. (1997). *Current practice in health sciences librarianship: Vol. 4. Collection development and assessment in health sciences libraries.* Lanham, MD: Medical Library Association and Lanham Press.

Acquisitions for Academic Medical and Health Sciences Librarians

Susan Suess

SUMMARY. Developing a library collection is one of the most important pursuits in medical librarianship. A library's collection is its foundation, and the collection is the central information resource upon which most library activities rely. Today's vision of the medical or health sciences collection must incorporate a broader range of materials, especially those in electronic and other nonbook formats. The increasing availability of information in electronic formats presents a new collection development challenge to librarians. *[Article copies available for a fee from The Haworth Document Delivery Service: 1-800-HAWORTH. E-mail address: <docdelivery@haworthpress.com> Website: <http://www.HaworthPress.com> © 2004 by The Haworth Press, Inc. All rights reserved.]*

KEYWORDS. Acquisitions, collection development, health sciences libraries, medical libraries, book selection

INTRODUCTION

Developing a library collection is one of the most important, if not the most important, of pursuits in medical librarianship. A medical library's collection

Susan Suess is Medical School Librarian, School of Osteopathic Medicine, Pikeville College, 147 Sycamore Street, Pikeville, KY 41501 (E-mail: ssuess@pc.edu).

[Haworth co-indexing entry note]: "Acquisitions for Academic Medical and Health Sciences Librarians." Suess, Susan. Co-published simultaneously in *The Acquisitions Librarian* (The Haworth Information Press, an imprint of The Haworth Press, Inc.) No. 31/32, 2004, pp. 101-109; and: *Selecting Materials for Library Collections* (ed: Audrey Fenner) The Haworth Information Press, an imprint of The Haworth Press, Inc., 2004, pp. 101-109. Single or multiple copies of this article are available for a fee from The Haworth Document Delivery Service [1-800-HAWORTH, 9:00 a.m. - 5:00 p.m. (EST). E-mail address: docdelivery@haworth press.com].

http://www.haworthpress.com/store/product.asp?sku=J101
© 2004 by The Haworth Press, Inc. All rights reserved.
10.1300/J101v16n31_09

is its foundation, and the collection is the central information resource upon which most library activities rely. And no library, especially a medical or health sciences library, can exist without constantly renewing its resources. This is the entire basis for acquisitions and collection development.

The traditional concept of a library is one of a collection of books and periodicals with circulation and reference services. The acquisition of monographs is one of the oldest functions in libraries. Indeed, until the beginning of scientific journals in the 17th century, a collection of monographs was the sine qua non of a library (Funk, 1996). Without the ordering and receipt of books, there was no library, and thus no need for cataloguing, reference, or any other services. Today's vision of the collection must incorporate a broader range of materials, especially those in electronic and other nonbook formats, and a greater sense of connectivity to include access to resources external to the library.

Just as the library's mission, objectives and goals should reflect those of its parent institution, library acquisitions should also reflect the character of the institution. The scope of acquisitions should parallel the extent of the institutional commitment to various activities and disciplines both internally and externally. A library's collections should be developed in a manner consistent with its overall goals, and collection development implies not only the selection of specific materials but also a master plan–a vision of how the library, responding to its unique set of circumstances and responsibilities, will build its collections and make the wisest use of its resources. Ultimately a medical library's collection in the aggregate is a selection from the vast universe of information in the medical and health sciences literature.

Selectors should know their institution and its internal and external interests, must understand the library's clientele and these clients' specific demands for information, and have knowledge of the collection, subject, and users. It makes a difference whether the institution serves high profile, intense research programs, has established centers of excellence in specific clinical or research areas, has specialized training programs with unique information requirements such as hospital, residency and fellowship programs, or has large-scale training grants.

Library budgets are becoming more restrictive at the same time as the output from the publishing industry is escalating exponentially, making selection more complex. Expenditures for the acquisitions of books, journals and audiovisual materials are exceeded in most library budgets only by personnel expenditures (Richards, 1997).

In the case of very specialized libraries, such as medical and health sciences libraries, it is not possible for a library to have in its local collection everything that its users may need. Health sciences library collections, in general, are developed to support one or more of five basic activities within that institution. These include clinical practice and health care services; research by faculty, staff and students; education and training of health care professionals; administration of health care services and educational programs; and, to a lesser degree than the others, the preservation of institutional publications and related materials.

There are many similarities in acquisitions and collection development processes in all types of libraries. Acquisitions and collection development are taking place in a rapidly changing environment. The nature of health science library collections is being altered as we attempt to resolve access versus ownership issues, and incorporate electronic and online formats with traditional print resources.

THE MEDICAL LITERATURE

In order to select appropriate items efficiently for a library collection, the librarian must first have an understanding of the role and purpose of the medical literature. Today, the definition of "literature" must incorporate new electronic and online formats as well.

The primary role of the literature in the scientific disciplines, including medicine, is to record and transmit discoveries and ideas that advance the state of knowledge within that discipline. At its most basic, this role can be defined as communication and is made manifest through publication of information. Publishing and scientific communication have been intertwined virtually since the issuance of the first scientific periodical in the 17th century (Richards, 1997).

There are differences between publication patterns among disciplines. For example, the scientist and the historian are divided not only by the language of their discipline but also by the form their works take. Historians communicate primarily through books while scientists communicate primarily through articles, largely because of the rapid pace of scientific discovery and the requirement that results be published and communicated quickly (Funk, 1996).

The principal challenge for acquisitions is to explore the medical literature in its broadest interpretation and to determine which segments or pieces of that literature are most appropriate to support the information needs of the group of users associated with the library. Medical and scientific literature is generally divided into three categories: primary, secondary and tertiary.

Primary level material includes source documents, such as journals, monographs, treatises, manuscripts, patient records, prints, portraits, and collateral reference items that contain original observations, annotated bibliographies, and dictionaries. Primary serials sources include journals containing original peer-reviewed articles and focus on a general or specialist audience.

Secondary level material includes reviews, state-of-the-art summaries, textbooks, interpretations of primary sources, and conclusions derived from primary sources. Secondary serial sources include those that publish review articles, summaries of current opinions, and news items. Tertiary level material includes the remainder of the synthetic literature, or repackaging of the primary literature for a purpose other than that intended by the author, such as popular treatments, annuals, handbooks, and encyclopedias. Tertiary serials sources include indexes and abstracts and other similar guides to serial literature (Richards, 1997).

Among the considerations for acquisitions decision making are the degree of importance of each level to the range of clinical, research, or educational activity supported by the library collection. In general, the greater the research effort the more the library should collect primary level materials. Similarly, the collection that primarily supports an education program will have a higher need for secondary and tertiary level material.

GROWTH RATES

Anyone who has ever visited a bookstore, or accessed websites such as Amazon.com or Barnes&Nobles.com, is aware of the incredible volume of publishing that takes place each year. Given today's publishing environment, it may be hard to believe that in 1800, there were approximately 90 scientific journals being published. By 1900, that figure has risen to more than 10,000. In 1994, there were more than 35,000 active periodical publications in the health sciences (Richards, 1997). According to *Bowker Annual Library & Book Trade Almanac*, approximately 6,200 new medical books are published each year (Bogart, 2002). To further confirm these publishing trends we can look at two studies that have been done in this arena.

DeSolla Price plotted growth rates of scientific literature over time and concluded that the literature of most scientific disciplines doubles every fifteen years. This growth rate has been relatively constant across scientific disciplines, including the health sciences (DeSolla Price, 1963). Lock, however, challenged DeSolla Price's explosion of literature theory calling it an illusion. Lock suggested that in fact the rate of expansion of the literature has been relatively constant at 5 to 7% per year (Lock, 1989). There is truth in each theory because each author justifies his view by examining the growth process from different perspectives. DeSolla Price examines all literature while Lock examines what he regards as the core periodical literature of various disciplines. Whichever measuring stick one uses, the growth rate for medical literature is significant and is something of particular importance to acquisitions librarians because it is from this publishing universe that library collections are selected. Factors affecting growth rates of the scientific literature include the increasing cost of science, especially instrumentation; the degree of specialization leading to fragmentation of disciplines; and the converse, an increase in interdisciplinary approaches to scientific disciplines.

With publishing in the medical field increasing each year, there are more items available than any single library can acquire. The world's largest medical library, the U.S. National Library of Medicine, has a collection of more than 6 million items and approximately 20,300 subscriptions (U.S. National Library of Medicine, 2002).

THE ACADEMIC MARKET

Certainly the academic market is a formidable one. *Statistical Abstracts of the United States* shows that in FY1998, academic libraries spent $4.6 billion on materials. With approximately 4,600 academic libraries in the United States, with budgets ranging from $100,000 to $1 million, these libraries represent an important part of the library world and a substantial market for publishers (U.S. Census Bureau, 2002; U.S. Center for Educational Statistics, 1998, Hoffert, 1998).

Academic medical librarians responsible for acquisitions face a challenging task. From a plethora of medical books published each year, academic medical librarians must select those most useful to their patrons. The few short core collection lists that are available are intended for use in the small hospital or internal medicine department library. As these are the only selection tools available, however, many academic medical librarians spend considerable time reviewing these collection lists and place heavy emphasis on acquiring books from these lists.

Selecting materials for inclusion in the collection of an academic medical library can be a complex process. As already stated, the needs of the library clientele, the current collection's strengths and weaknesses, the demands of cooperative collection agreements, the need to preserve historically important documents, the available space, and the budgetary limitations must all be considered.

A selection source designed for academic medical libraries would identify the most useful groups of texts for academic library patrons. Calls for the production of such selection sources have been heard intermittently. There is also some feeling that the level of specialization in the sciences minimizes the potential number of readers, which makes scientific book publishing a more risky economic enterprise. Consequently medical librarians are left with several short lists of standard authoritative medical reference works.

OVERVIEW OF SELECTION TOOLS

Numerous selection tools are available to librarians. However, few of these tools are specifically intended to assist academic medical librarians with selection. Below are the most common types of selection tools.

"Core" lists are highly selective guides to the literature that can be very helpful tools to the librarian selecting items for a library collection. One of the most recognized names in selection and most commonly used sources is the *Selected List of Books and Journals for Small Medical Libraries*, compiled by Alfred Brandon and Dorothy Hill and known familiarly as the Brandon/Hill List. This selection tool began biennial publication of a list of standard resources for the small hospital library in 1965 and continued to be published in the April issue of the *Journal of the Medical Library Association* in odd-numbered years. Starting with 2003, the Brandon-Hill Medical list will be published online only at www.brandonhill.com. This list offers a recommended list of books and periodicals, organized primarily by subject, and is designed as a selection guide for small and medium sized health sciences libraries. A new feature since the 15th edition in 1993 is the inclusion of a "minimal core list" chosen from the overall list.

A study by Murphy and Buchinger (1996) was designed to determine how the Brandon/Hill list was used during the general collection development activities of academic health sciences librarians in the United States and Canada. The survey found that inclusion on the Brandon/Hill list was the fourth most important factor, ranking below "recommendations from primary clientele," "circulation history of previous edition" and "frequency of interlibrary loan requests." Inclusion on the list was ranked as more important in the selection process than recommendations from librarian colleagues.

In addition to the Brandon-Hill Medical List there are also lists in Nursing and Allied Health. Professional societies and organizations often provide core lists or "opening day" collection guides. Examples of these types of lists would be *Ambulatory Surgery Center Core Library Collection* (AORN, 2001), *Osteopathic Medicine: An Annotated Bibliography and Guide to the Literature* (Elam, 1998), and *Opening Day Book Collection* (Association of Vision Science Librarians, 2002). Many disciplines have prepared lists that can be useful checklists for collection development and assessment.

Other commonly used sources for librarians include publishers' and vendors' catalogues, cataloguing records from NLM, acquisitions lists from other medical libraries, and reviews in medical and library journals. Specialty journals such as *JAMA*, *New England Journal of Medicine*, *Annals of Internal Medicine* and *Doody's Health Sciences Book Review Journal* often include reviews of books and journals in selected issues each year. Other resources targeted specifically for librarians include *Serials Review, Ulrich's International Periodical Directory, The Serials Directory, Books in Print,* and *Medical Books and Periodicals in Print.*

The challenge is to obtain the information as quickly as possible, with the least effort, avoiding redundancy but missing little. The number of sources used will depend on how comprehensive, or conversely how selective, the collection is. The depth of collecting for different topics within a library may vary; the sources used to identify materials will also vary accordingly.

JOURNALS

Serials are the core of health sciences library collections. In contrast to books, serials provide a rapid channel for the dissemination of information on specific topics. For this reason, they are ideally suited to the kinds of information exchange required by the volatile and highly specialized arena of biomedicine, fully exploiting the flexibility of the serials format, from the clinical case study to the review article, from the highly structured clinical trial report to the preliminary finding from the laboratory bench.

The trend in serials acquisitions is towards a hybrid of print and electronic serials products. Negotiating licensing agreements and knowledge of computer networks are fast becoming commonplace requirements for librarians who deal with serials. Document delivery trends are also blurring the traditional serials versus interlibrary loan lines. As technology makes it easier to acquire requested articles, libraries are reconsidering annual subscriptions, going from title-level acquisitions to article-level acquisitions.

ELECTRONIC/ONLINE

The increasing availability of information in electronic formats presents a new challenge to librarians in acquisitions and collection development. Electronic and online information compete with traditional print sources for budget dollars and now consume a larger percentage of library budgets than ever before. Whether the format is CD-ROMs, interactive video disks, or hypertext programs, librarians must be aware of the special characteristics, benefits, and disadvantages of each and be familiar with the format structure, characteristics and technical requirements. Special considerations include technical requirements and licensing. Will the product be mounted on a single workstation, a library or institutional LAN, or accessed through global networks such as the Internet?

The selection of electronic publications parallels that of monographs and serials in many ways. The fundamental difference between these resources and traditional resources is that the library is purchasing a license to use the software or product rather than purchasing outright ownership. Librarians will need to embrace the concept of access rather than ownership. For electronic publications to completely replace print resources, they will need to be commonplace, convenient and cheap (Richards, 1997).

HOSPITAL LIBRARIES

The acquisitions process in hospital libraries is not dramatically different from acquisitions in academic or other types of medical libraries, though some important distinctions can be drawn. The hospital librarian generally has a keener knowledge of the library's collection as well as a more detailed knowledge of the user groups. There is usually a substantial difference in the level of financial resources available for library purchases and there is a greater reliance on resource sharing in responding to information needs of the user group. Brandon and Hill have observed that collection development in hospital settings is different because errors in selection are relatively more costly and certainly more obvious than in a large medical center library (Brandon, 1965). Hospital libraries tend also to have a greater involvement of library users in the selection process, frequently in the form of a library committee that provides input to a process coordinated by the librarian. An intimate knowledge of the clinical and research programs of the hospital is critical to the process.

CONCLUSION

Libraries of all sizes are affected by the same realities: shrinking budgets, rising costs, expanding information sources and, for health sciences libraries, a radically changing health care environment. In a challenging economic environment, as acquisitions budgets dwindle and the number of available titles grows, libraries must make certain that acquisitions dollars are spent on materials that patrons actually use. Libraries' rate of acquisitions for the general collection will decrease and the rate of information obtained for specific end-users, either via the library or bypassing it completely, will increase.

REFERENCES

Ambulatory surgery center core library collection. (2001). Retrieved January 6, 2003, from the Association of Operating Room Nurses Web site: http://www.aorn.org/ Library/corelib.htm.

Bogart, D. (Ed.). *Bowker annual library & book trade almanac.* (2002). Medford, NJ: Information Today.

Brandon, A. N., & Hill, D. R. (1965). Selected list of books and journals for the small medical library 1965. *Bulletin of the Medical Library Association*, 53, 329-64.

DeSolla Price, D. (1963). *Little science, big science*. New York: Columbia University Press.

Elam, C. S. (1998). *Osteopathic medicine: An annotated bibliography and guide to the literature*. Chicago: Medical Library Association.

Fact sheet–The National Library of Medicine. (2002). Retrieved January 6, 2003, from the National Library of Medicine Web site: http://www.nlm.nih.gov/pubs/factsheets/nlm.html.

Funk, M. E. (1996). Monograph acquisitions. In Morse, D. H. (Ed.) *Acquisitions in health sciences libraries*. Lanham, MD: Medical Library Association and The Scarecrow Press.

Hill, D. R., & Sticknell, H. N. (2001). Brandon/Hill selected list of print books and journals for the small medical library. *Bulletin of the Medical Library Association*, 89, 131-153.

Hoffert, B. (1998.) Book report, part 2: What academic libraries buy and much they spend. *Library Journal*, 123, 144-6.

Lock, S. P. (1989). "Journalology": Are the quotes needed? *CBE Views*, 12, 57-59.

Murphy, S. C., & Buchinger, K. (1996). Academic health sciences librarians' use of the Brandon-Hill selected list in book selection activities; results of a preliminary descriptive study. *Bulletin of the Medical Library Association*, 84, 427-432.

Opening day book collection. (2002). Retrieved January 6, 2003, from the Association of Visual Sciences Librarians Web site: http://www.opt.indiana.edu/guideline/appB.html.

Richards, D. T. (1997). *Collection development and assessment in health sciences libraries*. Chicago: Medical Library Association.

U.S. Census Bureau. (2002). *Statistical abstract of the United States*. Washington, DC: Author.

U.S. Department of Education, Office of Educational Research and Improvement. *Academic libraries: 1998*. (2001). Retrieved January 6, 2003, from the National Center for Educational Statistics Web site: http://nces.ed.gov/surveys/libraries/highlights.asp#academic.

Collection Development in Public Health:
A Guide to Selection Tools

Lisa C. Wallis

SUMMARY. Public health librarians face many challenges in collection development because the field is multidisciplinary, the collection's users have varied needs, and many of the essential resources are grey literature materials. Further, little has been published about public health selection tools. However, librarians responsible for these areas have a number of resources available for their use. As in any subject area, each has its strengths and weaknesses, and users will have to consider their individual collection's needs when deciding which tools are most valuable to them. *[Article copies available for a fee from The Haworth Document Delivery Service: 1-800-HAWORTH. E-mail address: <docdelivery@haworthpress.com> Website: <http://www.HaworthPress.com> © 2004 by The Haworth Press, Inc. All rights reserved.]*

KEYWORDS. Collection development, public health, selection tools, grey literature

Due to its multidisciplinary nature, the field of public health can pose a challenge to librarians responsible for developing a supporting collection. In addition to its obvious connections to health and medical subjects, the public health

---

Lisa C. Wallis is Senior Assistant Librarian, San Francisco State University, J. Paul Leonard Library, 1630 Holloway Avenue, San Francisco, CA 94132 (E-mail: lwallis@sfsu.edu).

[Haworth co-indexing entry note]: "Collection Development in Public Health: A Guide to Selection Tools." Wallis, Lisa C. Co-published simultaneously in *The Acquisitions Librarian* (The Haworth Information Press, an imprint of The Haworth Press, Inc.) No. 31/32, 2004, pp. 111-120; and: *Selecting Materials for Library Collections* (ed: Audrey Fenner) The Haworth Information Press, an imprint of The Haworth Press, Inc., 2004, pp. 111-120. Single or multiple copies of this article are available for a fee from The Haworth Document Delivery Service [1-800-HAWORTH, 9:00 a.m. - 5:00 p.m. (EST). E-mail address: docdelivery@haworth press.com].

http://www.haworthpress.com/store/product.asp?sku=J101
10.1300/J101v16n31_10

literature draws from numerous other fields in the sciences and social sciences. Some of these include biology, chemistry, physiology, economics, law, education, psychology, geography, and, increasingly, computer science. In contrast to the biomedical literature, which generally is distinct and has a structured system of access, important works in public health are fundamentally diverse and to a great extent disorganized (O'Carroll, Cahn, Auston, & Selden, 1998).

Further complicating collection development is that fact that public health practitioners hold a variety of different job titles, ranging from health educators and public health nurses to social workers and epidemiologists. Lasker (1998), in her contribution to *Accessing Useful Information: Challenges in Health Policy and Public Health*, a forum co-sponsored by the New York Academy of Medicine and the National Library of Medicine, noted:

> Professionals in [public health and health policy] fields are extremely diverse in terms of discipline, extent of training, and work environment. Even more important, the information they need to carry out their work encompasses a broad range of subjects and sources. (p. 780)

For academic programs training future public health practitioners, the needs of their library users will be just as diverse.

This essay is designed to assist selectors in public health who may not be familiar with the field or who simply want new ideas to supplement their current tools. It will not cover the biomedical literature, which will be a significant part of any public health collection. Plenty of other resources are available for those needs, such as the "Brandon/Hill Selected List of Print Books and Journals for the Small Medical Library" (Hill & Stickell, 2001). Nor will it include the rapidly growing field of public health informatics, which has increasingly been the focus of leading public health agencies such as the Centers for Disease Control and Prevention (see Yasnoff, O'Carroll, Koo, Linkins, & Kilbourne, 2001) and the National Library of Medicine (see Selden, Humphreys, Yasnoff, & Ryan, 2001). Instead it will offer tools for selecting general public health materials; that is, resources that support curricula in the five core and seven supplemental fields of public health as identified by the Association of Schools of Public Health (ASPH): (a) health services administration, (b) biostatistics, (c) epidemiology, (d) behavioral sciences/health education, (e) environmental health sciences, (f) international/global health, (g) public health dentistry, (h) biomedical and laboratory practice, (i) nutrition, (j) public health practice and program management, (k) maternal and child health, and (l) occupational safety and health (ASPH, n.d./2002). The intended audience is librarians in schools of public health or at colleges and universities that offer undergraduate and graduate degrees in community health or related fields.

While most of the tools aid librarians in identifying and evaluating books, a number of the tools listed will help librarians find the grey literature. Grey literature is "that which is produced on all levels of government, academics, business and industry in print and electronic formats, but which is not controlled by commercial publishers" (GreyNet, 1999). It has also been described as fugitive information (Lynch 1998; New York Academy of Medicine [NYAM], 2002b), a term that reveals the difficulty librarians face in tracking down and collecting the materials. This segment of the literature is essential to a well-rounded public health collection as it is often the only source of current statistics, which are the basis for practitioners' needs analyses and program development plans. In addition, grey literature is published much more quickly than formally published literature, such as journal articles, making it the first source of much information.

ELECTRONIC TOOLS

In terms of convenience, it is hard to argue with the value of public health book publishers' web sites for selecting materials electronically. Many publishers offer free e-newsletters that notify subscribers whenever new titles are available, and these e-newsletters can often be edited so librarians can specify the subject areas in which they want notification. However, as the business of the publishers is to sell their products, users will have to look elsewhere for objective reviews. Still, these web sites allow visitors the next best thing to holding the books in hand. Most contain electronic tables of contents as well as author biographies and some even offer free sample chapters and integrated web sites. Holmberg (2000) writes of the many benefits of using publishers' sites for reference development that would apply to the main circulating collection as well. These include on-demand accessibility, the ability to quickly identify the newest edition of a title, and a much more extensive list of offerings than those provided by traditional review sources.

Identifying existent public health publishers can be tricky, as it is more common to label publishers as biomedical or general health publishers–which often indicates a concentration on clinical or consumer health resources. For the purposes of this essay, a review of the upcoming American Public Health Association (APHA) Annual Meeting Virtual Exhibition (n.d./2002) was helpful in narrowing the scope of publishers to those who have a direct interest in the field of public health. The assumption is that publishers who spend the time and money staffing a booth at the Annual Meeting feel their materials are relevant to the field of public health (Table 1).

TABLE 1. Book Publishers Appearing at the 2002 American Public Health Association Annual Meeting

Publisher	Home Page
American Academy of Pediatrics	http://www.aap.org/pubserv/
Hazelden Publishing & Educational Services	http://hazeldenbookplace.org/
Institute for Healthcare Advancement	http://www.iha4health.org/
International Life Sciences Institute	http://www.ilsi.org/
Jones and Bartlett Publishers	http://www.jbpub.com/
Jossey-Bass	http://www.josseybass.com/
Kluwer Academic Publishers	http://www.wkap.nl/
National Academies Press	http://www.nap.edu/
Sage Publications	http://www.sagepub.com/
Springer Publishing Company	http://www.springerpub.com/
Springer-Verlag New York	http://www.springer-ny.com/
Taylor & Francis Group	http://www.taylorandfrancis.com/
World Health Organization	http://www.who.int/pub/en/

Note: The American Public Health Association is itself a publisher, with an online presence at http://www.apha.org/media/.

Objective book reviews are increasingly available in electronic format. One electronic presence that specializes in the health sciences is *Doody's Book Review Service*, the electronic version of the *Doody's Health Sciences Book Review Journal*. Unlike the print equivalent, which is published every two months, subscribers to the electronic service receive weekly e-mail updates on new books in the health-related areas they specify. Clinicians working in academic settings write reviews, which are provided for around 70% of new titles. Primarily for biomedical librarians and professionals, the service does include a few relevant subject areas like public health, health care administration, epidemiology, and others. The book review service is offered as a member benefit to members of the APHA and other professional organizations, but a subscription that includes a journal literature review service is available to librarians for an annual fee (Doody Publishing, n.d./2002).

A free book review resource that is worth a look is *E-Streams: Electronic Reviews of Science and Technology References, covering Engineering, Agriculture, Medicine and Science*. It is an electronic-only publication edited by H. Robert Malinowsky, a collections librarian at the University of Illinois at Chicago. Published monthly, users may view the issues in HTML or PDF format, or they may register to receive a monthly text-only e-mail. In contrast to Doody's service, the reviews that appear in this publication are written by both librarians and professors with expertise in their review subjects. In each issue reviews are arranged by subject heading, and any given issue may or may not contain public health-related titles. However, the Web site does offer Boolean full-text searching of all past issues (Malinowsky, n.d./2002).

Finally, the online catalogs of some of the prominent public health libraries should not be overlooked when selecting library materials. Of course there will be a bit of a time lag between a resource's publication and its appearance in the catalogs, but these online catalogs can be a terrific source for rare and otherwise hard-to-find materials. National libraries, in particular, strive for comprehensive holdings in their subject areas. The most relevant catalog in terms of public health collection will, of course, be the National Library of Medicine's (NLM) LOCATORplus (n.d./2002a). Unfortunately, NLM does not offer a new materials list of any kind, but limiting a search to the current year will provide a complete, though lengthy, list of recently published materials. The subject search uses Medical Subject Headings (MeSH), not Library of Congress Subject Headings (LCSH), but a free online MeSH browser is available to find desired headings (NLM, n.d./2002b). Other catalogs to consider would be those of National Agriculture Library (n.d./2002) and the World Health Organization (n.d./2002), as well as any of the libraries of the accredited schools of public health in the United States, a list of which is available at http://www.asph.org/.

PRINT TOOLS

Book reviews in public health journals are clearly the best print source for selection no matter the size or type of the library. Librarians can be assured that the materials are relevant, as editors have already made that decision by choosing to review titles in the first place. Further, reviews provide the objective information not available in publishers' catalogs, whether in print or online. However, there may be a lag time between the publishing date and the appearance of the review. As some journals only publish book reviews irregularly, the number of reviews published in a given time period may not be enough to support the needs of a library selector.

At the APHA Annual Meeting in November 2000, a small group of public health librarians met to discuss the feasibility of developing a core list of public health journals–similar to the well-known Brandon-Hill lists (Wilcox, 2002). Response was positive, and while still in progress, the project has developed a preliminary core list of journals that are essential for any public health collection. This list was the basis for the journal titles presented in Table 2. A review of journals published to date since 2001 found that over half of the titles on the list publish book reviews at least occasionally. A distinction is made between titles that publish book reviews as a regular feature of nearly every issue and those that publish them only from time to time, as regular publishing will be of greater value to collection developers.

Core book lists are often used to select subject-specific materials for a library. However, such lists are not available for public health in general. A thorough search of the published literature and the World Wide Web revealed only one such list (Kronenfeld, Watson, Macera, & Kronenfeld, 1985), which was published in 1985 and is now, of course, outdated. On the other hand, the search did uncover numerous lists and bibliographies focused on subtopics

TABLE 2. Core Public Health Journals That Publish Book Reviews

Frequency	Journal Title
Regular feature	*American Journal of Epidemiology*
	British Medical Journal: BMJ
	Bulletin of the World Health Organization
	Journal of Epidemiology and Community Health
	Health Affairs
	International Journal of Epidemiology
	JAMA: Journal of the American Medical Association
	Journal of Health Politics, Policy and Law
	Journal of Public Health Policy
	Lancet
	Nature
	New England Journal of Medicine
	Science
	Statistics in Medicine
Irregular feature	*American Journal of Preventive Medicine*
	Emerging Infectious Diseases
	Environmental Health Perspectives
	Epidemiology
	Health Policy and Planning
	Inquiry
	Journal of Occupational and Environmental Medicine
	Public Health Reports
	Social Science and Medicine

Note: Thirty-eight titles appear on the essential core list. More information about the project, including its history and current status, is available at http://info.med.yale.edu/eph/library/phjournals/.

within public health such as diseases, public health specialties, and populations. Similarly, selectors may wish to consult the "Brandon/Hill Selected List of Print Books and Journals in Allied Health" (Hill & Stickell, 2000). While intended to be a resource for collections supporting health personnel at the assistant and technologist level, some materials on the list–namely within the subject categories AIDS/HIV, alternative/complementary therapies, and nutrition–would be appropriate for public health collections.

Due to the lack of well-established resources for selecting public health materials, librarians will need to be creative in tracking down other potential tools. This could include scanning reference sources in the health sciences. In the recently published and highly acclaimed *Encyclopedia of Public Health* (Breslow, 2001), for example, the editors have included a brief annotated bibliography listing some of the classic works in the field. This would be a valuable resource for anyone wanting to buy historical materials that have had a lasting influence on public health practice. In addition, each entry includes its own bibliography. A standard text for medical librarians, Roper and Boorkman's *Introduction to Reference Sources in the Health Sciences* (1994) contains numerous entries that would be valuable additions to a public health collection, particularly those in the "Medical and Health Statistics" chapter. Unfortunately, this book is a bit outdated, but plans for a new 4th edition are currently being discussed (J. Boorkman, personal communication, October 22, 2002).

GREY LITERATURE

As mentioned, the grey literature is a vital part of any public health collection. Currently one of the best free sources for tracking it is *The Grey Literature Report*, an online publication posted quarterly by the National Academy of Medicine. Unfortunately the reports are not indexed by topic, but the list is a significant timesaver as each issue compiles publications from nearly 100 organizations and government agencies (NYAM, 2002a). Each entry includes links to the electronic publications when available, or at the very least links to ordering information and the publisher's web site. Coverage is in no way limited geographically, though there are, of course, a significant number of publications from the New York area.

A major portion of the grey literature is comprised of government publications at all levels. *The Grey Literature Report* does include local, state, national, and even international documents. Librarians who do not work in libraries that are government document depositories may want to use additional tools to select and acquire health-related materials published by government bodies. In the United States the Government Printing Office (GPO) is the central federal document publisher, providing access to documents both in print and online via *GPO Access.* To keep up with the voluminous amount of literature published by the government, GPO does offer e-mail list notification of new titles, including lists specifically for health publications and government statistics (GPO, n.d./2002).

GENERAL SELECTION SOURCES

Choice is the primary collection development tool for most academic libraries, and it definitely should supplement the previously mentioned tools for selection in public health. According to the most recently published "*Choice*'s Selection Policy" (2001), public health reviews are published in the Health Sciences subject area. However, what is considered a public health title is often a matter of opinion. Nonetheless, the reviews appearing in the section are not limited to the R to RZ Library of Congress call number ranges. A review of a single year's issues (October 2001 to October 2002) revealed a small number of reviews from the fields of psychology, social welfare, history, and life sciences, to name a few. On average eighteen Health Sciences titles are published in each issue, and the May 2002 issue featured a separate 34-page supplement focusing on health.

The Amazon.com web site has become an increasingly popular selection tool for librarians. A marketplace for much more than just books, the site does include a number of features that make it a valuable tool for selection in public health. Users can search by keyword or use the advanced search or power search options available to search title, author, and subject, and publisher fields. Further, results can be sorted in a number of ways, including reviewer ratings. Best of all, most books include the full text of reviews not only from readers, but also from respected review sources like *Publishers' Weekly* and *Booklist.* On the other hand, results will include a number of publications that are irrelevant for academic libraries, as it is not possible to limit to ages other than baby through teen or to limit by intended audience. The Amazon.com database probably is used best as a tool for finding reviews on a specific item.

CONCLUSION

Public health librarians have an assortment of tools available to help them build their collections whether they prefer print or electronic format. These range from specialized book reviews in the journal literature to general tools like the Amazon.com web site. Though it may be challenging at times to meet the needs of the multidisciplinary users of these collections, with a little creativity and an ability to think beyond the phrase "public health," academic librarians can build an effective collection of monographs and grey literature.

REFERENCES

American Public Health Association. (n.d./2002). *APHA Annual Meeting 2002: Exhibits* [WWW document]. URL http://apha.expoplanner.com/.

Association of Schools of Public Health. (n.d./2002). *Core areas of study in public health* [WWW document]. URL http://www.asph.org/aa_section.cfm/3/53.

Breslow, L. (Ed.). (2001). *Encyclopedia of public health* (Vols. 1-4). New York: Macmillan Reference USA.

Doody Publishing. (n.d./2002). *About Doody Publishing* [WWW document]. URL http://www.doody.com/Rev400WebScripts/AboutDEJ.asp?ShoppingCartID=0D EJUAP1016-102902-180241-0.

Government Printing Office. (n.d./2002). *LISTSERV provided by the Government Printing Office* [WWW document]. URL http://listserv.access.gpo.gov/.

GreyNet. (1999, October). *GL '99: New Frontiers in Grey Literature.* Fourth International Conference on Grey Literature, Washington, DC.

Hill, D. R. & Stickell, H. N. (2000). Brandon/Hill selected list of print books and journals in allied health. *Bulletin of the Medical Library Association, 88*(3), 218-233.

Hill, D. R. & Stickell, H. N. (2001). Brandon/Hill selected list of print books and journals for the small medical library. *Bulletin of the Medical Library Association, 89*(2), 131-153.

Holmberg, M. (2000, Winter). Using publishers' Web sites for reference collection development. *Issues in Science and Technology Librarianship* [Online], 25. Available: http://www.library.ucsb.edu/istl/00-winter/article3.html

Kronenfeld, M. R., Watson, J. E., Macera, C. A. & Kronenfeld, J. J. (1985). A recommended core book list for public health libraries. *Medical Reference Services Quarterly, 4*(2), 39-52.

Lasker, R. D. (1998). Challenges to accessing useful information in health policy and public health: An introduction to a national forum held at the New York Academy of Medicine, March 23, 1998. *Journal of Urban Health, 75*(4), 779-784.

Lynch, C. (1998). The retrieval problem for health policy and public health: Knowledge bases and search engines. *Journal of Urban Health, 75*(4), 794-806.

Malinowsky, H. R. (Ed.). (n.d./2002). *E-Streams: Electronic reviews of science & technology references covering engineering, agriculture, medicine and science* [WWW document]. URL http://www.e-streams.com.

National Agriculture Library. (n.d./2002). *AGRICOLA online public access catalog* [Electronic database]. URL http://www.nal.usda.gov/ag98/english/catalog-basic.html.

National Library of Medicine. (n.d./2002a). *LOCATORplus* [Electronic database]. URL http://locatorplus.gov/.

National Library of Medicine. (n.d./2002b). *MeSH browser* [Electronic database]. URL http://www.nlm.nih.gov/mesh/MBrowser.html.

New York Academy of Medicine. (2002a, August). *Grey literature report, 4*(3) [WWW document]. URL http://www.nyam.org/library/greylit/glrv4n3.shtml.

New York Academy of Medicine. (2002b). *What is grey literature?* [WWW document]. URL http://www.nyam.org/library/greylit/whatis.shtml.

O'Carroll, P. W., Cahn, M. A., Auston, I., & Selden, C. R. (1998). Information needs in public health and health policy: Results of recent studies. *Journal of Urban Health, 75*(4), 785-793.

Selden, C. R., Humphreys B. L., Yasnoff, W. A., & Ryan, M. E. (2001). *Public health informatics* (Current Bibliographies in Medicine 2001-2). Bethesda, MD: National Library of Medicine.

Wilcox, M. (2002, June 2). *Core public health journal project* [WWW document]. URL http://www.phha.mlanet.org/corejournal.html.

World Health Organization. (n.d./2002). *WHOLIS* [Electronic database]. URL http://unicorn.who.ch/uhtbin/webcat.

Yasnoff, W. A., O'Carroll, P. W., Koo, D., Linkins, R. W., & Kilbourne, E. M. (2001). Public health informatics: Improving and transforming public health in the information age. *Topics in Health Information Management, 21*(3), 44-53.

Selection in Exercise, Sport and Leisure

Mary Beth Allen

SUMMARY. This paper discusses techniques for selection of library materials in the subjects of exercise, sport and leisure. Details are shared about utilizing standard review sources, locating subject-specific publishers, searching indexes and abstracts as sources of reviews, and tapping into the work of professional organizations. *[Article copies available for a fee from The Haworth Document Delivery Service: 1-800-HAWORTH. E-mail address: <docdelivery@haworthpress.com> Website: <http://www.HaworthPress.com> © 2004 by The Haworth Press, Inc. All rights reserved.]*

KEYWORDS. Exercise, kinesiology, leisure, recreation, sport

INTRODUCTION

Newcomers to the process of selecting materials in exercise, sport and leisure have an interesting challenge. As librarians at university libraries or in public libraries, they are typically given selection responsibility in a number of additional subjects also, so the time allocated for each subject is quite limited. Though exercise, sport and leisure are relevant to nearly everyone and very ac-

Mary Beth Allen is Applied Life Studies Librarian and Associate Professor of Library Administration, University of Illinois at Urbana-Champaign, 146 Library, 1408 West Gregory Drive, Urbana, IL 61801 (E-mail: m-allen3@uiuc.edu).

[Haworth co-indexing entry note]: "Selection in Exercise, Sport and Leisure." Allen, Mary Beth. Co-published simultaneously in *The Acquisitions Librarian* (The Haworth Information Press, an imprint of The Haworth Press, Inc.) No. 31/32. 2004. pp. 121-127; and: *Selecting Materials for Library Collections* (ed: Audrey Fenner) The Haworth Information Press, an imprint of The Haworth Press, Inc., 2004, pp. 121-127. Single or multiple copies of this article are available for a fee from The Haworth Document Delivery Service [1-800-HAWORTH, 9:00 a.m. - 5:00 p.m. (EST). E-mail address: docdelivery@haworthpress.com].

cessible to persons who are not necessarily specialists, selectors may have few leads and little direction about where to begin. And though the subjects are interesting and relevant to anyone, there is a specialized literature. Add to this the fact that many interdisciplinary elements come to play in the subjects, and what results is a very complex assignment. Library users interested in exercise, sport and leisure can arrive at these subjects from any number of avenues: clinical medicine, behavioral medicine, immunology, psychology, sociology, gerontology, history, education, economics, business and law. To learn more about these unique disciplines, new selectors may begin by browsing the current journals as they are received in the library, thus learning a great deal about the subject matter and looking for relevant reviews of important books and other resources. The obvious strategy at this point is to order materials that are reviewed in any of the journals received. This may work well for some time, with the primary benefit that one's knowledge of the breadth and depth of the subject matter will grow significantly by exposure to the current literature. However, one difficulty with this method is that by the time reviews are published, the materials may already be out of print or difficult to acquire. Also, only a small percentage of the total universe of published material is ever reviewed in this manner. Granted, browsing the current journals is an excellent way to learn about research trends and become familiar with library users' potential interests, either in an academic institution or in a public library. When critical new research is published in a discipline's major journals, users will likely be interested in reading more about the topic. So being knowledgeable about new developments will help selectors respond to this need for additional literature. But in the long run, selectors must also utilize more timely and efficient means for identifying appropriate materials to acquire in exercise, sport and leisure.

STANDARD REVIEW SOURCES

There are a number of standard review sources that can be useful to a selector with responsibility in exercise, sport and leisure. A signed review in a standard source includes valuable information about a work's intended audience as well as the appropriateness of its content and the type of library for which it will be best suited. Fortunately, sport and associated disciplines are universally popular subjects and are typically given good attention in standard review sources.

Choice and ChoiceReviews.online include a category called "Science and Technology–Sports and Physical Education," and also review sport reference sources in the "Reference-General" category. A quick scan of these two locations in each issue will very efficiently locate some of the best new books for the circulating collection as well as the reference shelf. High quality, mainstream sources are reviewed, usually five or so titles related to exercise, sport and leisure in each monthly issue. Reviews are signed and the reviewer's institutional affiliation is indicated. A good review in *Choice* nearly always ensures that the work is of fine quality and is appropriate for most academic and public libraries, although notes are included in the reviews that indicate specific qualifications to the level and type of collection that are appropriate for the source.

American Reference Books Annual is another excellent source for thorough reviews of reference works. *ARBA* is published by Libraries Unlimited, and each annual compilation includes a chapter called "Recreation and Sports." Within the chapter, there is a section of general works, and these are further categorized by type of sources, such as indexes, dictionaries and encyclopedias, handbooks and yearbooks, biography, etc. Additional sections are focussed on a particular sport or activity such as baseball, hockey, tennis, or card games. The signed reviews in *ARBA* provide the basic bibliographic information about titles, including price, and include several paragraphs of description for each title. A typical "Recreation and Sports" chapter in the yearly *ARBA* contains reviews of over thirty major reference sources.

Booklist also offers a range of excellent reviews, especially intended for public libraries, but perfectly appropriate for most libraries which build and maintain sport collections. The "Recreation & Sports" category in the Adult–Nonfiction section usually contains at least ten to fifteen signed reviews of important books on sport and recreation topics. These usually tend toward the more popular genres, and include many biographies, autobiographies, essays and histories. Basic bibliographic information is presented, along with price, and a paragraph of descriptive detail to summarize the content. The online version of *Booklist* is available at: www.ala.org/booklist.

Reference Reviews, and its online version available via Emerald full-text journal service, offers a "leisure and sport" category and one usually finds three to five resources reviewed in this category in each issue. However, they define "leisure and sport" more broadly than usual, to include topics such as food, wine and cosmetics. For more information, see: www.emeraldinsight.com/rr.htm.

In addition, when searching for books on exercise, sport and leisure in the online *Books in Print* database, there are often links to reviews of the sources. These can be useful when evaluating sources and making selection decisions.

SPECIALIZED PUBLISHERS

There are a number of specialized publishers in the fields of exercise, sport and leisure, each of which has established a reputation of excellence in its own defined area. Including such publishers on a carefully defined approval plan profile will ensure that the library acquires these critical materials in a timely fashion. If an approval plan is not possible, requesting catalogs from these publishers and visiting their websites regularly will help identify many appropriate materials for acquisition.

Human Kinetics Publishers is based in Champaign, Illinois, with additional international offices in Canada, England, Australia, and New Zealand. This growing publisher advertises that it is "The Information Leader in Physical Activity," and if its title list is any indication, this is certainly true. The subjects covered range from sports science, sports medicine, fitness and health, to dance, recreation and aquatics. Human Kinetics publishes approximately one hundred and forty books and twenty journals each year, plus a growing number of videos and course software. It offers distance education courses; and it organizes conferences, often partnering with and supporting relevant sport organizations such as Sport for All, American Master Teacher Program, the YMCA, and the National Strength and Conditioning Association. The list of books includes textbooks, consumer or popular interest titles, as well as professional and academic, research titles. Human Kinetics produces twenty-six different catalogs, all available upon request via their website. Online ordering is also available directly from their website at: www.HumanKinetics.com.

Another specialized publisher is Sagamore Publishing, also based in Champaign, Illinois. Sagamore's range of subjects focuses primarily on parks, leisure and recreation, including therapeutic recreation, commercial recreation and tourism, administration and management of recreation, with a lesser emphasis on sport and fitness. Sagamore has published over one hundred and forty books and continues to publish two periodicals: *Management Strategy* and the *Journal of Park and Recreation Administration*. Online ordering is available directly from their website at: www.sagamorepub.com.

Venture Publishing, Inc. is another publisher that concentrates on materials in the fields of leisure and recreation. They offer general recreation and leisure titles, but also cover the health aspect with materials in therapeutic recreation, long-term care, and activity programming. Based in State College, Pennsylvania, their catalog is published twice a year, and is also available to download from their website at: www.venturepublish.com.

Island Press covers multidisciplinary topics that provide an important environmental perspective to recreation and leisure. Their title list includes some four hundred books on topics such as ecotourism, ecosystems research, sustainability of communities, environmental policy, environmental health and conservation. Their catalog is available online at: www.islandpress.org/index.html.

Frank Cass Publishers is a UK-based venture with North American offices in Portland, Oregon. They publish books and journals in broad-based areas of social science and politics and have a very unique and growing series called "Sport in the Global Society." They currently list over seventy-five titles in this international sport series alone, and they produce a separate catalog for sports studies. Their website offers more detail at: www.frankcass.com.

Fitness Information Technology is another specialized publisher that lists titles primarily in social aspects of sport: marketing, sociology, psychology. They offer textbooks, series of trade books and also produce the journal *Sport Marketing Quarterly*. Their online catalog is available at: www.fitinfotech.com.

Meyer & Meyer Sport is a German publisher with over nine hundred titles on its title list, many in English and some in a multi-lingual format. They also publish periodicals, videos and CD-ROMs to accompany their books. Meyer & Meyer is a partner with many sport governing bodies and German sport organizations to support international sport. Their catalog is available through their website at: www.meyer-meyer-sports.com.

Many other publishers, large and small, offer important series on aspects of exercise, sport and leisure. For example, Routledge offers a sports science series and currently has eighty titles listed in this category on its website at: www.routledge-ny.com. CABI Publishing, publisher of *Leisure, Recreation & Tourism Abstracts*, presently contains fifty-one books in its "Leisure/Tourism" section. For their online catalog, see: www.cabi-publishing.org. Lippincott Williams & Wilkins publishes books and journals, including textbooks, in the field of sports medicine, and offers many titles in the categories of exercise science, physical therapy, massage therapy and occupational therapy. Their website can be found at: www.lww.com. Publishing giant Elsevier, with its imprints Mosby, Churchill-Livingstone, Butterworth-Heinemann, Saunders, and others, is a major player in health science publishing, including many sports medicine and exercise science books and journals. In its allied health section, Slack Incorporated offers materials in athletic training, occupational therapy and physical therapy. Sage Publications publishes on the social aspects of sport and leisure. And CRC Press offers an excellent series on nutrition in exercise and sport, as well as many other titles on related health issues such as aging and disability. Most major publishers, from Academic to Wiley, cover these subjects to some degree, and with increased societal interest in health and wellness strategies, the quantity of literature available is growing at a racing pace.

INDEXES AND ABSTRACTS

Excellent subject-specific indexing and abstracting tools exist for exercise, sport and leisure, and these can be utilized routinely for retrieving book reviews as well as periodical citations. Though none of the following offer full-text articles online, two of the three provide an abstract that contains adequate information for making a selection decision. The major subject-specific indexes and abstracts that include book reviews are *Leisure, Recreation & Tourism Abstracts*, *SPORTDiscus*, and *Physical Education Index*. In all three, there is a separate section for book reviews or they can be retrieved separately from other types of documents. All three are available in an electronic format, but only *LRTA* and *PEI* are also available in print.

LRTA is published by CAB International, in association with the World Leisure and Recreation Association. It is a quarterly print journal, derived from the CAB Abstracts database; over one hundred and twenty high quality, scholarly serials are cited in the journal; both author and subject indexes are included and content is also arranged by broad subject categories for easy browsing. The content is available electronically via the CAB Abstracts database, or through another CABI product called "leisuretourism.com."

Developed by the Sport Information Resource Centre in Ottawa, Ontario, Canada, in cooperation with a number of international sport organizations, the well-respected *SPORTDiscus* is a comprehensive, international database. Covering all aspects of sport and exercise, and most of the leisure and recreation literature, it provides bibliographic information and usually an abstract describing the source. Thousands of book reviews and references to books on exercise, sport and leisure can be found by limiting to this document type. References to other print material types, as well as videos, CD-ROMs and URLs can be found in the same manner.

Physical Education Index, formerly published by BenOak Publishing, is currently produced by Cambridge Scientific Abstracts. A standard in most academic libraries, the print version is issued quarterly, with a hardbound annual cumulative edition. An electronic version is available. Only citations are provided, but it is arranged by broad subject categories for browsing, and also indexes content by author, subject and geographic area, with separate sections for book reviews and patents.

ORGANIZATIONS AND OTHER SOURCES

An excellent selection source for the novice and the experienced selector alike is *Nasline*, the Newsletter of the North American Sport Library Network (ISSN 1480-5162). The online edition of this newsletter is sent to members of the group. For non-members and the general public, it is also archived in an online full text format from No. 5+ at the organization's web site, hosted by the Sport Information Resource Centre's SPORTQuest: http://www.sportquest.com/naslin/.

Nasline's editor, Gretchen Ghent, is also Chair of NASLIN and a founding member of the group. Ms. Ghent does a phenomenal job of not only reporting news of the sport library and information world, but also listing new and forthcoming publications on physical education and sport, defined broadly. In the September 2002 issue alone, over 150 books and publications are listed, usually with basic bibliographic information, plus price and additional details such as the publisher's web site, to make ordering unique materials easy. *Nasline*'s extremely thorough "publications update" is divided into the following categories: new and forthcoming books; new editions and reprints; olympiana; reference works; local interest; biography; conference proceedings; serials–new title, title changes; special issues of periodicals; and fun stuff/pictorial works.

Finally, there are numerous additional sources of assistance with selection decisions. More generic library professional associations, such as ALA's RUSA, develop lists of "best sources." ALA also produces the *Guide to Reference Books, Best Books for Young Adults*, and *Reference Sources for Small and Medium-sized Libraries*. Within the subject disciplines themselves, many excellent organizations exist to organize and inform the public they serve and these groups often produce the seminal documents of a field and sell publications via their presence on the Web. Visit the websites of organizations like the American Alliance of Health, Physical Education, Recreation and Dance (AAHPERD); National Recreation and Parks Association (NRPA); American College of Sports Medicine (ACSM); or the International Council of Sport Science and Physical Education (ICSSPE). Additionally, major college and university libraries with good kinesiology and leisure studies programs and major public libraries with comprehensive collection policies will often publish their lists of new acquisitions on the Web. Knowing what other libraries are buying can keep a selector informed, even when a generous budget for collecting in these subjects is not available.

Collection Development
in a Maritime College Library

Jane Brodsky Fitzpatrick

SUMMARY. Collection development in the highly specialized area of
the United States merchant marine, which includes navigation, marine engineering, shipping, naval architecture and shipbuilding, and seamanship,
requires familiarity with the national and international organizations, governmental and other, which regulate and oversee the marine industry. This
article discusses sources for core monographs and serials which are required for the study of and employment in the maritime industry. Standard
review sources and collection development tools are inadequate as selection tools in the field. *[Article copies available for a fee from The Haworth Document Delivery Service: 1-800-HAWORTH. E-mail address: <docdelivery@haworth
press.com> Website: <http://www.HaworthPress.com> © 2004 by The Haworth Press,
Inc. All rights reserved.]*

KEYWORDS. Merchant marine, marine engineering, naval architecture, navigation, seamanship, shipping, shipping safety

Jane Brodsky Fitzpatrick is Head of Technical Services and Acquisitions at the
Maritime College, State University of New York, Throggs Neck, NY 10465 (E-mail:
jfitzpatrick@sunymaritime.edu).

[Haworth co-indexing entry note]: "Collection Development in a Maritime College Library." Fitzpatrick,
Jane Brodsky. Co-published simultaneously in *The Acquisitions Librarian* (The Haworth Information Press,
an imprint of The Haworth Press, Inc.) No. 31/32, 2004, pp. 129-138; and: *Selecting Materials for Library
Collections* (ed: Audrey Fenner) The Haworth Information Press, an imprint of The Haworth Press, Inc.,
2004, pp. 129-138. Single or multiple copies of this article are available for a fee from The Haworth Document
Delivery Service [1-800-HAWORTH, 9:00 a.m. - 5:00 p.m. (EST). E-mail address: docdelivery@haworth
press.com].

STEPHEN B. LUCE LIBRARY AT SUNY MARITIME COLLEGE

As Head of Acquisitions and Technical Services at the State University of New York (SUNY) Maritime College, one of my main duties is collection development. This highly specialized college is one of only five state merchant marine academies in the United States. There is also one federal academy. The biggest challenge is to keep the maritime titles up to date, with a small budget and support staff. In this article, I will be discussing the acquisition of monographs, and some serials, in the specialized subject areas of merchant marine, navigation, naval architecture and marine engineering. Most of these core titles are located in the reference collection.

The Stephen B. Luce library is named in honor of Admiral Stephen Bleecker Luce (1827-1917), author of the classic textbook *Seamanship* (1898), and an advocate for the establishment of state nautical schools for training merchant marine officers. The Luce library is located in a 19th century pentagonal fort in the Throg's Neck section of the Bronx. The library has over 84,000 volumes, and currently subscribes to approximately 375 periodicals. The library's mission is to support the curriculum, to train men and women to operate and manage commercial ships as officers in the United States merchant marine. The Maritime college faculty recently approved a curriculum which does not require students to qualify for merchant marine licenses, but most of the students still choose the license program. Students (cadets) participate in a military style regiment, wear uniforms, and receive hands-on experience aboard the training ship *Empire State VI*. Cadets are required to complete three summer cruises, which last approximately two months, and generally sail to European and Mediterranean countries. Developing leadership skills is an important element of the academic mission. The college grants bachelors degrees in marine engineering, marine environmental science, marine transportation, naval architecture, and international trade and transport. There is a humanities major as well. In addition to earning a bachelor's degree, students must pass a U.S. Coast Guard examination in order to qualify either as third assistant engineer or third mate, the entry level officer ranks in the U.S. merchant marine. A small percentage of graduates join the United States Navy, Marines, or Coast Guard upon graduation. The Maritime College also offers a masters degree program in the business of international transportation and trade. To support the Maritime College general education requirement, the library maintains a standard academic core collection. Unfortunately, due to the high cost of maritime titles, and budget constraints, the general collection has become dated. The library has been a selective federal depository since 1948.

The subjects of merchant marine, navigation, naval architecture and marine engineering are very specialized. Related core subjects include oceanography and meteorology, but this article will be restricted to analyzing the acquisition of the merchant marine related titles. Although international in scope, the number of people involved in the maritime industry is relatively small compared to other industries, resulting in a small targeted audience for publications. Consequently, most titles are very expensive. A great number are published abroad.

Most published monographs about the United States merchant marine are selected for the collection, even if the books have not had very good reviews. Such titles, which include self-published memoirs, are invaluable because so little is written in this area, and good literary style must sometimes be sacrificed. The collection should be as comprehensive as the budget will allow. As a result, maritime monographs with a non-American emphasis have lower priorities.

ACQUIRING CORE TITLES: NATIONAL RESOURCES

The maritime industry is subject to both national and international rules and regulations for safety, ship construction, navigation, licensing, and related procedures. As a selective federal depository library, the Luce library receives titles which are required for students in the merchant marine license program. The United States Coast Guard enforces safety regulations for the maritime industry, and also administers the examinations required for officers' licenses. The library receives the Code of Federal Regulations (CFR), marine accident reports, and congressional hearings related to the maritime industry along with other government documents relating to navigation and shipping safety. The cadets must be familiar with, and know how to use, several CFR titles specific to transportation and shipping, in order to pass the Coast Guard examinations and work onboard ships. The library also receives publications relating to the Maritime Administration (MARAD) which is the agency within the United States Department of Transportation which oversees merchant marine affairs. MARAD's website (http://www.marad.dot.gov) lists statistical publications which are no longer distributed in print format, but can be accessed either on the Web or in PDF format. Receiving all these items free is critical for the collection, keeping it up to date with federal documents necessary to support the license curriculum. Without depository status, searching for and paying for these documents would be time consuming as well as prohibitively expensive.

The American Bureau of Shipping (ABS) is a classification society which oversees standards for shipbuilding. Classification societies set standards for shipbuilding that are used by insurance underwriters. The major ABS titles are rules and regulations for classifying and building various types of vessels, and are generously donated to the library by the ABS. A printed list of titles arrives each year with the loose-leaf rules volumes. I go through the list by searching multiLIS, the online catalog, to be sure that the latest edition of each title is in the collection. Some titles are now searchable online, and available as free downloads from http://www.eagle.org/company.html.

Many core titles are updated irregularly. Cornell Maritime Press, a small company which publishes basic titles such as *The Merchant Officers' Handbook*, *American Merchant Seaman's Manual*, and the *Modern Marine Engineer's Manual*, does not have a website. Cornell sends out an annual printed catalog, with occasional postcards announcing new titles or update editions. Since these titles are updated irregularly, vigilance is required to make sure that the library always has the latest edition. For example, Volume I of *The Modern Marine Engineer's Manual*, a two-volume essential reference, was updated to the 3rd edition in 1999. The 3rd edition of Volume II was not published until 2002. Publications are often delayed months after they are announced. The Maritime college bookstore forwards faculty book requests to me each semester which I review and compare to the collection. Since faculty who teach the license courses are up to date with the maritime industry standards and regulations, these forms are a helpful tool for discovering new editions of core titles. Also helpful for finding new or updated titles are the printed new accessions lists from the United States [federal] Merchant Marine Academy in New York and the World Maritime University in Sweden, which I receive by mail.

ACQUIRING CORE TITLES: INTERNATIONAL

For international regulations, there are publishers whose monographs and serials are routinely added to the collection. The International Maritime Organization (IMO) is a United Nations agency that publishes protocols and standards for shipping safety. IMO mails printed flyers to announce new titles and updates. I also search the IMO website several times a year to update titles or to purchase new ones. The IMO no longer mails out a printed catalog. Instead, there is a downloadable PDF format list of all publications at the IMO website (http://www.imo.org), which is searchable by various categories. Problems arise when trying to determine if publications are actual updates, contain new information, or are just compilations of already published rules and regulations. Discrete items have their own ISBN's, but every item does not have an ISBN. Loose-leaf volumes may have inserts of just a few pages, sometimes additional pages, sometimes replacement pages (updates) and even corrections. All items have IMO sales numbers, but IMO numbers often stay the same when titles are updated. The cataloger has made the IMO sales number searchable in the Luce library's online catalog, which makes it easier to avoided duplicating titles. IMO supplies titles relating to the International Safety Management Code (ISM), Standards of Training, Certification, and Watchkeeping for Seafarers (STCW), International Convention for the Prevention of Pollution from Ships (MARPOL), and the International Convention for the Safety of Life at Sea (SOLAS). The library must have the latest versions of all these rules and regulations which govern the shipping industry, since these publications have a great impact on the Maritime college curriculum, and are essential for the library collection.

In order to maintain maritime serials, despite budget constraints, some titles are reordered with decreased frequency, but essential core titles such as *Lloyd's Register of Shipping* must be updated every year. Alternating similar titles is often a compromise. For example, the library now alternates *The Fairplay World Shipping Directory* with *Lloyd's Maritime Directory* even though both are annual publications. An in-house database of standing order serials is the best tool for tracking the order frequency, and it is updated with the next order date when volumes are received.

INTERNET ORDERING OF FOREIGN PUBLICATIONS

The Internet has expedited shopping for foreign publications. Additionally, using the SUNY American Express card, I can purchase foreign publications directly without having to order foreign currency checks, saving time and the cost of the foreign drafts. There are a few nautical books sites that I browse about twice a year in order to update the core maritime collection. It is important to be vigilant, since there are many updates that can be missed if these sites are not diligently searched.

Warsash Nautical Books (http://www.nauticalbooks.co.uk), Witherbys (http://www.witherbys.com/), and to a lesser extent Brown, Son & Ferguson (http://www.skipper.co.uk/) are three major British sources for professional and technical maritime monographs. Witherbys has a link to "New Publications" or a link to the "Online Bookstore," where there are categories subdivided by overlapping subjects such as annuals, safety, crime at sea, etc. There is also a quick search feature for locating a specific title. These publishers' websites are best searched simultaneously with the online catalog to compare titles with the library's holdings. When the library owns every previous edition of a title, I automatically order it. Some title runs have gaps, due either to budget restrictions, or because the title may be important, yet marginal, so that it would not be necessary to own every edition. Witherbys is an excellent source that sells only established authoritative titles. Witherbys also publishes and sells titles produced by various maritime organizations such as Oil Companies

International Marine Forum (OCIMF), Society of International Gas Tanker and Terminal Operations Ltd (SIGTTO), and International Association of Classification Societies (IACS). There are often discrepancies and confusing information about editions on the website and in the printed catalog. As a recent example, an IACS title is listed as a new first edition published in 2002 in the Witherbys printed catalog, while the catalog inset lists the same title as a second edition, published in 2002. The library holds the identical title third edition, published in 1995! A lot of careful research is involved in efficiently updating the collection, without duplicating the many publications with very similar titles.

Brown, Son & Ferguson's, Ltd, another nautical publisher, is located in Glasgow Scotland. According to the website (http://www.skipper.co.uk/home.htm), "We have been nautical publishers, printers and ships' stationers since 1832. In our site you will find nautical textbooks both technical and non-technical, books about the sea, historical books, information on old sailing ships and how to build model ships." The website features either latest editions or current catalogues, which leads to a subject list. Some monographs, however, have neither ISBN nor publication date listed. Many of Brown, Son & Ferguson's publications are also available through Witherbys or Warsash. As mentioned above, there are often errors at these sites, which require careful examination. For example, *Collisions and their Causes* is listed by Warsash as a second edition, yet it has the 2002 publication date and ISBN of the third edition as listed at the Nautical Institute site.

Alphabetical lists are more efficient to scan, since the subject headings on all three sites do not use controlled vocabularies, and tend to be confusing. The sites are searchable by ISBN, title, and author. Warsash has links, within the record of each title, to other books in the same category. A title search can then link to other books in Warsash's subject headings. Most links bring up good bibliographic information including title, author, and ISBN. However, the records often do not show publication dates or edition information, and it is unclear whether these are reprints, updates, or completely new editions. Usually an e-mail to the publisher or vendor gets the answer. Titles are frequently presented as second revised editions, where the ISBN matches a cataloging record of the second edition, and is probably just a reprint.

The Nautical Institute (http://www.nautinst.org), located in London, publishes *Seaways*, a monthly journal, as well as nautical monographs dedicated to "high standards of qualification, competence and knowledge among those on or concerned with the sea," as stated on their homepage. Categories are listed as clickable subject links, which confusingly takes you to a slightly different list of titles than when selecting the publications link. The descriptions are accurate however, and although date of publication is absent, edition information is usually listed. It is easier to browse the Nautical Institute publications by subject headings, since they are all listed on one page, unlike Warsash and Witherbys, which require clicking back and forth between subjects and titles.

The Institute of Marine Engineering Science and Technology (IMarEST), (http://www.imarest.org/eshop/) located in London, is another excellent source of maritime monographs. I select almost all of their publications, with the exception of those that are specific to training and procedures for the British merchant navy. Professions training, marine safety and navigation titles are IMarEST's specialty. The books are authoritative, and written by known experts in the maritime field. Clicking on publications yields a complete list of IMarEST books, in no discernible order. The Marine Engineering Practice (MEP) series is an invaluable set of marine engineering monographs. However, their enumeration system is very confusing, and it is very difficult to determine which titles have been updated and need to be ordered. The hyperlinked titles bring up a record with title, ISBN, but not always a date of publication. IMarEST conference proceedings are important monographs which are part of a combined annual subscription to their periodical *Marine Engineer's Review (MER)*, and therefore do not need to be ordered separately.

Drewry, a British shipping consulting company (http://www.drewry.co.uk), and Ocean Shipping Consultants (http://www.osclimited.com) publish reports about the international business aspects of merchant shipping. Prohibitively expensive, these monographs typically cost between $650 and $1,500 apiece. Although each company sends out a multitude of flyers, the websites feature the latest studies. The market analyses and forecasts deal with various business aspects of the maritime industry such as cruise ships, tankers, bulk carriers, containerization, ports, and trade, etc. These titles are ordered very selectively, most often using an annual collection development grant which focuses on international trade and the business of shipping.

There has been some consolidation in the maritime publishing world. Lloyds of London Press (LLP) was merged into Informa, which publishes books, newspapers and serials, and runs international business conferences, many of which relate to the maritime industries. Informa owns Cargo Systems, a publisher of several important maritime directories and annuals. Cargo Systems also publishes industry business reports, which, along with Informa's conference proceedings and reports, are selectively added to the collection when the budget allows. While LLP once had a distribution warehouse in Queens, New York, now all titles are shipped from the United Kingdom. Informa's paper mailings are endless, as are their reminder letters for new editions and expiring subscriptions, which continue to arrive in the mail even after orders have been placed. It is very easy to order duplicate titles mistakenly, especially when pre-publication announcements can sometimes arrive many months in advance of actual publication. Additionally, Informa often misses their target release dates. Monographs, important books, conference proceedings, serials and periodicals all require different contacts, making it difficult to order from this very important publisher.

Fairplay Publications Limited and Lloyd's Register's Maritime Information Publishing Group also merged, to form a new company called Lloyd's Register/Fairplay. The company distributes Fairplay periodicals, such as the indispensable magazine *Fairplay International Shipping Weekly*, as well as *Lloyd's Register of Ships*, which has been published since the mid-eighteenth century. Serial titles have changed to reflect the merger. For example, the *Fairplay World Shipping Directory* is now called *Lloyd's Register Fairplay World Shipping Directory*. These important directories and registers are reordered through pro-forma invoices from LR/Fairplay, based on ordering cycles that are entered into the in-house database of standing order serials. The few monographs that Fairplay published in the 1980s have not been updated.

SELECTING FOR CIRCULATING COLLECTIONS

The Robert W. Gove Memorial Collection of literature of the sea is a special circulating collection. The collection of almost 600 titles is dedicated to "fostering a better understanding of the seagoing profession and life at sea." The collection was established in memory of Robert W. Gove (class of 1978) who was lost at sea when the freighter he was working on, the S.S. Poet, disappeared in 1980. The library receives an annual donation from the Gove family. Many of the titles which fit the Gove collection guidelines come from the Naval Institute Press, which publishes excellent histories about the navy, marines, coast guard, merchant marine, and the interactions of these services. Most of Naval Institute Press new titles are purchased for the Gove collection. I can select new titles from their annual printed catalog, which always has a new book section, or on the website, http://www.usni.org, where there is a list of new and forthcoming titles. The website is also searchable by eleven categories, such as Biography and Memoirs, Fiction, and Ship Reference, with a drop down selection of subjects better than most maritime and naval publishing sites, including a merchant marine section. Often, their military titles are relevant to the collection, since the Maritime College has a naval ROTC program, and there is also a close relationship between the Coast Guard and the merchant marine.

The California based Glencannon Press is a small publisher of "books on ships and the sea . . . for anyone who served in the merchant marine, or the Navy or the Coast Guard . . ." according to their website (http://www.glencannon. com/). I usually order from their flyers, since they have a very small number of titles (less than fifty), most of which are already in the Gove collection. Although Glencannon does not include dates in the book descriptions, either on the printed flyer or on the website, there are ISBNs. It is not as much of a problem to check titles against the online catalog since there are so few titles. The opening webpage lists new publications, and there is a subject list for browsing the backlist. Other small presses which publish titles which fit our collection profile include Conway Maritime Press, Ensign Press and Brassey's, a military publishing house (http://www.brasseysinc.com/) which also sells the Conway Maritime titles. Brassey's website has good bibliographic information and subject areas. Conway Maritime publishes maritime history reference titles. Most relevant to the Luce Library is the *History of the Ship* series. Conway's titles are also available from the Naval Institute Press. Ensign Press, located in Camden, Maine, is a very small publisher of maritime history titles. Ensign mails new book announcements from which I usually choose titles, although they do have a website http://www.ensignpress.com/. The Luce library owns all of the titles listed on the website.

The Gove collection also has a large maritime fiction section, which is transferred to the training ship each year for the annual summer sea term. *Library Journal* and *Choice* are good sources for Gove titles, which include more popular fiction titles such as the Patrick O'Brian series of 19th century sea stories, and true adventures including Sebastian Junger's *A Perfect Storm*, and books about legendary ships such as Titanic, Lusitania, Andrea Doria, and other merchant ships, renowned or not.

The library receives standing orders from several other publishers in the maritime field, very specialized companies that publish directories, registers, and other annuals that are ordered either through pro-forma invoices, or by running a query from an in-house Microsoft Access database. The database contains publication frequency and ordering cycle information, as well as updated vendor and price information.

BOOK REVIEW SOURCES

There are several publications for maritime-specific book reviews. The *Mariner's Mirror*, published by the Society for Nautical Research, has lengthy scholarly reviews of historical rather than technical monographs. The titles reviewed tend to be mostly British, or at least have a British perspective, so there are usually only two or three titles at most that I select from any issue. Additionally, the reviews often appear long after publication. For example, in the November 2002 issue, two reviewed titles had been added to the library collection in February of 2001 and 2002. The *Mariner's Mirror* is most helpful for discovering titles that have otherwise been missed, or for quoting reviews in the annotated New Accessions list.

TR News, is a bi-monthly publication of the Transportation Research Board of the National Academies, which publishes and sells monographs focusing on the transportation aspects of shipping which includes containerization, intermodalism, and port use. Logistics and economics are the emphasis of these publications. *TR News* also abstracts, but does not review, a small number of related books that they do not publish. *Ocean Navigator* and *The Woodenboat* are two other periodicals which feature short reviews, and useful new book announcements.

Often, working at the reference/circulation desk is a collection development opportunity. While checking books in or out, I am alerted to old and out-of-date titles. I will go online either to the publisher, or to a vendor, to see if the title has been updated, or if there is something else newer that has been published in the specific subject area. In the case of maritime-related titles, if no updated edition has been published, and the book is seriously out of date, it will be transferred to our Maritime History collection. All older editions of merchant marine related titles are retained in this special collection

CONCLUSION

In sum, the maritime collection is kept up to date through a combined use of standing orders, website searching and printed catalogs and flyers received from various publishers. The World Wide Web has certainly made finding and ordering foreign, rare, and out of print titles easier and more economical, but I still rely on printed catalogs and announcements, and even standard review sources such as *Choice*, for collection development. Experience with and knowledge of the specialized information needs of the maritime industry and the related publishers and agencies is, in the end, however, the most valuable tool of all.

Collecting the Dismal Science:
A Selective Guide
to Economics Information Sources

Deborah Lee

SUMMARY. This article provides an introduction to the major information resources in the field of economics. The essay evaluates the major selection tools in the area of business and economics, as well as selected core reference titles. The article also includes suggestions for developing and evaluating economics collections, as well as a listing of online economics collection development policies. *[Article copies available for a fee from The Haworth Document Delivery Service: 1-800-HAWORTH. E-mail address: <docdelivery@haworth press.com> Website: <http://www.HaworthPress.com> © 2004 by The Haworth Press, Inc. All rights reserved.]*

KEYWORDS. Collection management, business reference, economics

INTRODUCTION

Economics is the study of how society uses scarce resources to choose among consumption and production alternatives. The literature of economics is generally divided along two general areas: microeconomics and macroeconomics.

Deborah Lee is Associate Professor and Reference Services Librarian, Mississippi State University Libraries, Reference Department, Mississippi State University, P.O. Box 5408, Mississippi State, MS 39762 (E-mail: dlee@library.msstate.edu).

[Haworth co-indexing entry note]: "Collecting the Dismal Science: A Selective Guide to Economics Information Sources." Lee, Deborah. Co-published simultaneously in *The Acquisitions Librarian* (The Haworth Information Press, an imprint of The Haworth Press, Inc.) No. 31/32, 2004, pp. 139-147; and: *Selecting Materials for Library Collections* (ed: Audrey Fenner) The Haworth Information Press, an imprint of The Haworth Press, Inc., 2004, pp. 139-147. Single or multiple copies of this article are available for a fee from The Haworth Document Delivery Service [1-800-HAWORTH, 9:00 a.m. - 5:00 p.m. (EST). E-mail address: docdelivery@haworthpress.com].

10.1300/J101v16n31_13

Macroeconomics is the study of the economy at an aggregate level–including concepts such as the money supply, gross domestic product, or inflation. Microeconomics is the study of individual economic agents (such as individuals, families or companies) and the decisions they make. Developing a comprehensive economics collection can present a challenge. Users range from novice researchers exploring investment decisions to sophisticated researchers conducting a comprehensive literature search. This article will provide the collection development librarian with an overview of economics resources and a brief introduction to some of the core Internet resources available.

One of the collection development challenges in the area of economics is the sheer breadth of information available. This information can be subdivided into distinct subfields. While there are a number of ways to subdivide the field of economics, Albert Rees suggests the following eight categories (Rees, 1968):

1. mathematical economics;
2. history of economic thought;
3. economic history;
4. industrial organization;
5. agricultural economics;
6. public finance;
7. labor economics;
8. international economics.

As with all collection development initiatives, information sources vary according to the user populations they serve. Users of economics data generally fall into three broad categories. The first is the general user, who is looking for basic information or investment-related research. Currency is frequently of prime importance to this group of users. The second type of user is the undergraduate or general researcher. These users need both current information and, at times, a more historical treatment of the topic. Because this group of users has not had extensive economics or mathematics training, they need access to materials written at an introductory or layman's level. The third group of users requires more in-depth information and has a significant background in economic theory and quantitative methods. This third group consists of specialists and practitioners in the field, graduate students (or perhaps undergraduate majors), and economic policy analysts. Often this group will need access to original data in either a cross-sectional or time series format and the information needed will be of a highly technical nature.

While the casual user and undergraduate student will need access to a broad range of materials, including monographs, journals, and online resources, the more sophisticated user will need access to journal articles and data sources.

This article will present an overview of some of the major selection tools available to the economics subject bibliographer. No effort has been made to provide a comprehensive listing of resources available. Rather, this selective overview will cover the major print and electronic resources. Items are listed in priority order within each section.

GENERAL SELECTION TOOLS

Journal of Economic Literature

The *Journal of Economic Literature* or *JEL* is one of the primary reference tools for economists. Published by the American Economic Association, the *JEL* contains important survey and review articles, book reviews, an annotated list of books published in the field, and an annual listing of dissertations completed in the field. To facilitate access to information, the *JEL* developed a classification system that is widely used throughout the field. Many journals and conference proceedings organize material based on the *JEL* classification system. (An online version of the system is available at http://www.aeaweb.org/journal/elclasjn.html.) The *JEL* is available as part of an individual or institutional membership with the American Economic Association. Access is also available through *JSTOR* and selected business databases such as Ebsco's *Business Source Premier* and *ABI-Inform*.

Choice

Choice, published by the Association of College and Research Libraries (ACRL), provides short reviews of both print and electronic resources. Items selected for review are typically of interest to those teaching undergraduate economics classes. Reviewers of subject specific materials (i.e., non-reference items) are usually instructors within the field. While most of the technical materials typically of use to economics researchers would not be reviewed in *Choice*, it supplies critical reviews of materials of interest to a more general audience.

Social Science Reference Source: A Practical Guide by Tze-Chung Li. Westpoint, CT: Greenwood Press, 2000.

Li provides an overview of social science reference sources, with a chapter devoted solely to economics resources. Sections are divided by resource type and extensive annotations are provided. Li also does a good job of providing a broader context for the collection of economics resources, making this an excellent source for bibliographers without an extensive background in economics. Most of the resources are core reference tools and most are print resources.

The Search for Economics as a Science: An Annotated Bibliography by Lynn Turgeon, editor. Lanham, MD: Scarecrow Press, 1996.

Textbooks play a crucial role in both undergraduate and graduate economics education. Indeed, textbooks such as Samuelson's principle textbooks have served as a defining element in how economics has been presented (at least at the undergraduate level) for the last fifty years. *The Search for Economics as a Science* attempts to provide a guide to the literature in economics, with a heavy emphasis on textbooks. Unfortunately, this bibliography has a number of flaws. The annotations were dated at the time of publication, with few works published after 1990 included. The annotations are inconsistent from one section to another, and little justification is given for presenting one edition of a text over another. Given these flaws, this is one of the few resources currently available that attempts to provide a guide to this type of literature. This resource would be especially helpful to subject specialists attempting to evaluate or weed their collection.

INDEXES AND DATABASES

EconLit

EconLit is the American Economic Association's electronic bibliography and index of economics information published around the world. *EconLit* serves as the primary indexing source for publications in economics; its citations include journal articles, working papers, books, chapters, and dissertations. Available as both a CD-ROM and an Internet database, *EconLit* utilizes the *JEL* subject descriptors. Citations are not full-text.

ABI-Inform

ABI-Inform serves as one the oldest and most well-known business databases. Providing indexing and selected full-text, *ABI-Inform* covers both economics and the more broadly defined business literature. While many of the working papers and dissertations found in *EconLit* are not indexed in *ABI-Inform*, this database provides access to a broader array of economics and business literature. The availability of full-text articles makes this a popular choice among researchers and students. *ABI-Inform* is produced by Proquest and is available in both Internet and CD-ROM formats.

Business Source Premier (BSP)

Developed and marketed by EBSCO Publishing, *Business Source Premier* (and its scaled-down cousin, *Business Source Elite*) has emerged as a major competitor to Proquest's *ABI-Inform*. Providing indexing and abstracting to over 3,300 journals, *BSP* includes full-text coverage for over 2,800 titles.

Social Science Citation Index (SSCI)

Produced by ISI, *SSCI* provides access to current and retrospective citations, which include cited reference searching. This allows the researcher to track the citation patterns of critical literature through over 1,700 scholarly social science journals. *SSCI*, unlike other indexes, allows researchers to search journal citations. It is available via the Internet (in ISI's Web of Science), in print, and on CD-ROM.

JCR: Journal Citation Reports *(Social Sciences)*

The *Journal Citation Reports* or *JCR* is produced by ISI and is available in a Science and a Social Science edition. *JCR* is a unique product that tracks the citation frequency of selected social science journals. Useful both for research and collection development activities, *JCR* allows users to track the citation patterns of journals and to conduct bibliometric studies.

WORKING PAPERS

Working papers represent a primary source of information for economists, with research appearing months or even years ahead of journal publications. There are a number of resources available, with many institutes or research centers maintaining, at the minimum, an index of papers on the Internet. Two of the more popular sources for working papers are *NBER* and *NetEc*.

National Bureau of Economic Research (NBER) Working Papers
http://www.nber.org/

NBER is a private, non-profit research organization devoted to the study of the economy at both the micro and macro level. The *NBER* working paper archive is one of the core research resources in economics. While the archive may be searched for free, access to the full text of the working papers is by subscription only. Subscriptions are available to the complete archive (in either a print/electronic combination or electronic only) or to a selected subset. *NBER* research associates are some of the leading economists in their subfields and their research frequently appears as *NBER* working papers long before appearing in the journal literature.

NetEc
http://netec.mcc.ac.uk/NetEc.html

Founded in 1993, *NetEc* provides online access to working papers in the area of economics and finance from around the world. *NetEc* provides a gateway to other online working paper archives, including *BibEc* (covering print titles) and *WoPEc* (covering electronic titles) as well as a general web resource known as *WebEc*. One advantage to using *NetEc* is the common search interface, which allows the user to search all of the various *NetEc* resources. While providing an excellent index to the working paper literature, *NetEc* does not necessarily provide access to the full text.

RELATED WEB RESOURCES

There are a large number of Internet resources available in this area, produced by educational, commercial, and governmental agencies. This section will discuss a few of the most important or useful.

Resources for Economists on the Internet (RFE)
http://rfe.org/

Sponsored by the American Economic Association and edited by Bill Goffe, *RFE* serves as a primary meta-site for Internet-based resources of interest to both practicing and academic economists. Providing access to over one thousand resources, most links are annotated and updated on a regular basis. Resources include data sources, links to conferences and economics publications, government web sources, working papers, and other economic information.

New Books at the Harvard Baker Library
http://www.library.hbs.edu/bakerbooks/recent/

Historically, a core collection development tool for any area of business was the *Harvard Business School Core Collection*. Unfortunately, this title ceased publication in 1999. While not nearly as comprehensive or useful as the print resource, the Baker Library at Harvard University does provide free access to a listing of new titles recently added to the Baker Library collection (one of the premier business collections in the United States). The web page provides access to the materials added within a given month, with new acquisitions divided into twenty-three subject areas, many of which are related to areas within the field of economics. Each title is linked to the Baker Online Catalog and selected titles are linked to Barnes&Nobles.com.

Economics Times Series Page
http://www.economagic.com/

A subsection of the web page *Economagic*, this site provides a listing of free economic time series data. There are more than 100,000 time series available, many of which support customized searching and all of which may be downloaded as spreadsheet files. Most of the data is produced by a governmental branch and relates to the United States.

American FactFinder
http://factfinder.census.gov

The *American FactFinder* web site is maintained by the U.S. Census Bureau and serves as the main web portal for Census data. Data is available via ftp and through pre-formatted tables. Data sets covered by this source include the 1990 and 2000 decennial census, the 1997 Economic Census, and the American Community Surveys. While there is any number of census sources on the Internet, the *American FactFinder* is an excellent source of information for both the novice and advanced user needing demographic or related census materials.

Economics Research Guides

A number of libraries have produced online research or subject guides. While not a substitute for developing collections based on local needs, these guides can provide the novice subject bibliographer with a useful overview of the field. Table 1 lists a small sample of such guides.

DEVELOPING AN ECONOMICS COLLECTION

As with all collection development activities, economics collections must be developed based on the information needs of the user base. When evaluating an economics collection, the subject bibliographer will need to analyze both print and electronic resources, as well as monographic versus journal holdings (Carpenter and Getz, 1995). In terms of journal collections there are a number of ways to evaluate journal holdings. Many economics departments utilize a system of ranking journals for promotion and tenure purposes; subject bibliographers may find these of use in evaluating journals (Mason, Steagall, and Fabritius, 1997). These rankings typically divide journals into categories–such as "A level journals," "B level journals," etc. . . . These categories reflect the weight the department or school gives to faculty publications in these journals. A number of factors may be considered by the department when developing these lists: the relevance of the journal to the fields supported by the department,

TABLE 1. Economics Subject or Research Guides

Boston University

http://www.bu.edu/library/research-guides/econweb/

Indiana University, Bloomington Libraries

http://www.indiana.edu/~libpoli/RR/econ_res.html

Mississippi State University Libraries

http://library.msstate.edu/resources/guides/Economics.asp

Tulane University

http://www.tulane.edu/~html/econ.htm

University of Massachusetts, Amherst Libraries

http://www.library.umass.edu/subject/economics/index.html

University of California, Santa Barbara

http://www.library.ucsb.edu/guides/econg.html

the prestige of the journal in the field, and the acceptance rate of the journal. Other journal evaluation options include faculty and chair evaluations (Mason, Steagall, and Fabritius, 1997). This approach consists of a survey of faculty members and asks them to either rank existing journal holdings (from the most useful to the least) or questions faculty in an open-ended format to specify the most useful resources for their research. These surveys can be developed in such a way as to both evaluate existing journal collections and to solicit information on new research areas (or new journals) that the collection does not currently support. Finally, impact and citation studies can be used to identify core economics journals in the field (Laband and Piette, 1994), although this approach does not necessarily incorporate local research needs or priorities.

COLLECTION DEVELOPMENT POLICY STATEMENTS

A number of academic libraries have placed their collection development policies online. A comprehensive listing of various types of collection development policies, for different types of libraries, is available online at the meta site ACQWEB (http://acqweb.library.vanderbilt.edu/acqweb/cd_policy.html). While not specifically focused on economics or business, this site provides examples of collection development policies for public, university, and college, special and governmental libraries. Table 2 lists examples of economics collection development policy statements available online.

TABLE 2. Online Collection Development Policy Statements

Boise State University	http://library.boisestate.edu/colldev/cdp/buseco.htm
Boston University	http://www.bu.edu/library/collections/cdeconomics.htm
New York University	http://www.nyu.edu/library/bobst/collections/cdps/social/economic.htm
Northwestern University	http://staffweb.library.northwestern.edu/cm/policystatements/Economics.pdf
Old Dominion University	http://www.lib.odu.edu/aboutlib/coldev/policies/econcd.shtml
Rice University	http://sparta.rice.edu/~keckker/policies/bus-econ.html
University of Pennsylvania	http://www.library.upenn.edu/services/collections/policies/econt.html
University of Texas–Austin	http://www.lib.utexas.edu/admin/cird/policies/subjects/economics/html
Wake Forest University	http://www.wfu.edu/Library/colldev/econ.pdf

CONCLUSION

Economics, as a discipline, includes a number of subfields. There are literally thousands of data sources and bibliographic resources available. Only a few of those resources have been included in this guide. One of the challenges in the field is the lack of a recent, comprehensive reference tool devoted solely to economics information sources. The resources covered in this guide provide a broad overview of the field of economics and will hopefully assist the economics or social sciences subject bibliographer in the development of a useful economics collection.

REFERENCES

Carpenter, D. and Getz, M. (1995). Evaluation of library resources in the field of economics: A case study. *Collection Management, 20* (1/2), 49-89.

Laband, D. N. and Piette, M. J. (1994). The relative impacts of economics journals: 1970-1990. *Journal of Economic Literature,* 32, 640-666.

Mason, P. M., Steagall, J. W. and Fabritius, Michael M. (1997). Economics journal rankings by type of school: Perceptions versus citations. *Quarterly Journal of Business Education, 36,* 69-79.

Rees, A. (1968). Economics. *International Encyclopedia of the Social Sciences, 4,* 472-480.

Collection Development Challenges for the 21st Century Academic Librarian

Susan Herzog

SUMMARY. In the down-sized academic library of the twenty-first century, many librarians with little or no formal collection development training or experience are being entrusted with large departmental budgets, occasionally without the collaboration of a department liaison. How do new librarians, or librarians new to a discipline, deal with this challenge? This article attempts to provide both tools and suggestions to help librarians make the best collection decisions and to build relationships with their department(s). The subject focus is psychology and includes links to sample online collection development policies for psychology as well as print sources for psychology and other disciplines. *[Article copies available for a fee from The Haworth Document Delivery Service: 1-800-HAWORTH. E-mail address: <docdelivery@haworthpress.com> Website: <http://www.HaworthPress.com> © 2004 by The Haworth Press, Inc. All rights reserved.]*

KEYWORDS. Collection development, collection management, collection development policy/policies, academic library/libraries, 21st century, academic librarian(s), weeding, acquisitions, approval plans, liaison(s), psychology

---

Susan Herzog is User Education Librarian, Eastern Connecticut State University, 83 Windham Street, Willimantic, CT 06226 (E-mail: herzogs@easternct.edu).

[Haworth co-indexing entry note]: "Collection Development Challenges for the 21st Century Academic Librarian." Herzog, Susan. Co-published simultaneously in *The Acquisitions Librarian* (The Haworth Information Press, an imprint of The Haworth Press, Inc.) No. 31/32, 2004, pp. 149-162; and: *Selecting Materials for Library Collections* (ed: Audrey Fenner) The Haworth Information Press, an imprint of The Haworth Press, Inc., 2004, pp. 149-162. Single or multiple copies of this article are available for a fee from The Haworth Document Delivery Service [1-800-HAWORTH, 9:00 a.m. - 5:00 p.m. (EST). E-mail address: docdelivery@haworthpress.com].

10.1300/J101v16n31_14

Have you looked at any academic library job postings lately? If you have, you may have noticed a new trend. While large research libraries still hire collection development librarians, many smaller institutions are seeking generalists who can work on the reference desk, teach information literacy instruction and collect for various subjects. A sample from *Library Job Postings on the Internet* on 12/20/02 reveals the following job description excerpts, all posted on 12/17/02 (Nesbeitt, 2002, 12/17/02):

- Instruction Librarian, Saddleback College, Orange County, CA: "Review and select print and electronic materials for library acquisition."
- Systems Librarian, Gustavus Adolphus College, Folke Bernadotte Memorial Library, St. Peter, MN: "The Systems Librarian will work as part of a team providing reference services, extensive instruction, building liaison relationships with academic departments, sharing responsibility for collection development, and the management of the library in a collegial environment."
- Faculty Librarian, South Mountain Community College, Phoenix, AZ: ". . . collaborating with other librarians in performing liaison activities with college departments and developing library collections."
- Reference Librarian, Sojourner Truth Library, SUNY New Paltz, New Paltz, NY: ". . . and assisting with collection development in assigned subject areas."

In addition, collection development subject areas are not necessarily assigned to librarians with degrees in that collection area. In many instances, the assignment defaults to the subject areas handled by the person the new librarian is replacing. To complicate the issue further, collection development courses are not required in every MLIS program (*Survey of Collection Development Courses at ALA Accredited Programs*, 2002). What can the conscientious new hire do to ensure that s/he does right by the departments entrusted to her/him? This article includes steps librarian can take to educate themselves, as well as useful tools and ideas for collecting in any discipline, with specific examples for collecting for psychology. The focus on online sources is intended to enable newly hired librarians to "hit the ground running" rather than to indicate that these sources are superior to print resources.

THE BASICS

Collection Development Policies

In addition to learning how much money a department has to spend and the name of the faculty liaison, there are a few basic questions you need to ask:

1. How many majors are there in the subject area? If the number of majors has increased/decreased, a re-calculation of the budget may be advisable. The most helpful information would include the following:

> The Department of Psychology is one of 18 teaching divisions in the College of Arts and Sciences. There are 26 faculty members, two adjunct professors, two instructors, and two professors emeritus in the department. Listed below are the number of degrees awarded to students in Psychology for the past five years. (*Psychology Collection Development Policy Statement*, 2002)

2. What degrees are offered? Are any graduate degrees offered/proposed?
3. Have any new courses been added/proposed?
4. Is there an existing collection development Policy?

Surprisingly, many academic libraries have yet to develop or update collection policies. While it may seem that the lack of a policy gives more freedom, in reality the opposite is true, especially for librarians with little collection development experience. A good collection policy will include the following critical information to help in making collection decisions:

a. Scope of coverage (languages, geographical focus, chronological periods)
b. Related subjects and interdisciplinary relationships
c. Format of materials collected (monographs, serials, conference proceedings, encyclopedias, dictionaries, handbooks, indexes, audiovisual materials, dissertations and theses, microforms, and electronic resources).

Equally important as what IS collected is what is NOT collected. Ask whether the library collects textbooks, psychological tests, juvenile literature, or popular literature (*Psychology Collection Development Policy Statement*, 2002). Does the department have a special collection focus, such as a "special interest in collecting materials related to emerging areas such as evolutionary psychology, environmental psychology, psychology of women, and psychobiology"? (Kirkpatrick, 2002). Ask also if there are other relevant on-campus or local resources or any cooperative collection agreements (Kirkpatrick, 2002).

The best collection development policies include a collection analysis covering existing strength of the collection and current collecting intensity by LC classification (*Psychology Collection Development Policy Statement*, 2002). The most specific sample I found online is *Collection Profile: Psychological & Brain Sciences* from the University of Louisville; try the link, "Current title/volume count," under "Classifications and Recommended Level of Development" (Laning, 2002).

The sample policies were the result of a Google search on "collection development policies" psychology (http://www.google.com). If working with another discipline, make the appropriate substitution to find good examples of policies. Current policies can also be found by consulting the following Web sites:

1. *Acqweb's Directory of Collection Development Policies on the Web* (http://acqweb.library.vanderbilt.edu/acqweb/cd_policy.html#college).
2. *Australian Libraries Gateway: Collection Development Policies,* which includes "guidelines to assist libraries that are about to formulate or revise a collection development policy" (http://www.nla.gov.au/libraries/resource/acliscdp.html).

Following is an abstract from the site: "Whitehead, D. (1989). How to write a collection development policy. *Acquisitions, 6*(2), 25-28. Positively the shortest useful article available; very practical and sensible. Suggests 'lifting' as much as possible from other policies to save reinventing any wheels."

Collection Management: Gifts and Weeding

Additional policies to locate are gift policies and weeding policies. Before there is a phone call from someone with several hundred books to donate, it is critical to know how the library handles donations. An excellent sample policy is *Making a Gift to the Library* by David Gray of Marshall University (http://www.marshall.edu/colldev/gifts.htm).

Weeding is an inherent part of collection management. A good collection development policy will include the department/library philosophy on weeding: "Continuous maintenance of the collection is based upon systematic evaluation of materials in all locations in relationship to curriculum shifts, use statistics, core bibliographies, physical space limitations and the availability of information in alternative formats. Current periodical titles are reviewed annually prior to their renewal. All other areas of the collection should be reviewed every three to five years. The collection maintenance process includes weeding materials no longer relevant to curriculum needs, elimination of superfluous titles where information is duplicated in more current or authoritative sources, and ordering replacement copies of damaged and heavily used items still relevant to curriculum needs" (Smokey, 2002). For detailed information on Collection Assessment techniques, the University of Wyoming Libraries provides extensive guidelines (http://www-lib.uwyo.edu/cdo/collass.htm).

Faculty Research

It's also critical to know whether the library collects titles for individual faculty research. Some libraries consider that part of their mission while others do not. At the State University of New York, University at Albany, "The University Libraries' collection development mission is to identify, select, manage and preserve collections that support the curricula and research of the faculty, students, and staff of the University at Albany and to facilitate access to a wide variety of electronic and other resources and services for their use" (*Collection Development Policy*, 1996).

THE TOOLS

Fortunately, there is no need to reinvent the wheel. Generous colleagues have provided significant information, much of it available online. In addition, vendors are continually developing new tools to make the process more efficient.

Websites

I am including pointers to only a few web sites. Most are megasites with links to hundreds of resources:

- "*AcqWeb* is a World Wide Web site providing links to information and resources of interest to librarians with acquisitions or collection development responsibilities. The scope is international" (Cook, 2002) (http://acqweb.library.vanderbilt.edu/).
- *ALCTS Publications Acquisitions Bibliography: A Selected Bibliography for Library Acquisitions, Fourth Edition*: "The guidelines for inclusion of recommended titles in this list are as follows. Books and articles were selected which offered breadth and depth of coverage, with broad applicability, rather than those dealing with highly technical or specific topics. Sources with comprehensive bibliographies were preferred. Finally, recent publications were preferred over less recent, with the exception of those publications which were considered to be standard references or 'classics.' Finally, the most important single criterion for selection was clarity of explanation and description" (Hall, 2000) (http://www.ala.org/alcts/publications/acqbib.htm).
- *Collection Development and the Internet: A Brief Handbook for Recommending Officers in the Humanities and Social Sciences Division at The Library Of Congress*, from the Library of Congress Acquisitions De-

partment, is intended "to provide practical guidance in using the Internet to extend the techniques we have traditionally used in the area of collection development" (Yochelson et al., 2000) (http://lcweb.loc.gov/acq/colldev/handbook.html).

- *Internet Library for Librarians: Acquisitions, Serials, and Collection Development* (http://www.itcompany.com/inforetriever/acqsercd.htm).
- *A Tool Kit of Links and Documents for Collection Development and Management Librarians* (http://ublib.buffalo.edu/libraries/units/lml/colldev/cdInternet.html).
- *Using the Web for Collection Development: Selecting Print and Audiovisual Materials* (http://www.paccd.cc.ca.us/library/lib101/Colldevbib.htm).
- For a directory of publishers and vendors tailored for specific disciplines, see *AcqWeb's Publisher Web Sites: Subject Directory* (Leiserson, 2002) (http://acqweb.library.vanderbilt.edu/acqweb/pubr.html#subj).

Approval Plans

Many academic libraries use approval plans to simplify collection responsibilities and make acquisition processes more efficient for everyone involved: selection, placing orders, paying the bills, cataloging the selections, and processing them for shelving. A good approval plan can save the library money and staff time. The most critical aspect of an approval plan is the profile; it is imperative to update the profile continually to fit department demands. A librarian in a new position must review the current approval plan to make sure that it reflects current needs. Links to the major North American approval plans may be found on the Web site, *A Tool Kit of Links and Documents for Collection Development and Management Librarians* (D'Aniello, 1999) (http://ublib.buffalo.edu/libraries/units/lml/colldev/cdInternet.html#approval).

ONLINE COLLECTION DEVELOPMENT TOOLS

Title Source II

I highly recommend the online collection development tools provided by Baker & Taylor. Baker & Taylor's *Title Source II* is an especially helpful tool, integrating selecting and ordering into "one-stop-shopping" (http://ts2d.informata.com/ TS2/). *Title Source II* is an inexpensive and versatile program that allows multiple search parameters. Reviews can also be searched on *Title Source II: CHOICE, Criticas, Doody's, ForeWord Magazine, Horn Book*, and *Kirkus*. Titles selected for purchase can be saved in a cart. One searcher can set up as many carts as are needed, to collect for more than one department, or to separate undergraduate orders from graduate. The cart may be e-mailed to faculty for review or to the person who places orders, cutting down significantly on paperwork. Another advantage of *Title Source II* is that each record includes the current inventory in the warehouse that services a particular campus. This function becomes especially useful as fiscal deadlines draw near; collection dollars will not be wasted while you wait to check availability. Baker & Taylor may be contacted for a free trial (E-mail: electser@btol.com).

ChoiceReviews.online

Most academic librarians are familiar with the print publication *CHOICE: Current Reviews for Academic Libraries*, which reviews significant current books and electronic media of interest to those in higher education. "Established in 1964, *CHOICE* publishes reviews of over 6,500 new books and Internet sources annually, making it one of the most comprehensive English language review journals available today. *CHOICE* is a publication of the Association of College & Research Libraries, a Division of the American Library Association" (*CHOICE*, 2002) (http://www.ala.org/acrl/choice/presssite.html).

Unfortunately, many librarians are not aware of the online version, which is an exceptional collection development tool. A library that subscribes to the print publication can add online access for a very small fee. "*ChoiceReviews.online* provides Web access to the entire database of *CHOICE* reviews published since September 1988. The database is updated monthly, generally at mid-month, with reviews that will be printed in the next monthly issue of *CHOICE*. Launched on the Web in April 1999, *ChoiceReviews.online* is currently in version 1.7. Subscribers to the library edition (accessible by password) receive access to the entire database, a monthly email bulletin announcing new items matching their profile, and a private workspace on the Web to view the current issue, create and maintain customized groups of citations and reviews, and e-mail copies of selected reviews to colleagues. See http://www.ala.org/acrl/choice/subscr.html for current subscription information. Free two-month trials of *ChoiceReviews.online* are available *ChoiceReviews.online*" (*About ChoiceReviews.online*, 2002).

The online version may be searched by the usual search parameters. A particularly helpful tool is the Profile feature. "Use Profile to indicate the subjects, topics, and readership levels of materials that match your interests. When the *ChoiceReviews.online* database is updated monthly, you will be sent an e-mail message of titles matching your profiled interests. The Monthly Update section also provides easy access to the list of matching titles" (*About ChoiceReviews.online*, 2002) (http://www.choicereviews.org/

Rev170ChoiceScripts/ProfileForm.asp?SCID=123102-225829-22020&Ne
wReg=ON).

PRINT TOOLS

In the "everything is on the Web" world, it is easy to forget the traditional tools of the librarian: books. Following is a list of selected print sources for collection management in general, as well as specific sources for psychology. In addition, be sure to consult *Contemporary Psychology: APA Review of Books*, the primary book review journal for psychology, containing critical reviews of books, films, tapes, and other media relevant to psychology.

Books

50 years of notable books. (1996). Chicago: Booklist Publications.

The best books for academic libraries. (2002). Temecula, CA: Best Books, Inc.

Bibliographic guide to psychology. (1975-). Boston: G. K. Hall.

Books for college libraries: A core collection of 50,000 titles. (1988). Chicago: American Library Association.

Bartlett, R. A. (1998). *Choice's outstanding academic books, 1992-1997.* Chicago: Association of College and Research Libraries.

Baxter, P. M. (1993). *Psychology: A guide to reference and information sources.* Englewood, CO: Libraries Unlimited.

Beers, S. E. (1996). *Psychology: An introductory bibliography.* Lanham, MD: Scarecrow Press.

Futas, E. (1995). Collection development policies and procedures. Phoenix, AZ: Oryx Press.

Gorman, G. E. & Miller, R.H. (1997). *Collection management for the 21st century: A handbook for librarians.* Westport, CT: Greenwood Press.

Hill, J. S., Hannaford, W. E., & Epp, R.H. (1991). *Collection development in college libraries.* Chicago, IL: American Library Association.

Nisonger, T. E. (1992). *Collection evaluation in academic libraries: A literature guide and annotated bibliography.* Englewood, CO: Libraries Unlimited.

Persson, D. M. (1990). *Psychology and psychiatry serials: A bibliographic aid for collection development.* New York: The Haworth Press, Inc.

Rupp-Serrano, K. (2000). *Collection management: Preparing today's bibliographies for tomorrow's libraries.* New York, NY: The Haworth Press, Inc.

Sandy, J. H. (1996). *Approval plans: Issues and innovations.* New York: The Haworth Press, Inc.

Wynar, B. S. (2002). *American reference books annual, 2002.* Englewood, CO: Libraries Unlimited.

Journal Articles

Dorner, D. G. (1994). A study of the collection inventory assessments for psychology in the Canadian conspectus database and an analysis of the conspectus methodology. *Library & Information Science Research*, 16, 279-97.

Gangl, S. D. (1991). Communication and cooperation in psychology collection development in a large university: The SCOPE project. *Behavioral & Social Sciences Librarian*, 11(1), 97-112.

Gilman, I. B. (1991). Evaluating research library collections in psychology: Beyond the conspectus. *Behavioral & Social Sciences Librarian*, 10(2), 27-56.

Jordan, R. P. (1991). Colloquium on collection coordination in psychology/psychiatry. *Behavioral & Social Sciences Librarian*, 11(1), 73-112.

Schoen, D. M., & Hino, S. M. (1998). Building psychology collections using core journal lists: An annotated bibliography. *Behavioral & Social Sciences Librarian*, 17(1), 55-61.

Segal, J. A. (1991). Psychology/psychiatry collection development: The social work branch library. *Behavioral & Social Sciences Librarian*, 11(1), 75-83.

Shontz, D. E. (1991). Coordinating collection development and use: Psychology at the University of Florida. *Behavioral & Social Sciences Librarian*, 11(1), 85-95.

Shontz, D. E. (1992). The serial/monograph ratio in psychology: Application at the local level. *Behavioral & Social Sciences Librarian*, 11(2), 91-105.

Sylvia, M. J. (1998). Citation analysis as an unobtrusive method for journal collection evaluation using psychology student research bibliographies. *Collection Building*, 17(1), 20-28.

Yang, E. L. (1990). Psychology collection review: A cooperative project between librarians and departmental faculty members. *Collection Management,* 13(3), 43-55.

THE LIAISON PROCESS

Most academic libraries have a liaison system where each librarian works with one or more departmental liaisons. This process varies wildly; in some libraries/departments, the librarian is a mere conduit, making sure that the liaison receives approval plan slips and catalogs, and reviewing the liaisons' request lists before they are sent to be ordered. At the other extreme, sole responsibility falls on the librarian to purchase all the books for the department. While some librarians prefer the latter, unfettered approach, be particularly careful in these circumstances to follow the collection development policy, or to insure that such a policy is created, so that everyone knows the parameters of selection. The last thing needed by a new hire, or by a librarian assigned to a new collection area, is to be accused of frivolously spending the precious dollars earmarked for the department. Ideally, there will be a separate policy covering liaisons; a good starting point is *Library Faculty Liaison Guide* by David Gray of Marshall University (http://www.marshall.edu/colldev/liaison_guide. htm). Bear in mind that this sample reflects a university with a collection development librarian, and that modifications would be necessary in a library where such a position does not exist. In addition, more specific information regarding deadlines would be especially helpful.

Many current library school collection development classes train librarians to view themselves as collection development experts. This is treacherous ground. The librarian's expertise must be integrated with that of the subject specialist, the teaching faculty member. Other problems may arise if a faculty member approaches the Acquisitions Department directly with requests, rather than going through the established channel of the faculty liaison. In this type of situation, the best tactic is to contact the liaison and review the requests with him/her. A proactive approach that may preempt various problems is to request time at a department meeting. If it is possible to meet face-to-face with the faculty, let them know the services the library can provide and ask them directly how they, as a department, prefer to work with their contacts. Be aware that being given time at a department meeting is a privilege; keep your remarks brief and distribute handouts outlining any areas that may be subject to misunderstanding. For additional proactive ideas, see *Brainstorming Ideas for Faculty Liaison* on the BRASS Business Reference in Academic Libraries Committee Web site (http://www.ala.org/rusa/brass/liaison.html).

LIBRARY INSTRUCTION

A great way to build a good relationship with a department is to handle its library instruction needs. I have found that when I work with faculty on their information literacy instruction requests, we develop a one-on-one relationship, built on respect. Developing only one or two such relationships per semester leads to results that are exponential.

CONTINUING EDUCATION

The title of a pre-conference scheduled at the ALA Annual Meeting 2003, *Real World Collection Development: What You Didn't Learn in Library School*, exemplifies issues addressed in this article. "Many librarians in all types of libraries find that their academic training did not teach them everything needed to successfully fulfill their collection development responsibilities. The ever-changing nature of their jobs has made this task even more challenging. Speakers will focus on 'real-world' issues, trends, and skills related to the major activities involved in (1) selecting high quality and appropriate materials in all formats; (2) collection maintenance; (3) collection management; and (4) collection evaluation (e.g., collecting statistics) to help participants improve their collections. The pre-conference will focus on very practical issues with various hands-on and learning events" (Neuhaus, 2002).

Various library listservs and publications regularly publicize Continuing Education opportunities, many available online.

ASK COLLEAGUES FOR HELP

In spite of efforts to develop positive, fruitful relationships with faculty liaison(s) and academic department(s), problems may still arise. Turn to library colleagues for help. Difficulties in working with a faculty member may be due to a history of which the new librarian is unaware. The supervisor or the library director may be able to provide background information. For outside help with collection development questions, the new hire reluctant to reveal his/her ignorance to new colleagues can use the library listservs.

COLLECTION DEVELOPMENT LISTSERVS

ACQNET-L: The Acquisitions Librarians Electronic Network

"ACQNET is a forum in which acquisitions librarians and others interested in acquisitions may exchange information and ideas, and find solutions to common problems. It started with a group of 25 librarians in December 1990 and as of

February 2002 has over 1,500 subscribers" (Cook, 2002). For subscription information, see http://acqweb.library.vanderbilt.edu/acqweb/acqnet.html.

COLLDV-L

COLLDV-L was created and is moderated by Lynn Sipe, University of Southern California. "While the initial idea for what became COLLDV-L originated with the Chief Collection Development Officers of Large Research Libraries Discussion Group, it has never been officially affiliated with ALA or CMDS. Informally it has been a frequently consulted medium for announcements of ALA meetings of interest to collection development staff" (*COLLDV-L*, 2002) (http://www.ala.org/alcts/organization/cmds/colldv.html). I initially joined this listserv to learn more about collection development. As it does not produce a lot of traffic, I have maintained my subscription and have found the members to be very helpful whenever I have questions.

There are also library listservs for specific subject areas; the web sites mentioned above have links to many of these lists.

CONCLUSION

Building a library's collection is very satisfying work and the most tangible aspect of library service for many librarians. It is very gratifying to see people looking at the new bookshelf or to have students or faculty express thanks that the library has provided a particular book. While collection development duties are challenging, hopefully the tools and suggestions provided here will help the new librarian rise to the challenge.

REFERENCES

About ChoiceReviews.online. (2002). Retrieved December 30, 2002, from http://www. choicereviews.org/Rev170choicescripts/AboutChoice.asp?SCID=&ReturnURL= MainMenu.asp.

Brainstorming ideas for faculty liaison. (2001). Retrieved December 30, 2002, from BRASS Business Reference in Academic Libraries Committee, ALA Midwinter Conference Web site: http://www.ala.org/rusa/brass/liaison.html.

CHOICE: current reviews for academic libraries. (2002). Retrieved February 14, 2003, from http://www.ala.org/acrl/choice/index.html.

Clayton, P. (1998). *Guidelines for the preparation of a collection development policy.* Retrieved December 8, 2002, from Australian Libraries Gateway, Collection Development Policies Web site: http://www.nla.gov.au/libraries/resource/acliscdp.html.

COLLDV-L. (2002). Retrieved December 30, 2002, from American Library Association, Association for Library Collections and Technical Services, Collection Management and Development Section Web site: http://www.ala.org/alcts/organization/cmds/ colldv.html.

Collection assessment. (2002). Retrieved December 30, 2002, from University of Wyoming Libraries, Collection Development Office Web site: http://www-lib.uwyo.edu/ cdo/collass.htm.

Collection Development Education Committee. (2002). *Survey of collection development courses at ALA accredited programs (2002).* Retrieved December 30, 2002, from American Library Association, Reference and User Services Association, CODES Collection Development and Education Section Web site: http://www.ala.org/ rusa/codes/cde_syllabi.html.

Collection development policy. (1996). Retrieved December 8, 2002, from University at Albany, State University of New York, University Libraries Web site: http:// library.albany.edu/subject/cdp/policy.html.

Cook, E. (2002). *ACQNET welcome message.* Retrieved December 31, 2002, from http://acqweb.library.vanderbilt.edu/acqweb/acqnet/welcome.html.

D'Aniello, C. (1999). *A tool kit of links and documents for collection development and management librarians.* Retrieved December 8, 2002, from State University of New York at Buffalo, Lockwood Memorial Library Web site: http://ublib.buffalo. edu/libraries/units/lml/colldev/cdInternet.html.

Gray, D. (1999). *Library faculty liaison guide.* Retrieved December 30, 2002, from Marshall University Libraries, Collection Development and Acquisitions Web site: http://www.marshall.edu/colldev/liaison_guide.htm.

Gray, D. (1999). *Making a gift to the library.* Retrieved December 8, 2002, from Marshall University Libraries, Collection Development and Acquisitions Web site: http://www.marshall.edu/colldev/gifts.htm.

Hall, B. (2000). *ALCTS publications acquisitions bibliography: A selected bibliography for library acquisitions, fourth edition.* Retrieved December 8, 2002, from American Library Association, Association for Library Collections and Technical Services Web site: http://www.ala.org/alcts/publications/web/acq/acqbib.html.

Kirkpatrick, M. (2002). Collection development policies: Psychology. Retrieved December 8, 2002, from Boston University Libraries, Mugar Memorial Library Web site: http://www.bu.edu/library/collections/cdpsych.htm.

Laning, M. (2002). *Collection profile: Psychological & brain sciences.* Retrieved December 8, 2002, from University of Louisville, University Libraries, Office of Collection Development Web site: http://library.louisville.edu/collmgmt/profiles/psychology. html.

Leiserson, A. B. (2002). *AcqWeb's publisher web sites: Subject directory.* Retrieved December 8, 2002, from http://acqweb.library.vanderbilt.edu/acqweb/pubr.html#subj.

Mazin, B. *Acqweb's directory of collection development policies on the web.* Retrieved December 8, 2002, from http://acqweb.library.vanderbilt.edu/acqweb/cd_policy. html#college.

Nesbeitt, S. L. (2002). *Library job postings on the Internet.* Retrieved December 20, 2002, from http://www.libraryjobpostings.org/postings.htm.

Neuhaus, P. (2002). *Real world collection development: What you didn't learn in library school.* Retrieved December 30, 2002, from American Library Association, Reference and User Services Association, CODES Collection Development and Evaluation Section Web site: http://www.ala.org/rusa/codes/cde_pre_conf.html.

Nyhan, C., & Lent, L. (2002). *Using the web for collection development: Selecting print and audiovisual materials.* Retrieved December 8, 2002, from Pasadena City College, Shatford Library Web site: http://www.paccd.cc.ca.us/library/lib101/Colldevbib.htm.

Psychology collection development policy statement. (2002). Retrieved December 8, 2002, from Louisiana State University, LSU Libraries Web site: http://www.lib.lsu.edu/collserv/colldev/policies/psychology.html.

Sha, V.T. (2002). *Internet library for librarians: Acquisitions, serials, and collection development.* Retrieved December 8, 2002, from http://www.itcompany.com/inforetriever/acqsercd.htm.

Smokey, S. (2002). *Collection development policy statement: Psychology and school psychology.* Retrieved December 8, 2002, from Rochester Institute of Technology, RIT Library Web site: http://wally.rit.edu/information/collection/Statements/Psychology.html.

Title Source II on the Web. (2002). Retrieved December 31, 2002, from http://ts2d.informata.com/TS2/.

Using profile. (2002). Retrieved December 30, 2002, from http://www.choicereviews.org/Rev170ChoiceScripts/ProfileForm.asp?SCID=123102-225829-22020&NewReg=ON.

Yochelson, A., Ammen, C., Guidas, J., Harvey, S., Larson, C. & Mcginnis, M. (2000). *Collection development and the Internet: A brief handbook for recommending officers in the humanities and social sciences division at the Library Of Congress.* Retrieved December 8, 2002, from The Library of Congress, Collection Development Web site: http://lcweb.loc.gov/acq/colldev/handbook.html.

Crossing Boundaries:
Selecting for Research, Professional Development and Consumer Education in an Interdisciplinary Field, the Case of Mental Health

Patricia Pettijohn

SUMMARY. Both the demand for, and supply of, mental health information has increased across all sectors. Academic, public and special libraries must locate, evaluate and select materials that support consumer education, academic teaching, interdisciplinary research, and professional credentialing. Selectors must navigate disciplinary barriers to develop materials in an interdisciplinary field that includes not just psychology, psychiatry, social work, sociology, gerontology, medicine, and neurology, but also public policy and law. *[Article copies available for a fee from The Haworth Document Delivery Service: 1-800-HAWORTH. E-mail address: <docdelivery@haworthpress.com> Website: <http://www.HaworthPress.com> © 2004 by The Haworth Press, Inc. All rights reserved.]*

KEYWORDS. Mental health, interdisciplinary, multidisciplinary, collection development, learning communities, materials selection, behavioral healthcare, research library

Patricia Pettijohn is Research Librarian, Louis de la Parte Florida Mental Health Institute Research Library, University of South Florida, 13301 Bruce B. Downs Boulevard, Tampa, FL 33612 (E-mail: ppettijohn@fmhi.usf.edu).

[Haworth co-indexing entry note]: "Crossing Boundaries: Selecting for Research, Professional Development and Consumer Education in an Interdisciplinary Field, the Case of Mental Health." Pettijohn, Patricia. Co-published simultaneously in *The Acquisitions Librarian* (The Haworth Information Press, an imprint of The Haworth Press, Inc.) No. 31/32, 2004, pp. 163-176; and: *Selecting Materials for Library Collections* (ed: Audrey Fenner) The Haworth Information Press, an imprint of The Haworth Press, Inc., 2004, pp. 163-176. Single or multiple copies of this article are available for a fee from The Haworth Document Delivery Service [1-800-HAWORTH, 9:00 a.m. - 5:00 p.m. (EST). E-mail address: docdelivery@haworthpress.com].

Since 1995, when the Secretary General of the United Nations designated mental health as a key U.N. priority for the next fifty years, a series of national and international initiatives has focused attention on the global burden of behavioral and substance use disorders (Desjarlais, Eisenberg, Good, & Kleinman, 1996). The release of *Mental Health: A Report of the Surgeon General* (U.S. Office of the Surgeon General, 1999) in the same year as the first White House Conference on Mental Health confirmed the growing importance of this interdisciplinary field to national policy.

Selecting materials in the broad field of mental health requires a consideration of the information needs of a diverse community of users. The information needs of mental health professionals, engaged in ongoing credentialing and professional development, differ from those of professionals looking for clinical information to support psychiatric treatment or behavioral interventions. The needs of scholars engaged in teaching differ from those of interdisciplinary research teams relying on grants and contracts for funding. Similarly, the information needs of behavioral healthcare consumers and their families differ from those of undergraduate and graduate students pursuing degrees in social work, gerontology, applied anthropology, criminal justice, nursing and public health.

Policymakers, government agencies, community organizations, and behavioral healthcare service providers need mental health information that translates evidence-based research. Research faculty and staff need resources that encourage collaborative research across a range of disciplines, while providing depth and specificity of resources within research topics. The study of mental health is developmentally focused as well, requiring resources that support the study of mental health in childhood and adolescence, adulthood, and old age. Thus, gerontology, pediatrics, and child and adolescent studies must be included in the disciplines relevant to mental health.

CROSSING DISCIPLINARY BOUNDARIES

To successfully conduct collaborative projects on such multidimensional and interdisciplinary topics, we have to think about what would happen if disciplinary barriers were taken away . . . Whether or not the final product of the collaboration has wide appeal across fields and disciplines (and funding agencies) is the ultimate test of successful collaboration. (Tsuya, 2002, p. 57)

Disciplines closely associated with the study of mental health include virtually all social sciences, and many of the biological sciences. The study of behavioral disorders is linked to the study of law, special education, social work, and nursing in part because the public systems of criminal justice, education, social welfare, and public health serve as primary points of contact with persons with behavioral and substance use disorders. Because public policy plays a critical role in determining institutional response to mental illness, the study of mental health law is equally concerned with policy.

The literature of mental health includes the perspectives of a number of academic disciplines besides psychology and psychiatry. Some disciplines, such as developmental neuroscience or genetics, contribute basic research findings to the behavioral healthcare knowledge base in ways that may dramatically shift both theoretical paradigms and applied practice in mental health. While all disciplines apply the methodologies and theories unique to their field to mental health services and research, the integration of interdisciplinary knowledge characterizes the study of mental health.

Dobson, Kushkowski, and Gerhard have outlined the major characteristics of interdisciplinary fields, and the special considerations these bring to library selection:

- The complete map of the intellectual field is much broader.
- Appropriate research methodologies in an interdisciplinary area are likely to vary more widely, requiring a broader array of library materials to adequately support research.
- Bibliographic control may be weak or lacking, making it difficult to identify appropriate materials for a given collection.
- Specialization and stratification are part of an interdisciplinary field from the beginning of its development (1996, p. 280).

BASIC SELECTION TOOLS–COMMERCIAL DATABASES

Interdisciplinary fields present a number of problems for collection development and acquisitions librarians. The most obvious is the need to consult general, multidisciplinary bibliographic databases, as well as specialized resources that index and abstract the literature of specific disciplines and modalities. Access to *PsycINFO* from the American Psychological Association (APA), considered the primary index to scholarly psychological literature, cannot guarantee comprehensive coverage of behavioral healthcare but does provide a basic selection tool. *PsycINFO* provides indexing and abstracting of over 1,300 books yearly, but cautions that coverage is representative, rather than comprehensive. Until the appearance of the APA-sponsored electronic journal *Psycoloquy*, *PsycINFO* and *Contemporary Psychology: APA Review of Books* were the only APA products to review or abstract books. *Psycoloquy*, freely available on the Internet, is an open archive of articles and peer commentary that includes book reviews and author-submitted précis.

More comprehensive behavioral healthcare collections require the use of specialized databases to develop collections in particular genres or topics. For example, the Buros Institute *Mental Measurements Yearbook*, the Educational Resources Information Center (ERIC) *Clearinghouse on Assessment and Evaluation* and *Health & Psychosocial Instruments (HAPI)* may be needed to identify, select and locate tests and measures. Subject-oriented databases with substantive mental health content include *Sociological Abstracts* (Cambridge Scientific Abstracts), *Ageline* (American Association of Retired Persons), *Criminal Justice Abstracts* (National Council on Crime & Delinquency), *CJPI: Criminal Justice Periodical Index*, *e-psyche*, and *Cumulative Index to Nursing & Allied Health Literature (CINAHL)*.

Proprietary databases that cover the larger field of social science are also useful, and multidisciplinary databases, like the Institute for Scientific Information (ISI) *Current Contents Connect*, provide an overview of books and journals in economics, education, health sciences, information sciences, rehabilitation, social work, social policy, anthropology and sociology. For international research, *International Bibliography of the Social Sciences (IBSS)*, with over two million bibliographic entries dating from 1951, provides comprehensive coverage.

BASIC SELECTION TOOLS–PUBLIC DATABASES

Libraries of all types, including public, research, and academic, will benefit by monitoring the web-based databases of government agencies and non-profit organizations, and by participating in the current awareness services they provide. For example, *JustInfo*, an electronic newsletter, alerts subscribers to new publications from the National Criminal Justice Reference Service (NCJRS), hyper-linked to their publications catalog to facilitate ordering. A similar service covering demographic reports is offered by the Population Reference Bureau *E-Library* alert service.

The *National Technical Information Service* (NTIS) provides access to documents from many U.S. government agencies, through an online database with an advanced search interface; brief documents are provided without cost, longer items at a nominal cost. The Substance Abuse and Mental Health Services Administration (SAMHSA) *National Mental Health Information Center* is of particular interest, providing access to a wide range of materials, from fact sheets to films, at no cost. Substantive materials for researchers include monographs, reports and topical bibliographies. Another source of research reports is the National Science Foundation (NSF) *Online Document Center*, where documents from the Directorate for Social, Behavioral and Economic Sciences (SBE), are located.

The ERIC clearinghouses (Educational Resources Information Center, 2002) are another important resource, particularly the *Clearinghouse on Adult, Career, and Vocational Education (ERIC/ACVE)*, the *Clearinghouse on Assessment and Evaluation (ERIC/AE)*, the *Clearinghouse on Counseling and Student Services (ERIC/CASS)*, and the *Clearinghouse on Disabilities and Gifted Education (ERIC EC)*. While the web-based ERIC databases are freely accessible, access to the full text of documents will require either payment of a nominal fee to the ERIC Document Reproduction Service (EDRS), or library access to *E*Subscribe* or the ERIC microfiche collection. Selected full-text summaries of ERIC documents are freely available online through *ERIC Digests* (Educational Resources Information Center, 2002). For international information, searches of *WHOLIS*, the World Health Organization (WHO) library database, *WHODOC*, the current bibliography of WHO documentation, or the *WHO Publications Catalogue* are profitable.

The importance of these Internet sites to collection development in the area of mental health cannot be overestimated, since new areas of research, new findings, national research policies and priorities, and translations of the latest evidence-based research, often are first published in the arena of publicly funded research. In mental health research, generative articles may appear first in technical reports and government documents, and only later in the peer-reviewed literature (Blackburn, 2001).

THE ROLE OF RESEARCH PRIORITIES

As the role of research and development in the intellectual and economic life of the modern university has expanded, the need for special collections and resources that support research funded by foundation and government grants and contracts, rather than supporting an academic curriculum, has grown. The National Institute of Mental Health (NIMH) *Blueprint for Change Report* emphasized interdisciplinary research as a national research priority:

First, interdisciplinary research activities will require that linkages be made and supported across a range of scientific disciplines and between scientists and practitioners. In particular, transnational research activities should incorporate (as feasible) perspectives drawn from diverse areas, including developmental neuroscience, genetics, epidemiology, behavioral science, economics, anthropology, education, social marketing, organizational/industrial psychology, informational science, prevention, treatment, or services research. (Hoagwood and Olin, 2002, p. 764)

The establishment of local, state and national research priorities has an impact on selection in a number of ways. Materials are needed to support research projects generated by the funding agency's statement of research priorities. These materials may be purchased by the library in response to faculty requests, or purchased by research departments as part of a contract. In addition, grants and contracts require dissemination of research findings, creating a body of technical reports, proceedings and government documents to be identified and acquired.

Although the primary means of disseminating research is through technical reports and academic journal articles, grants and contracts often require that research findings be presented in formats useful to consumers. This translation of research has generated a large body of literature aimed at behavioral healthcare consumers and their families. These materials, ranging from topical information packets to comprehensive consumer collections, are available in print, electronic, and multi-media formats through government agency websites.

Materials are available on specific behavioral and substance use disorders through the NIMH, the SAMHSA, the NCJRS, and the National Institute on Alcohol & Alcoholism (NIAAA), among others. However, when the President's New Freedom Commission on Mental Health concluded, "America's mental health service delivery system is in shambles," fragmentation of mental health services and research among multiple agencies was cited as a key barrier (Eichenauer, 2002). This same barrier complicates the search for mental health information, which is widely dispersed among state and federal agency websites.

THE ROLE OF FOUNDATIONS, ASSOCIATIONS AND ORGANIZATIONS

Private foundations offering technical assistance, bibliographies, publications, consumer information, and in some cases significant donations of materials, include the Robert Wood Johnson Foundation and the Annie E. Casey Foundation. Other foundations and non-profit organizations target specific behavioral disorders, such as the John Maxwell Biasco Foundation for Children with Autism, which not only provides bibliographies on autism for children and their families, but also donates materials and matching funds to organizations willing to establish an autism resource center.

Professional associations and societies publish reports, monographs and proceedings, and offer current awareness services, electronic forums, mailing lists and subject-specific Internet portals and pathfinders. These range from non-profit organizations concerned with particular populations or issues, such as the National Resource Center on Homelessness and Mental Illness, to associations focused on particular professions, such as the American Academy of Child and Adolescent Psychiatry. Associations of library and information professionals specializing in mental health and substance abuse are among the best resources for a selector new to the behavioral healthcare field. These include the Association of Mental Health Librarians (AMHL), the Medical Library Association Mental Health Special Interest Group (MLA-MHSIG), and the Substance Abuse Librarians & Information Specialists (SALIS).

One of the most useful resources for selectors in the area of mental health policy is *PIE Online*, the Policy Information Exchange (PIE) searchable online database of primary source materials in mental health policy (Missouri Institute of Mental Health, 2002). In addition to technical reports and other documents on a range of behavioral healthcare issues, *PIE* includes a number of topical annotated bibliographies of recommended resources. Another source of publications in the area of mental health policy is the National Association of State Mental Health Program Directors (NASMHPD) National Technical Assistance Center for State Mental Health Planning (NTAC). The Bazelon Center for Mental Health Law publishes books, policy briefs, legal interpretation, law manuals, and technical assistance guides aimed for professionals and consumers.

CORE LISTS AND GUIDES–PRINT SELECTION TOOLS

Many of the basic selection tools and methods of acquiring monographs are limited in their usefulness when selecting in interdisciplinary areas (Llull, 1991). Approval plans and standing orders may not be practical. Writing about acquisitions at the RAND research library, Scheiberg (2001) notes:

> There is no approval plan in place; the research needs are too specific and time delimited to make an approval plan a viable option. This increases the burden on the selectors, who must keep abreast of both current and future research topics and trends within RAND's scope. Furthermore, the majority of RAND's research is valuable for its timeliness; this means that the selectors also have to strike a balance between classic and current literature, and decide whether proactive or reactive collection development is more applicable. (2001, p. 395)

Fortunately, a number of guides to the literature and topical core lists have been developed, although many are in need of updating. While some of these serve as guides to the social sciences generally, and others focus more narrowly on specific disciplines or topics, no single interdisciplinary guide to mental health resources is available. The annotations and recommendations of books and videos in *The Complete Mental Health Directory* (Mars & Stotland, 2001) are more relevant to consumer than academic collections. *Library Services in Mental Health Settings* (Johnson, 1997) includes a number of selected topical bibliographies. Of particular interest is the selective guide to clinical information resources in psychiatry, which identifies a core collection (Epstein, Saghafi, Foster, Dill, Fischerkeller and Tedjeske, 1997). The Brandon-Hill selected lists *Small Medical Library* and *Nursing* (Hill and Stickell, 2001, 2002) include core selections in neurology, psychiatry, and psychiatric nursing. Combining core lists from Saghafi et al. and the Brandon-Hill lists with *Core Readings in Psychiatry: an annotated guide to the literature* (Sacks, Sledge and Warren, 1995), generates a list of recommended titles useful in assessing and developing a core collection in clinical psychiatry.

Bibliographies and guides that address the intersection of mental health and specific disciplines include works on psychology (Reed & Baxter, 1992; Baxter, 1993) sociology and anthropology (Driver, 1972), consumer research and economic psychology (Earl, 1999), and managed behavioral healthcare (Center for Mental Health Services, Substance Abuse and Mental Health Services, 2000). For current multi-disciplinary reviews of materials in all formats, the *Behavioral & Social Sciences Librarian* is an especially useful resource (Stover, 2002).

INCLUSIVE AND DIVERSE MATERIALS

Another consideration complicating selection in the field of mental health is the need to provide resources that include information and data on ethnic and racial minorities, and that support the study of racial and ethnic disparities in health care. Annotated bibliographies on mental health and specific minority populations are included in *Mental Health: Culture, Race and Ethnicity* (2001), a supplement to the U.S. Surgeon General's groundbreaking 1999 report. Keita and Petersen's *Blacks in the United States: abstracts of the psychological and behavioral literature, 1987-1995* (1996) is useful for enhancing mental health collections retrospectively.

Inclusion of information and data on both men and women, and of works that consider the role of gender in behavioral healthcare problems and programs, poses additional challenges in developing either research or consumer collections. The U.S. Department of Health and Human Services Office on Women's Health (OWH) has created the National Women's Health Information Center–Women with DisAbilities (NWHIC-WWD) website, with consumer information, statistics, and publications for and about women with learning, developmental, neurological, psychiatric, and substance abuse disabilities (2002). A guide to core books and journals in print developed by the Women's Studies Section of the Association of College & Research Libraries (ACRL-WSS) includes a frequently updated bibliography, *Mental Health* (Smith, 2002). Global information on gender disparities is available through the World Health Organization (WHO) Department of Mental Health and Substance Abuse.

CONCLUSION

Selecting materials in the field of mental health requires an awareness of publicly funded research, interdisciplinary selection tools, and specialized databases. Resources supporting both applied fields and academic disciplines must be included when developing mental health collections. Fortunately, much is freely available on the Internet, including full text publications and guides to the literature.

LIST OF SELECTION RESOURCES

American Academy of Child and Adolescent Psychiatry. Retrieved December 3, 2002, from http://www.aacap.org/index.htm.
American Association of Retired Persons (2002). *Ageline*. Retrieved November 23, 2002, from http://research.aarp.org/ageline/home.html.
American Psychological Association (1987-1990). *PsycBOOKS: books & chapters in psychology*. Arlington, VA: Author.
American Psychological Association (2002). *Contemporary psychology: APA review of books*. Washington, DC: Author.
American Psychological Association (2002). *PsycINFO*. Retrieved November 30, 2002, from http://www.apa.org/psycinfo/.
American Psychological Association (2002). *Psycoloquy*. Retrieved November 29, 2002, from http://psycprints.ecs.soton.ac.uk/.
Anderson, C.W. & Adley, A.R. (Eds.) (1997). *Gay & lesbian issues: Abstracts of the psychological and behavioral literature, 1985-1996*. Washington, DC: American Psychological Association.
Annie E. Casey Foundation. (2002). Retrieved November 11, 2002, from http://www.aecf.org/.

Baxter, P.M. (1993). *Psychology: A guide to reference and information sources.* Englewood, CO: Libraries Unlimited.

Buros Institute of Mental Measurements (2002). *Mental measurements yearbook.* Highland Park, NJ: Buros Institute of Mental Measurements, University of Nebraska Press. Retrieved December 1, 2002, from http://www.silverplatter.com/catalog/mmyb.htm.

Cambridge Scientific Abstracts (2002). *Sociological abstracts.* Retrieved December 11, 2002 from http://www.csa.com.

Center for Mental Health Services, Substance Abuse and Mental Health Services and Administration (2000). *Annotated bibliography for managed behavioral health care: 1989-1999: Special report.* Retrieved November 1, 2002 from http://purl.access.gpo.gov/GPO/LPS17844.

CJPI: Criminal justice periodical index. (2002). Ann Arbor, MI: Bell & Howell Information and Learning Co. Retrieved November 12, 2002, from http://www.umi.com/.

Cumulative index to nursing & allied health literature (2002). Glendale, CA.: CINAHL Information Systems. Retrieved November 1, 2002, from http://www.cinahl.com.

Driver, E.D. (1972). *The Sociology and anthropology of mental illness: A reference guide.* (Rev. ed.). Amherst, MA: University of Massachusetts Press.

e-psyche (2002). Albuquerque, NM: Database Access Group. Retrieved December 11, 2002, from http://www.e-psyche.net/.

Earl, P.E. & Kemp, S. (1999). *The Elgar companion to consumer research and economic psychology.* Cheltenham, UK; Northampton, MA: Edward Elgar.

Educational Resources Information Center (2002). *ERIC clearinghouse on adult, career, and vocational education (ERIC/ACVE).* Retrieved November 11, 2002, from http://ericacve.org/.

Educational Resources Information Center (2002). *ERIC clearinghouse on assessment and evaluation (ERIC/AE).* College Park, MD: National Library of Education, U.S. Department of Education and Department of Measurement, Statistics, and Evaluation, University of Maryland. Retrieved November 8, 2002 from http://ericae.net/.

Educational Resources Information Center (2002) *ERIC clearinghouse on counseling and student services (ERIC/CASS).* Greensboro, NC: University of North Carolina at Greensboro, School of Education. Retrieved November 5, 2002 from http://ericcass.uncg.edu.

Educational Resources Information Center (2002). *ERIC clearinghouse on disabilities and gifted education (ERIC EC).* Reston, VA: The Clearinghouse. Retrieved November 14, 2002 from http://ericec.org/.

Educational Resources Information Center. (2002). *ERIC clearinghouses.* Washington, D.C.: Office of Educational Research and Improvement, U.S. Dept. of Education, Retrieved December 2, 2002, from http://www.eric.ed.gov/.

Educational Resources Information Center (2002). *ERIC digests.* Washington, DC: ERIC Clearinghouses, Office of Educational Research and Improvement (OERI), U.S. Department of Education. Retrieved October 11, 2002, from http://www.ed.gov/databases/ERIC_Digests/index/.

ERIC Clearinghouse on Disabilities and Gifted Education (ERIC EC). (2002). *Minibibs: ERIC EC minibibliographies.* Retrieved December 2, 2002, from http://ericec.org/factmini.html.

Epstein, B.A., Saghafi, E., Foster, A.G., Dill, D.M., Fischerkeller, J.H., Tedjeske, J.M. (1997). Clinical information resources in psychiatry: A selective guide. In Mary E. Johnson (Ed.) *Library services in mental health settings* (pp. 125-172). Lanham, MD & London: Medical Library Association and The Scarecrow Press.

Feinberg, S., Feldman, S., & Jordan, B. (1996). Building a family support collection: Guidelines. In S. Feinberg & S. Feldman (Eds.), *Serving families and children through partnerships: A how to do it manual for librarians* (pp. 117-29). New York: Neal-Schuman.

Goldman, B., Busch, J.C., Egelson, P.E., Saunders, J.L. & Mitchell, D.F. (Eds.) (1997). *Directory of unpublished experimental mental measures.* (Vols. 1-7, 1974-1997). Washington, DC. American Psychological Association; New York: Human Sciences Press.

Harvard University (1972). *The Harvard list of books in psychology, compiled and annotated by the psychologists in Harvard University.* Cambridge: Harvard University Press.

Health & psychosocial instruments (2002). Pittsburgh: Behavioral Measurement Database Services. Retrieved November 15, 2002, from http://www.ovid.com/.

Hill, D.R. & Stickell, H. (2001). *Print books and journals for the small medical library 2001.* New York: Mount Sinai School of Medicine. Retrieved January 14, 2003 from http://www.brandon-hill.com/small_medical/index.shtml.

Hill, D.R. & Stickell, H. (2002). *Print nursing books and journals 2002.* New York: Mount Sinai School of Medicine. Retrieved January 12, 2003 from http://www.brandon-hill.com/nursing/index.shtml.

Institute for Scientific Information. (2002). *Current contents connect.* Retrieved December 11, 2002, from http://www.isinet.com/isi/index.html.

International bibliography of the social sciences (2002). Retrieved December 1, 2002, from The London School of Economics and Political Science Web site: http://www.lse.ac.uk/collections/IBSS/.

John Maxwell Biasco Foundation for Children with Autism (2002). Retrieved October 30, 2002, from http://www.maxie.org/.

Johnson, Mary E. (Ed.) (1997). *Library services in mental health settings.* Lanham, MD & London: Medical Library Association and The Scarecrow Press.

Jordan, B. (1996). Building a family support collection: print and non-print resources. In S. Feinberg, S. Feldman, & B. Jordan (Eds.), *Serving families and children through partnerships: A how to do it manual for librarians* (pp. 131-58). New York: Neal-Schuman.

Keita, G.P. & Petersen, A.C.O. (1996). *Blacks in the United States: Abstracts of the psychological and behavioral literature, 1987-1995.* Washington DC: American Psychological Association.

Llull, H.P. (1991). Meeting the academic and research information needs of scientists and engineers in the university environment. *Science & Technology Libraries, 11*, 83-90.

Maddox, T. (Ed.) (1997). *Tests: A comprehensive reference for assessments in psychology, education, and business.* Austin, TX: Pro-Ed.

Mars, L. & Stotland, N. (Eds.) (2001). *The complete mental health directory: A comprehensive source book for individuals and professionals.* (Third Ed.) Millerton, NY: Grey House Publishing; Gale Research.

Medical Library Association Mental Health Special Interest Group (2002). Retrieved December 3, 2002, from http://www.miami.edu/mhsig/.

Missouri Institute of Mental Health, Policy Resource Center. (2002). *PIE online: Policy information exchange (PIE).* Retrieved November 4, 2002, from http://www.mimh.edu/mimhweb/pie/.

National Alliance for the Mentally Ill (NAMI). (2002). Retrieved October 1, 2002, from http://www.nami.org/.

National Alliance for the Mentally Ill [NAMI] Literature Committee (2002). *NAMI book reviews.* Retrieved October 1, 2002, from National Alliance for the Mentally Ill [NAMI] Web site: http://www.nami.org/advocate/bookreviews. html 2002.

National Association of State Mental Health Program Directors (NASMHPD) and Substance Abuse and Mental Health Administration (SAMHSA) (2002). *National technical assistance center for state mental health planning (NTAC).* Retrieved October 23, 2002, from http://www.nasmhpd.org/ntac/.

National Council on Crime and Delinquency and SilverPlatter Information, Inc. (2002). *Criminal justice abstracts.* Sage Publications, Inc. 2002.

National Criminal Justice Reference Service (2002). *JustINFO.* Retrieved November 2, 2002, from http://puborder.ncjrs.org/listservs/subscribe_JUSTINFO. asp.

National Criminal Justice Reference Service abstracts database. (2002). Retrieved November 2, 2002, from National Criminal Justice Reference Service Web site: http://abstractsdb.ncjrs.org/content/AbstractsDB_Search.asp.

National Institutes of Health, U.S. Department of Health and Human Services (2002). *National Institute of Mental Health (NIMH).* Retrieved November 1, 2002 from http://www.nimh.nih.gov/.

National Institutes of Health, U.S. Department of Health and Human Services (2002). *National Institute on Alcohol Abuse and Alcoholism (NIAAA).* Retrieved November 1, 2002 from http://www.niaaa.nih.gov/.

National Resource Center on Homelessness and Mental Illness Policy Research Associates, Inc. (2002). *National Resource Center on Homelessness and Mental Illness.* Retrieved November 12, 2002, from http://www.nrchmi.com/.

National Science Foundation (NSF) (2002). *National Science Foundation online document center.* Retrieved December 2,2002, from http://www.nsf.gov/ pubsys/ods/index.html.

National Technical Information Service (NTIS), U.S. Department of Commerce (2002). *National Technical Information Service.* Retrieved December 1, 2002, from http://www.ntis.gov/.

Office on Women's Health (OWH), U.S. Department of Health and Human Services (2002). *National Women's Health Information Center women with dis-Abilities website.* Retrieved November 3, 2002 from http://www.4woman. gov/wwd/index.htm.

Population Reference Bureau (2002). *E-library.* Retrieved November 9, 2002 from http://www.prb.org/.

Reavis, P.A., Epstein, B.A., & Piotrowicz, L.M. (1995). Selected books on mental illness and treatment for patients and their families. *Psychiatric Services, 46* (12), 1292-1302.

Reed, J.G., & Baxter, P.M. (1992). *Library use a handbook for psychology.* Washington, DC: American Psychological Association.

Robert Wood Johnson Foundation (2002). Retrieved December 1, 2002, from http://www.rwjf.org/

Sacks, M. H., Sledge, W. H., & Warren, C. (1995). *Core readings in psychiatry: An annotated guide to the literature.* Washington, DC: American Psychiatric Press.

Smith, K.R. (2002). Mental Health. In Megan Adams & Bernice Redfern (Eds.). *Core lists in women's studies.* Chicago: Association of College & Research Libraries, Women's Studies Section. Retrieved December 18, 2002, http://www.library.wisc.edu/libraries/WomensStudies/core/crmental.htm.

Substance Abuse and Mental Health Services Administration (SAMHSA) and Center for Mental Health Services. (2002). *SAMHSA's national mental health information center.* Retrieved January 23, 2002, from http://www.samhsa. gov/search/search.html.

Substance Abuse and Mental Health Services Administration (SAMHSA) and U.S. Department of Health & Human Services (2002). *SAMHSA.* Retrieved December 4, 2002, from http://www.samhsa.gov/.

Substance Abuse Librarians & Information Specialists (2002). Retrieved November 18, 2002, from http://www.salis.org/.

U.S. Office of the Surgeon General (1999). *Mental health: A report of the Surgeon General.* Rockville, Md.: Dept. of Health and Human Services, U.S. Public Health Service. Retrieved November 2, 2002, from http://www.surgeongeneral. gov/library/mentalhealth/home.html.

U.S. Office of the Surgeon General (2001). *Mental health: Culture, race, and ethnicity: A supplement to mental health: A report of the Surgeon General.* Rockville, Md.: Dept. of Health and Human Services, U.S. Public Health Service. Retrieved November 2, 2002, from http://www.surgeongeneral.gov/library/mentalhealth/cre/.

VandenBos, G. R. (Ed.) (2000). *Videos in psychology: A resource directory.* Washington, DC: American Psychological Association.

World Health Organization (2002). *Current bibliography of WHO documentation (WHODOC).* Retrieved December 12, 2002, from http://www.who.int/library/database/whodoc/index.en.shtml.

World Health Organization (2002). *WHOLIS World Health Organization library database.* Retrieved December 1, 2002, from http://www.who.int/library/database/index.en.shtml.

World Health Organization (2002). *World Health Organization publications catalogue 1991-2003.* Retrieved December 1, 2002, from http://www.who.int/dsa/cat98/zcon.htm.

REFERENCES

Blackburn, N. (2001). Building bridges: Towards integrated library and information services for mental health and social care. *Health Information and Libraries Journal, 18,* 203-212.

Desjarlais, R., Eisenberg, L., Good, B. & Kleinman, A. (1995). *World mental health: Problems and priorities in low-income countries.* New York: Oxford.

Dobson, C., Kushkowski, J.D. & Gerhard, K.H. (1996). Collection evaluation for interdisciplinary fields: A comprehensive approach. *The Journal of Academic Librarianship, 22* (4), 279-284.

Eichenauer, H.S. (2002, October 29) *Letter to President George W. Bush, President's New Freedom Commission on Mental Health interim report to the President.* Retrieved December 2, 2002, from http://www.mentalhealthcommission.gov/reports/interim_letter.htm.

Hoagwood, K., & Olin, S.S. (2002). The NIMH blueprint for change report: Research priorities in child and adolescent mental health. *Journal of the American Academy of Child and Adolescent Psychiatry, 41* (7), 760-67.

Scheiberg, S.L. (2001). Acquiring minds: Acquisitions in two contexts: Comparison of the University of Southern California and the Rand Corporation. *Library Collections, Acquisitions, and Technical Services, 25* (4), 389-399.

Stover, M. (Ed.) (2002). *Behavioral & social sciences librarian.* Binghamton, NY: The Haworth Press, Inc.

Tsuya, N.O. (2002). Panel on best collaborative practices: A synthesis. In N.O. Tsuya & J.W. White (Eds.) *Collaboration and comparison in international social science research.* New York: Social Science Research Council.

Retrospective Collection Development: Selecting a Core Collection for Research in "New Thought"

John T. Fenner
Audrey Fenner

SUMMARY. The New Thought movement is the focus of an exercise in developing a core collection to support research in a defined subject area. The authors outline the New Thought movement's conceptual and historical development and apply this outline to the selection of library resources. A sample collection development policy is included; such a policy is the framework for selection decisions. Special problems and concerns of gathering resources are presented, including library mishandling of this subject in the past. Titles in the core collection are presented, incorporating several types and formats of materials and varied points of view. Lists are given of the contacts, source material and bibliographic references used in assembling this New Thought core collection. *[Article copies available for a fee from The Haworth Document Delivery Service: 1-800-HAWORTH. E-mail address: <docdelivery@haworthpress.com> Website: <http://www.HaworthPress.com> © 2004 by The Haworth Press, Inc. All rights reserved.]*

John T. Fenner is Business and Information Consultant, 2123 Forest Edge Drive, Greensboro, NC 27406 (E-mail: johnfenner@worldnet.att.net). Audrey Fenner is Head, Acquisition Department, Walter Clinton Jackson Library, University of North Carolina at Greensboro, P.O. Box 26170, Greensboro, NC 27402-6170 (E-mail: fafenner@uncg.edu).

[Haworth co-indexing entry note]: "Retrospective Collection Development: Selecting a Core Collection for Research in 'New Thought.' " Fenner, John T., and Audrey Fenner. Co-published simultaneously in *The Acquisitions Librarian* (The Haworth Information Press, an imprint of The Haworth Press, Inc.) No. 31/32, 2004, pp. 177-215; and: *Selecting Materials for Library Collections* (ed: Audrey Fenner) The Haworth Information Press, an imprint of The Haworth Press, Inc., 2004, pp. 177-215. Single or multiple copies of this article are available for a fee from The Haworth Document Delivery Service [1-800-HAWORTH, 9:00 a.m. - 5:00 p.m. (EST). E-mail address: docdelivery@haworthpress.com].

10.1300/J101v16n31_16

KEYWORDS. Collection development, collection management, core collection, historical research, library selection, metaphysical religions, New Thought, research collection, retrospective selection

SUMMARY OF CONTENTS

- Brief Description of the Library, Subject, and User Group
- Tracing the New Thought Lineage: Biographical Sketches
- Collection Development Policy for the New Thought Collection
- Problems and Considerations in Selection for the New Thought Core Collection
- The Core Collection
- Contacts, Source Material and Bibliographic References

BRIEF DESCRIPTION OF THE LIBRARY, SUBJECT, AND USER GROUP

The Library Environment

A new faculty member at a wholly fictitious academic institution has a research interest in the New Thought movement: its origins, its place in the history of American religions, its philosophy and theology, its organizational history, and the psychology of its formative leaders and members. The institution's library has almost no resources available on New Thought that can support the work of this faculty researcher and her students. A collection of materials must be gathered, a collection of sufficient breadth and complexity to satisfy the needs of academic researchers. Because much of the research to be conducted is historical, primary sources rather than secondary sources will comprise the bulk of the collection. The library's initial focus in selection will be on retrospective collecting rather than on purchasing new titles.

Subject Area

"New Thought" refers to an American religious movement that developed in the 19th century and was at its height between 1875 and 1920. It existed and was popular contemporaneously with spiritualism, theosophy, and Christian Science. This movement focused initially on the healing of disease. It evolved into a group of religions that defined themselves as "metaphysical," sharing a common philosophy that human nature is essentially divine, that religious faith has directly practical applications and benefits, and that health, happiness and material success can be attained by the movement's adherents. From this intensely optimistic and characteristically American doctrine came leaders, ideas and teachings whose influence continues to the present day. Interestingly for scholars of religion, many pioneers and leaders of the New Thought movement, past and present, are women.

TRACING THE NEW THOUGHT LINEAGE: BIOGRAPHICAL SKETCHES

An attempt to trace the lineage of New Thought influence and conceptual development is a necessary prerequisite for collection development decisions for this institution's New Thought collection. In the following section we list the major leaders in New Thought and identify the people who influenced them. This section serves to represent the role of the subject bibliographer in a research library. Sometimes it is very difficult to separate the functions of bibliographer and scholar; the work of one cannot be done without the expertise of the other.

There is no single document or publication that we have found that succinctly and clearly identifies lines of historical development across New Thought personalities and organizational boundaries. Unfortunately, current cataloging practices do not support the tracing of conceptual development beyond providing for a simple shelf adjacency. Where lineage is not specified in this list, an author and/or organization has an affiliation with an ecumenical New Thought organization. Writings of some of these major leaders have not been included in the core collection due to resource constraints.

Martha Baker co-founded, with her husband Frank, the Wisdom Institute of Spiritual Education.

Annie Cecilia Bulmer Bill claimed to be Mary Baker Eddy's successor. She founded the Parent Church of Christ, Scientist, which later became the Church of Universal Design.

Nona Brooks, along with her sisters Fannie Brooks James and Alethea Brooks Small, and Malinda Cramer, co-founded Divine Science Federation International. Nona Brooks and her sisters earlier founded the Divine Science College. Brooks was influenced by Mrs. Frank Bingham, a student of Emma Curtis Hopkins, and ordained by Malinda E. Cramer.

Emilie Cady wrote the textbook that The Unity School of Christianity used as its main instructional vehicle.

Nicol C. Campbell founded the School of Practical Christianity, which later became the School of Truth.

Arthur Corey was a prominent Christian Science practitioner who left the first Church of Christ, Scientist in Boston. He founded the Farallon Foundation. He was taught by Bicknell Young, and was asked by Ernest Holmes to lead the Church of Religious Science. Corey's extensive collection of Christian Science material was donated to Southern Methodist University.

Malinda E. Cramer co-founded, with the three Brooks sisters, the Divine Science Federation International which has centers on several continents. Earlier she founded the Home College of Divine Science and the Divine Science Church, and she was also a prominent healer.

John Valentine Dittemore was a senior member of the Board of Directors of the First Church of Christ, Scientist. He left the Church to follow Annie Bill, founder of the Parent Church.

John W. Doorly was a Christian Science practitioner and lecturer. He was President of the Mother Church but fell from favor and became a leading dissident. He was taught by Bicknell Young.

Horatio Dresser was the son of Julius A. Dresser. He edited the writings of Phineas P. Quimby and accused Mary Baker Eddy of plagiarizing Quimby's work.

Julius A. Dresser and Mary Baker Eddy were the star pupils of Phineas P. Quimby. When Quimby died, Eddy wanted Dresser to lead the New Thought movement.

Henry Drummond influenced Friend Stuart, who founded the Church of the Trinity, and Ernest Holmes, who founded the Church of Religious Science.

Mary Baker Eddy founded the Christian Science movement. Christian Science is a registered name of The First Church of Christ, Scientist in Boston, commonly called the Mother Church. According to followers of New Thought, Phineas P. Quimby heavily influenced Eddy's metaphysical teaching.

Herbert Willoughby Eustace was a prominent member of the Board of Trustees of the Christian Science Publishing Society. He led the Board of Trustees in their legal challenge against the Board of Directors of the First Church of Christ, Scientist in Boston. He taught many Christian Science practitioners.

Warren Felt Evans was an early follower of Phineas P. Quimby. His writings pre-date those of Mary Baker Eddy. Evans was originally a Swedenborgian clergyman.

Charles Fillmore co-founded The Unity School of Christianity. He was taught by J. S. Thatcher, an early Christian Scientist, and was further influenced by Eugene B. Weeks and Emma Curtis Hopkins. He was ordained by Hopkins at her Christian Science Theological Seminary.

Myrtle Fillmore co-founded The Unity School of Christianity with her husband, Charles Fillmore. Like her husband, she was taught by J. S. Thatcher and also was influenced by Eugene B. Weeks and Emma Curtis Hopkins.

Emmet Fox was ordained in Divine Science. He served as clergyman in the Church of the Healing Christ. He regularly preached at Carnegie Hall in New York City and for many years had the largest congregation of any New Thought leader.

Joel S. Goldsmith was a long-time Christian Science practitioner who later left the Church and began his own practice and teaching. He became the spiritual leader of Infinite Way.

Leon Greenbaum founded the Primitive Church of Christ, Scientist, based on a congregational system of governance.

Albert C. Grier founded the Church of Truth.

Henry Thomas Hamblin founded Science of Thought.

Ernest Shurtleff Holmes was a founding leader of the International New Thought Alliance. He founded the Institute of Religious Science, which eventually became the United Church of Religious Science. He was influenced by W. W. Atkinson (a.k.a. Swami Ramacharaka), Christian D. Larson, Henry Drummond, Mary Baker Eddy, and Thomas Troward.

Fenwicke Lindsay Holmes was the brother of Ernest Shurtleff Holmes. He was influenced by W. W. Atkinson (a.k.a. Swami Ramacharaka), Christian D. Larson, and Thomas Troward. He and his brother Ernest co-founded the Metaphysical Institute.

Emma Curtis Hopkins was second in command to Mary Baker Eddy in Christian Science before a falling out. Hopkins went on to start her own highly successful metaphysical training school, where she taught the founders of The Unity School of Christianity, Divine Science, Religious Science, and Home of Truth. This earned her the title "teacher of teachers." She served as editor of the *Christian Science Journal* under Mary Baker Eddy and later founded the

Emma Curtis Hopkins College of Christian Science. Many consider her the founder of organized New Thought.

Fannie B. James co-founded the Divine Science Federation International. Earlier, James and her sisters founded the Divine Science College and Divine Science Church. James was influenced by Mrs. Frank Bingham, a student of Emma Curtis Hopkins.

H. B. Jeffery founded the Christ Truth League. His teachings are similar to those of Emma Curtis Hopkins.

Lewis Johnson founded the Antioch Association of Metaphysical Science, which serves a predominantly African-American population.

Max Kappeler was a prominent and prolific independent European Christian Scientist. He was influenced by John W. Doorly. The Kappeler Institute continues to disseminate his published works in all formats.

Edward A. Kimball was a member of the first Board of Education of the Massachusetts Metaphysical College and was, at one time, the practitioner most favored by Mary Baker Eddy. She transferred copyrights to all her work to him during the Woodbury slander trial. He was a member of the committee that reviewed the final revision of Eddy's book *Science and Health*. After Kimball and Eddy died in the same year, the Christian Science church establishment repudiated Kimball's teachings.

Margaret Laird was a prominent Christian Science practitioner and teacher who later left the church. She founded the Margaret Laird Foundation, a Christian Science research organization. She was taught by Bicknell Young.

George Mamishisho Lamsa, a speaker for The Unity School of Christianity, founded the Calvary Missionary Church. His monistic view is derived from Aramaic Bible sources, namely the Eastern Peshitta Bible.

Christian D. Larson had primary influence on Ernest Shurtleff Holmes. He wrote a major New Thought curriculum and edited a New Thought journal.

Carolyn Barbour Legalyon, a former Christian Science practitioner, founded Church of the Science of Religion centers around the world. Ernest Shurtleff Holmes and Charles Fillmore influenced her teaching.

Rabbi Morris Lichtenstein founded Jewish Science, the Jewish equivalent of Christian Science.

Brother Mandu (a pseudonym) was the founder of World Healing Crusade.

Annie Rix Militz was a student of Emma Curtis Hopkins and later taught at Hopkins' seminary. She founded the Home of Truth, which grew into several centers. Militz published *Mastermind*, an influential New Thought magazine.

Catherine Ponder founded Unity Worldwide.

Phineas Parkhurst Quimby was the originator of New Thought. None of his writings were published during his lifetime. His star pupils were Mary Baker Eddy and Julius Dresser.

Frederick L. Rawson founded the Society for the Spread of the Knowledge of True Prayer. He was influenced by Mary Baker Eddy and was a member of the First Church of Christ, Scientist until he was excommunicated for his unorthodox opinions.

Frank B. Robinson was the founder of Psychiana. Emilie Cady, Ernest Shurtleff Holmes, and Robert W. Collier influenced him. A merger of his organization with Ernest Shurtleff Holmes' Church of Religious Science was considered but did not take place.

Oliver C. Sabin. Jr. founded the Evangelical Christian Science Church.

Ervin Seale was the most successful clergyman in the Church of Truth. He regularly preached in Philharmonic Hall in New York City. He was a President of the International New Thought Alliance.

Alethea Brooks Small was a co-founder of the College of Divine Science and its first President. She was later head of the healing department of the College. Small was influenced by Mrs. Frank Bingham, a student of Emma Curtis Hopkins.

Robert Sterling founded Unity Universelle in France.

Augusta Emma Simmons Stetson was the most powerful and successful leader in the Christian Science movement next to Mary Baker Eddy. Possibly she would have succeeded Eddy had Eddy not taken steps to discredit her.

Friend Stuart founded the Church of the Trinity, often called the Invisible Ministry. His teachings are similar to those of James Allen, Henry Drummond, Emmett Fox, and The Unity School of Christianity.

Hugh Anketell Studdert-Kennedy, a former Episcopal clergyman, was a long-time staff member of the newspaper *Christian Science Monitor*.

Masaharu Taniguchi, a former devotee of Omoto, introduced New Thought into Japan by founding the Seicho-No-Ie, which publishes an English language magazine of the same name. Taniguchi's philosophy was influenced chiefly by Fenwicke Holmes.

Elizabeth Towne was the publisher of the long-running and widely read New Thought journal, *Nautilus*. She was a President of the International New Thought Alliance.

Thomas Troward, the most prominent English exponent of New Thought, was a major influence on Ernest Shurtleff Holmes. He was a Vice President of the International New Thought Alliance.

Erma Wiley Wells founded several churches of the denomination Church of the Truth. She later served as President of the International New Thought Alliance.

James H. Wiggin edited Mary Baker Eddy's book *Science and Health*. He is credited by some with making the work readable and consistent.

Bicknell Young was a liberal student of Edward Kimball, and enjoyed a similar reputation within Christian Science. He taught the famous 1910 Normal Class. His lecture notes still are widely disseminated.

COLLECTION DEVELOPMENT POLICY FOR THE NEW THOUGHT COLLECTION

Preface

The following collection development policy is an adaptation and synthesis of two collection development policies:

1. The Ohio State University Libraries Collection Development Policy for the History of Christianity (Alt and Shiels, 1987).
2. St. Olaf College's Proposed Collection Development Policy for Religion (ALA and ACRL, 1981).

Definition of New Thought

For the purpose of developing and maintaining this collection, the following definition of New Thought will be used:

> New Thought is a mind-healing movement that originated in the United States in the 19th century, based on religious and metaphysical presuppositions (i.e., concerning the nature of ultimate reality). New Thought principles emphasize the immanence of the divine, the divine nature of humanity, the immediate availability of divine power to humanity, the spiritual character of the universe, and the principle that sin, human disorders, and human disease are basically matters of incorrect thinking.

Purpose of the Collection

The prime mandate of the New Thought collection is to serve the research needs of the university's faculty and students. Only as resources permit will the needs of other groups and individuals be supported.

Levels of the Collection

The collection will serve three main user groups. For purposes of resource allocation, they are ranked in importance.

Primary user group:	university students and faculty
Secondary user group:	researchers from outside this university
Tertiary user group:	New Thought church organizations, clergy, practitioners, and individual members or adherents

Principles of Resource Selection

The initial focus will be on purchasing published primary source materials written from the 1860s through the mid to late 20th century. Some secondary sources and reference titles will also be purchased. Additional secondary source materials and current writings on New Thought will be added as resources permit.

The collection will focus on the following groupings of New Thought materials, in the priority shown below:

1. authorized textbooks, including hymn books, of New Thought organizations
2. seminal literature of the New Thought movement in prose and poetry
3. New Thought coursework, instructional guides and curricula
4. biographies of New Thought leaders
5. histories of New Thought organizations
6. critical, analytical, and scholarly works on New Thought
7. current periodicals of New Thought organizations
8. local congregational and organizational materials
9. support materials for New Thought organizations (e.g., congregational aids, children's materials, and audiovisual materials).

New Thought fiction will not be acquired, although bibliographies of such material will be made available.

Scope and Limits of Coverage

New Thought concepts can be found in a variety of Western philosophies, including the writings of Plato, Hegel, Swedenborg, and Emerson, and in such Eastern philosophies as Jnana Yoga and Vajrayana Buddhism. This collection, however, will begin with the contributions of Phineas P. Quimby and follow the historical development of his ideas and teachings through the mid to late 20th century.

Formats of Materials Collected

Materials that meet the guidelines for inclusion in the collection can be in any format. In the event of multiple format availability the following priority will be followed: printed, digital, audiovisual, microform. This applies in all cases except for periodicals and general reference works, like concordances, for which digital formats will be preferred over printed formats. For printed materials, hardbound materials will be purchased whenever possible; however, paperback materials will be purchased if they are of more recent publication and are more easily available. When core, seminal materials are available only in paperback editions, the library will bind them. Other materials will not be bound but may, at the discretion of the Collection Development Librarian, be placed in other types of protective coverings or in a controlled environment.

Number of Copies

The library will purchase only one copy of New Thought reference resources, unless the Collection Development Librarian specifically and formally approves multiple copies. Additional copies for lending will be purchased only when significant borrowing demand is voiced. The definition of "significant" will be left to the Collection Development Librarian.

Budget and Policy Review

The budget for the New Thought collection and the collection development plan will be submitted annually for review by the Library Director. This collection development policy must be submitted every three years for review by the Library Director.

Censorship and Coverage

The collection will attempt to cover the entire spectrum of early and formative New Thought. In setting priorities for acquisitions, the weighting of various classes of materials will be by the influence of the materials over the development of New Thought. All titles meeting the selection criteria and priorities outlined in this policy will be collected without judgment regarding particular individual or organizational authorship or sponsorship.

Language Priorities

Because the majority of original sources were written in English, the collection will initially include only English-language materials.

Chronological Priorities

The collection should reflect the entire early history of New Thought, beginning with Phineas P. Quimby. For core, seminal metaphysical materials, there is to be no priority given to any one period. However, some time periods may be more represented than others due to the distribution of New Thought publishing over time.

Retrospective Additions

Periodicals, when selected, should begin with the current issue: no expensive retrospective additions of periodicals should be acquired unless they are received as gifts or approved by the Collection Development Librarian. This restriction is justified as an economy measure.

Gifts

Gifts will be subject to the same selection criteria as new orders. The library will not retain materials not fitting the needs of the library. Duplicates of materials already held will not be added to the main reference collection but may be added to the circulating collection, if justified by demand and if space allows.

Rare Materials

The library will not seek rare materials, unless they are offered as gifts. However, the library may choose to photocopy rare materials for reference and/or lending whenever copyrights have expired or copyright permission is obtained.

Selection Criteria

The Collection Development Librarian will make use of all available bibliographies, reviews, library catalogs, publishers' catalogs, as well as personal contact with experts in the field, in researching and selecting materials for the collection.

Delegation of Authority

Final responsibility for library planning including budgeting, collection development, administration, and maintenance rests with the Collection Development Librarian.

Weeding

The relevance of materials in the collection may change over time. Periodic weeding of the collection will be necessary to identify items that no longer fit the criteria for selection or inclusion. Materials for which there is no longer adequate demand should be withdrawn. Older editions of some titles may be retained for their historical value even though later editions have been purchased.

Preservation

Titles that are not weeded are in fact chosen for permanent status in the collection. These materials should be inspected periodically to be certain that they are in a useable condition. They may require binding, rebinding, replacement, or other protective and/or preservation techniques. Such maintenance is an essential part of collection development and insures against the needless use of funds for replacements at a later date, and against the complete loss of significant titles for which no replacement in any form is available.

Digitization will be considered as a means of both preserving and providing access to rare and/or fragile materials.

PROBLEMS AND CONSIDERATIONS IN SELECTION FOR THE NEW THOUGHT CORE COLLECTION

Budgetary Limitations/Technology

We first had to estimate the size of the budget for the New Thought core collection. A reasonable budget for such a small research collection may be well under US$2500.00. This precludes the purchase of some very desirable materials. Presumably the library can provide online access and computer equipment for its users. There are many software products, both shareware and standard distribution, that could be of use to the New Thought collection should its budget be increased. For example, there are several Bible and author concordance software packages available. One that would be desirable for the New Thought collection is *Concord*, published by The First Church of Christ,

Scientist in Boston. This concordance package includes the Old and New Testaments as well as the major published writings of Mary Baker Eddy. Another electronic title is *Journal Search*, available from The Bookmark. This CD-ROM product includes the full text of articles that appeared in the *Christian Science Journal* from its inception in 1883 through 1910, as well as the complete published writings of Mary Baker Eddy.

Expected Use of the Collection

In determining the core collection, the librarian must balance conflicting demands: should the material reflect the current, expected, or potential user base? For this exercise, we have chosen to reflect the expected user base from which use of the collection may be drawn.

Organizations have power, prestige, and marketing strength. Because of these facts, the core collection is biased toward authors who have had some organizational backing. Consequently, unaffiliated authors with no organization supporting their work are generally omitted from this collection. One would hope eventually to expand the collection with more resources.

Christian/Secular Balance

New Thought uses both secular and Christian language to communicate its message. Some groups, including a majority of the members of the International New Thought Alliance, prefer secular language. Others, especially The First Church of Christ, Scientist and The Unity School of Christianity, prefer Christian language. The collection has been balanced to reflect both preferences.

The Test of Time/Contemporary Balance

For the core collection, we had to choose between the desire to include contemporary, unproven New Thought material and the need to include well-regarded, widely distributed, proven New Thought works. This collection reflects a research orientation by including only those authors and materials that have proven themselves or reached institutional status. This decision was aided by the fact that almost no independent, unbiased reviews of this material exist. The major theological journals ignore New Thought and the popular press regards it as a niche market. The core collection recognizes that some authors are well received across several generations, across organizations, and across languages. Because of this, there are some exceptions to the general policy in this core collection of including only one representative work of any one writer.

Syncretism and Collection Integrity

Syncretism is an enormous problem for New Thought in general and for the International New Thought Alliance in particular. The INTA presently has difficulty separating New Age from New Thought, principally because their membership code guarantees free expression. This is less of a problem with The Unity School of Christianity, which has exercised strong central control in some areas; it is certainly not an issue in Christian Science, where materials and communications have been very tightly controlled.

The Christian Science organization with headquarters in Boston does not consider itself to be a New Thought denomination, nor does it acknowledge any debt to New Thought in its history or doctrinal development. After studying a number of sources, however, we decided that a case could be made for including Christian Science, at least in its earlier days, as part of the broad, mind-healing movement.

Much material uncovered in the initial screenings for the core collection had to be discarded because the authors blended New Thought with other popular, contemporary concepts. This has been true for as long as New Thought has existed. For example, we have chosen not to include such derivative past and present writers as Norman Vincent Peale, Dale Carnegie, Charles Allen, Barbara Marx Hubbard, Robert Schuller and Catherine Ponder because of their syncretistic tendencies. The weeding of syncretistic authors was the most time-consuming part of developing the New Thought lineage and determining what to include in the core collection.

Lineage Integrity

"New Thought" is a rather arbitrary label we applied to a definition upon which few can agree completely. Arguments can be made to begin New Thought in the West with Plato, Ralph Waldo Emerson, G. W. F. Hegel, Emanuel Swedenborg, George Berkeley, Phineas Quimby, Warren Evans, or Mary Baker Eddy, or in the East with the monist ideas of Jnana Yoga or Vajrayana Buddhism. We have chosen to begin with Quimby and we can trace the writers in the core collection back to him. Some major contributors to New Thought have left one New Thought organization for another under acrimonious circumstances, with the result that the original organization has dropped coverage of, reference to, and publication of the works of the person who left. This caused problems in determining the significance of the author and in finding citations for his/her materials.

Types and Priority of Materials

As stated earlier, the collection is intended to support research into the New Thought movement by university faculty and students. Primary source materials are necessary to this type of research. These include published and unpublished diaries, letters, personal accounts, other manuscripts, monographs, treatises and original journal articles. Secondary sources, which are accounts or interpretations of past events written much later, will be given less emphasis in the initial stages, as the core collection is being assembled. Our fictitious university is unlikely to acquire many unpublished, original New Thought materials, unless they are donated. The core collection will, however, include published primary sources, often in reprinted editions. Reprints will be of considerable importance to the acquisition process. Fortunately inexpensive reprints of New Thought books are readily available from several sources to be enumerated later.

The core collection is small; consequently, some types of materials had to be excluded altogether. Priority was given to core, seminal New Thought authors and titles, which could be shown to have influenced the development and dissemination of the movement. The collection is somewhat biased toward the first works of major New Thought figures.

The core collection must cover the subject areas for which New Thought is best known: metaphysics, healing, mysticism, prayer, prosperity, and meditation.

Research studies in New Thought may be undertaken with a view to placing present attitudes or practices in historical context. Research may include interviewing members and adherents of New Thought groups and organizations, to examine how their teachings have been formed and shaped by historical events. New Thought web sites may also include online bibliographies that may list publications of interest, and may use terminology that can be used in searching more traditional resources. Digitized archival material may be found online that would be of value for analysis in research projects.

For all of these reasons the library will consider certain freely available web resources to be part of the New Thought collection, and will catalog web sites of selected New Thought organizations that may be of value to faculty and student researchers. These web sites will be readily accessible through the library's online public catalog. The selection of web sites to be included will be made by librarians and catalogers, and will include sites that may be recommended by researchers. Often individuals maintain New Thought web sites on a voluntary basis, and this presents concerns in adding them to a library catalog. However dedicated and knowledgeable these volunteer webmasters may be, the sites may not have sufficient organizational support to guarantee that they will remain stable, be frequently updated, or even continue to exist.

Any movement, especially in its earliest days, attracts individuals and groups that have their own agendas. There are true believers, sycophants, and debunkers. Scoffers and debunkers may be leaders of offshoot groups, rivals for leadership, or disaffected former believers. As with other religious movements, early New Thought writers demonstrate all these objectives in their work. Depending upon their circumstances at the time, they wrote doctrinal works, apologetics, histories, criticisms, polemics, textbooks, curricula, autobiographies, and political statements. Our core New Thought collection had to recognize these differences of intention among the materials we located. Certain titles were deemed not useful, often because of lack of objectivity, for researchers at an academic institution.

There is a bias to monographs in the core collection. This is due, to a large extent, to the limited budget and small size of the collection, and the fact that print formats were the prime means of disseminating New Thought teachings for most of the movement's history. Time, a more generous budget, and/or gifts to the library may change this situation substantially, making it possible to purchase more widely in non-print formats.

We decided that it would be better to have relatively complete coverage in a few key categories than to have a random, incoherent smattering of materials in all categories. We felt that the core collection must include the authorized materials of major New Thought organizations, principally the authorized periodicals, textbooks, and hymn books used by each organization. Hymn books were included because they exemplify organizational theology. The decision to focus on a few key categories meant that several categories in which there is no shortage of New Thought material had to be omitted. The categories that we reluctantly excluded were religious reference materials of a general nature in which New Thought was given only incidental coverage, and certain materials in which New Thought was the prime focus. These latter included New Thought fiction, poetry, theses, biographies, bibliographies, pamphlets, correspondence, histories, essays, devotional aids, criticism, children's materials, concordances, and both spoken and music audio materials. Examples of these were, however, consulted in choosing the New Thought core collection and examples of materials of these types are included in the bibliography. Although the librarian responsible for selection would need to access many of these materials, particularly bibliographies and concordances, the New Thought collection in this academic library would have less need of them because of its focus on supporting research. Furthermore, the library's collection development policy specifically states that digital concordances are to be preferred over print. Given the limited resources available and the incomplete, developing nature of the core collection, no concordances were purchased although they will be a high priority item for gifts and/or next year's budget.

The recognition of the difference between the needs of the library and the needs of the researcher is often difficult to determine. The collection development policy offers help in making difficult decisions.

This core collection serves primarily a research-support function in an academic library. Its small size precludes it initially serving as a lending library for New Thought ministers, practitioners, organizations, members, or inquirers.

Library Indifference and Mismanagement

Few libraries have given much continuous attention to New Thought materials, and subject classification of these materials has been haphazard at best. On January 12, 2003 a keyword search for "New Thought" in OCLC WorldCat yielded 3,308 hits, 3,051 of those for English-language titles. Scanning those titles soon made it clear that many did not concern the New Thought movement in any way. In contrast, searching "New Thought" as a descriptor in WorldCat yielded only 22 hits.

Catalogs of academic or theological libraries may have few New Thought entries. One example is the shared catalog of Weldon Library at the University of Western Ontario, and the libraries of Huron University College and Brescia University College. All are located in London, Ontario. There are approximately 3.1 million bibliographic records in this combined catalog (K Marshall, personal communication, Feb. 3, 2003). A subject search of the catalog for "New Thought" resulted, on January 23, 2003, in only thirty-one hits. Several of these titles were duplicated among the three libraries; some copies were in storage. Some of the thirty-one hits were bibliographic records for Internet resources. A search on the same date of the catalog of Walter Clinton Jackson Library, University of North Carolina at Greensboro, brought similar results: fourteen hits for titles given the "New Thought" subject heading, and two under the subdivision "New Thought–History." This reflects very limited holdings in New Thought in a library catalog that includes approximately 900,000 bibliographic records (A. I. Wreath, personal communication, January 30, 2003).

There are libraries with relatively large holdings of New Thought titles. On January 23, 2003 we did subject searches for the term "New Thought" in the web catalogs of several other libraries. There were 571 occurrences of this heading in the catalog of Southern Methodist University (SMU), 565 in the Library of Congress catalog, and 93 in the catalog of the Mary Baker Eddy Library for the Betterment of Humanity. New Thought materials can also be identified in library catalogs under form subdivisions for publication types and genres (dictionaries, history, fiction, poetry, and so on), and under headings for individual denominations. Personnel at the library of The Unity School of

Christianity said during a telephone conversation that there are over 1,500 titles in that library's collection. This is essentially a New Thought collection, although it includes a considerable amount of general interest material.

There are no known major private collections of New Thought materials still in existence anywhere in the English-speaking world.

Generally, current religious reference titles used in libraries ignore or give scant coverage to New Thought.

Many early volumes of New Thought periodicals have been lost through the failure of libraries to maintain continuous subscriptions or to purchase back issues. We sadly point out that, as it now reads, the New Thought collection development policy of our fictitious academic library would bring about the same result.

Libraries, particularly public libraries, have routinely weeded their New Thought collections, treating the material as popular genre or polemical literature of passing interest.

Some major collections have been purchased by organizations seemingly to prevent widespread public access to the material they contain. The Dittemore and Carpenter collections are examples; they were acquired by The First Church of Christ, Scientist. Evidently no academic or research libraries realized the significance of these collections and access to them is now controlled and restricted.

Many early New Thought books are still available for purchase; they may be reprinted privately and in small runs. Publishers often want to label New Thought material with more saleable labels such as "Applied Psychology," "Prosperity," "Health," etc., with the result that library catalogers may not recognize the literature as requiring a "New Thought" classification. Furthermore, some reference sources limit the category "New Thought" to those organizations that belong to New Thought associations. This severely distorts the listings, since major organizations such as Christian Science and The Unity School of Christianity, though they can be considered part of the "metaphysical" movement, are not members of New Thought associations. Other smaller New Thought organizations and some individuals have distanced themselves from ecumenical New Thought associations for reasons of personalities, power, politics, and doctrine. Another problem in locating New Thought literature is the generally poor bibliographic control of New Thought material in libraries that have holdings in this subject. For example, a collection given the designation "New Thought" in the SMU libraries was simply a collection of sermons by an earlier writer; they were not related in any way to the New Thought movement. Because of inconsistent bibliographic treatment, we had to seek New Thought materials under many different keywords, descriptors and subject classifications.

Concordances, Catalogs, Bibliographies and Bibles

Concordances can be helpful in identifying relationships among New Thought writers. There are particularly good concordances available to the works of Fillmore, Holmes, and Eddy. The best among these are in digital rather than print format, and our collection development policy states a preference for digital concordances. Given the small size of the core collection, concordances would not be extremely useful at this point.

There are several good denominational and distributor catalogs for New Thought materials.

A big disappointment in bibliographies was the International New Thought Alliance's *How to build a library of New Thought books* (INTA, 1992), which includes significant numbers of New Age and general interest titles. Even the initial lists of basic books are not entirely New Thought but include peripheral material.

The only Bible included in the core collection is that translated from the Syriac by George Lamsa, because it is a textbook of a major New Thought organization. In general, we assumed that users of the New Thought collection would have access to Bibles in the general library collection. The core collection would focus on the major New Thought authors and organizational materials (i.e., the standard textbooks and current periodicals of the different New Thought organizations). Again, digitized Bibles in many translations are available, but cost constraints preclude purchase at this time.

Copyright and Public Domain

Many of the titles in the core collection are reprinted works, and some of the material is no longer under copyright. Because of the importance of this early material, much of it has been republished by several smaller presses, often with subtle title changes. This makes it difficult to determine if similar-sounding works referred to in different bibliographies have identical content. Some books may have new introductions, prefaces, and/or indexing. It is also difficult to determine which edition of a title is most likely to be available.

Sources Not Examined

There are two titles that we were unable to examine directly that would prove useful in the further development of the New Thought core collection. One is a bibliography on New Thought written by Sam Ronnie and published in an unidentified periodical. The other is a bibliography entitled *A Christian Science Library* by Ernest J. Brosang that includes over 700 titles.

In addition, one major holder of New Thought material identified in *Subject Collections: A guide to special book collections and subject emphases . . .* (7th ed.) (R.R. Bowker, 1993) could not be reached by phone or fax at the time of writing.

THE CORE COLLECTION

The New Thought core collection is first to serve the needs of faculty and students doing academic research. To support this focus, the core collection must have relatively complete coverage in a few categories but may omit many others entirely.

The author and organizational lineage of New Thought identified earlier formed the basis for choosing the materials listed.

The meager resources available to the library limit its ability to extend coverage beyond the breadth or depth identified below. The bibliography includes many titles that, if resources were available, would have been included in the core collection.

We have listed the most recent known publisher and publication date to aid in the acquisition of the material. Sometimes the publication date of the material chosen for the collection will be subsequent to the date cited in the source. This reflects changes in publishers.

Authorized Hymn Books

Christian Science hymnal. (1960). Boston: The Christian Science Publishing Society. Hymn book of Churches of Christ, Scientist throughout the English-speaking world.

Wings of song. (1984). Unity Village, MO: Unity Books. Songbook of Unity churches throughout the English-speaking world.

Authorized Active Periodicals (Active)

Active service: A magazine devoted to the spreading of the knowledge of divinely scientific thinking.

Society for Spreading the Knowledge of True Prayer, Box 29, Woking, Surrey GU21 4AR England. Bimonthly. First published in 1916.

The Christian Science journal. (ISSN: 0009-5613)
    The Christian Science Publishing Society, 1 Norway Street, Boston, MA
    02115; 617-450-2000. fax: 617-450-2930. Monthly. First published in
    1883. Official organ of The First Church of Christ, Scientist.

Creative thought for each day. (ISSN 1045-6139)
    Religious Science International, West 1636 First, Spokane, WA 99204.
    Monthly.

Healing thoughts.
    P.O. Box 5619, Plainfield, NJ 07060; telephone: 201-756-4669. Organ of
    the largest independent Christian Science organization.

The individual Christian Scientist.
    P.O. Box 128, Ahwahnee, CA 93601. Only periodical directed to unaffiliated
    Christian Scientists.

New Thought. (ISSN: 0146-7832)
    International New Thought Alliance, 5003 East Broadway Road, Mesa, AZ
    85206; 480-830-2461. Quarterly. First published in 1914.

New Thought journal.
    P.O. Box 700754, Tulsa, OK 74170; fax: 918-742-7883. Monthly. First
    published in 1992. Best source for communication among the various New
    Thought organizations.

Path of Truth.
    School of Truth, P.O. Box 6116, Johannesburg 2000, South Africa;
    011-838-6954. Monthly. First published in 1937.

The review.
    Science of Thought Press, Bosham House, Bosham, Chichester, West Sussex,
    England P018-8PJ; 0243-572109. Bimonthly. First published in 1921.

Science of Mind. (ISSN: 0036-8458)
    United Church of Religious Science, Box 75127, Los Angeles, CA 90075;
    213-388-2181. Monthly. First published in 1927.

Unity, a way of life. (ISSN: 0162-3567)
    The Unity School of Christianity, Unity Village, MO 64065; 816-524-3550;
    816-251-3550 (fax). Monthly. First published in 1889.

Authorized Textbooks

Bill, A. C. B. (1930). *The science of reality: Its universal design and practical
    application.* Washington, DC: A.A. Beauchamp.
    Textbook of the Church of Universal Design.

Cady, E. H. (1955). *Lessons in truth: A course of twelve lessons in practical Christianity*. Lees Summit, MO: The Unity School of Christianity. Textbook of The Unity School of Christianity.

Campbell, N. C. (1953). *My path of truth*. Johannesburg: School of Truth. Text of the School of Practical Christianity.

Cramer, M. E., and James, F. (1957). *Divine science: Its principles and practice*. Denver, CO: Colorado College of Divine Science. Textbook of the Divine Science Church. This book is a composite of M. E. *Cramer's Divine science and healing* and F. James' *Truth and health: Science of the perfect mind and its law of its expression: The College textbook*.

Eddy, M. B. (1906). *Science and health with key to the scriptures*. Authorized edition. Boston: The First Church of Christ, Scientist. Textbook of The First Church of Christ, Scientist in Boston.

Eddy, M. B. (1936). *Church manual of the First Church of Christ, Scientist in Boston, Massachusetts*. Authorized edition. Boston: The First Church of Christ, Scientist. Textbook/organizational manual for Christian Science churches.

Goldsmith, J. S. (1947). *The infinite way*. Los Angeles: Willing Publishing. Textbook of The Infinite Way study groups.

Hamblin, H. T. (n.d.). *Within you is the power*. Chichester, England: Science of Thought Press. Textbook of Science of Thought.

Holmes, E. S. *The science of mind*. (1988). New York: G.P. Putnam's Sons. Textbook of the United Church of Religious Science.

The Holy Bible from ancient Eastern manuscripts. Containing the Old and New Testaments. (1957). (G. M. Lamsa, Trans.). Philadelphia: A.J. Holman. Textbook of the Calvary Missionary Church.

Hopkins, E. C. (1958). *Scientific Christian mental practice*. Cornwall Bridge, CT: High Watch Fellowship. Textbook of the College of Christian Science.

LeGalyon, C. B. (1963). *All things new: The science of religion textbook*. New York: Analysts' Publisher. Textbook of the Church of the Science of Religion.

Lichtenstein, M., Rabbi (1925). *Jewish science and health*. New York: Jewish Science Publishing. Textbook of Jewish Science.

Rawson, F. L. (Ed.). (1914). *Life understood from a scientific and religious point of view*. London, England: Crystal Press. Textbook of the Society for the Spread of the Knowledge of True Prayer.

Robinson, F. B. (1943). *Your God power*. Moscow, ID: Psychiana.
Textbook of Psychiana.

Sabin, O. C. (1905). *Christian Science instruction: An exposition of evangelical Christian Science teaching with rules, formulas and instructions*. 1st ed. Washington, DC: News Letter Press.
Textbook of the Evangelical Christian Science Church.

[Schuchman, H.] (1975). *A course in miracles*. Tiburon. CA: Foundation for Inner Peace.
Textbook of *A Course in Miracles* study groups.

Collections and Collected Works

Holmes, E. S. (Ed.). (1941). *Mind remakes your world*. New York: Dodd Mead.
This book contains articles written by 36 leaders from 18 New Thought organizations. Best example of New Thought ecumenical activity to date.

Dresser, H. W. (Ed.). (1961). *The Quimby manuscripts*. New York: Julian Press.
Posthumously published writings of Phineas P. Quimby, here considered the originator of New Thought. The rare early edition includes correspondence between Quimby and Mary Baker Eddy.

Eustace, H. W. (1985). *Christian Science: Its "clear, correct teaching" and Complete writings*. Berkeley, CA: The Trustees for the Complete Writings of Herbert V. Eustace, C.S.B.
This book has appeared in several editions, the first published in 1934. It describes Eustace's techniques of mental healing, which differ from those of authorized Christian Science, and which are used by Eustace-trained practitioners.

Stetson, A. E. (1992). *Sermons and other writings on Christian Science*. Cuyahoga Falls, OH: Emma Publishing Society.
Contains the author's justification for being the first Christian Scientist to practise outside of an established organization.

Dictionaries

Fillmore, C. (1942). *Metaphysical Bible dictionary*. Kansas City, MO: Unity Books. Encyclopedic dictionary of metaphysical definitions of terms used in the Bible.

Fillmore, C. (1985). *The revealing word*. Unity Village, MO: The Unity School of Christianity. Definitions of over 1,200 New Thought words and phrases.

Holmes, E. S. (1986). *New Thought terms and their meanings: A dictionary of the terms and phrases commonly used in metaphysical and psychological study*. New York: Dodd Mead.

Directories

Beebe, T. (1977). *Who's who in New Thought: Biographical dictionary of New Thought personnel, centers, and authors' publications*. Lakemont, GA: CSA Press.
Invaluable aid to determining lines of historical development.

Doctrinal Works and Handbooks

Evans, W. F. (1875). *The mental cure*. Boston: Colby and Rich. Appeared simultaneously with Mary Baker Eddy's *Science and health*. Evans' second book after *Mental medicine*, published in 1872. Earliest published techniques of mental healing.

Holmes, F. L. (1969). *Law of mind in action: Being and becoming*. Seal Beach, CA: Truth in Action Publications.
F. L. Holmes' first and most successful book.

Jeffery, H. B. (1967). *The principles of healing*. Fort Worth. TX: Christ Truth League.
Covers techniques used by Christ Truth League practitioners.

Kappeler, M. (1969). *The spiritual principle of prayer*. London: Foundational Books.
Covers New Thought teachings on prayer.

Melton, J. G. (Ed.). (1991). *American religious creeds* (Vol. 3). New York: Triumph Books.
This book includes an extensive collection of statements of belief and doctrine from many New Thought organizations.

Militz. A. R. (1937). *Prosperity through the knowledge and power of mind*. (8th ed., rev.). Los Angeles: DeVorss & Co.

Palmer, C. (n.d.). *You can be healed*. Unity Village, MO: Unity Books.
Covers techniques used by The Unity School of Christianity practitioners for treatment of various types of diseases.

Taniguchi, M. (1963). *Recovery from all diseases: Seicho-no-Ie's method of psychoanalysis*. Tokyo, Japan: Seicho-no-Ie Foundation.
Describes techniques used by Seicho-no-Ie practitioners.

Trine, R. W. (1989). *In tune with the infinite: Fullness of peace, power, and plenty.* London, England: Unwin Paperbacks.
Trine's book has sold over a million copies. Unfortunately, it is seldom assigned the descriptor "New Thought" by publishers or librarians.

Troward, Thomas. (1917). *The Edinburgh lectures on mental science.* New York: R. M. McBride.
Troward's first and best-known work.

Instructional Materials

Corey, A. (1970). *Christian Science class instruction* (3d rev. ed.). Santa Monica, CA: DeVorss & Co.
Originally published by the Farallon Foundation in 1945, this is the earliest published Christian Science class instructional material by an authorized teacher of Christian Science, as Corey was at one time. The First Church of Christ, Scientist, does not authorize publication of such material.

Foundations of Unity (n.d.). Unity Village, MO: Unity.
Home study course of The Unity School of Christianity.

Wells, E. W. (1942). *The fine art of living: A correspondence or home study course in truth fundamentals.* Spokane, WA: Church of Truth.
Home study course of the Church of Truth.

Web Sites

Affiliated New Thought Network (http://www.newthought.org/)

Association for Global New Thought (http://www.agnt.org)

Association of Unity Churches (http://www.unity.org)

Christian Science Foundation (http://www.christianscience.org)

Divine Science Federation International (http://home.earthlink.net/~edmag/dsfed/)

Foundation for Inner Peace (http://64.77.6.149/index.html)

International New Thought Alliance (http://websyte.com/alan/online.htm)

Kappeler Institute for the Science of Being, Inc. (http://www.kappelerinstitute.org)

Mary Baker Eddy Institute (http://www.mbeinstitute.org)

Religious Science International (http://www.rsintl.org/)

United Church of Religious Science (http://www.religiousscience.org/)

Unity School of Christianity (http://www.unityworldhq.org)

CONTACTS, SOURCE MATERIAL
AND BIBLIOGRAPHIC REFERENCES

Associations, Foundations and Institutions

In compiling the core collection titles, it was necessary to consult practitioners and followers of New Thought. They were the experts and the people most able to direct us to current sources. Many groups went out of their way to assist us. These included the Christian Science Foundation, the Foundation for Inner Peace, the Kappeler Institute, and the New Thought Alliance. Unfortunately, the spokespersons for these groups did not always have a sufficiently comprehensive knowledge of New Thought to be of much help in directing us to sources of appropriate materials.

Some groups were difficult to locate. For example, the Kappeler Institute has different distribution arms for printed and audio materials, and different distributors in different countries. Not all sources can be reached easily by telephone. Some groups and organizations have web sites while others do not.

Most of the individual New Thought groups gladly supplied us with complimentary printed materials.

Names and addresses of New Thought organizations we consulted are listed below. E-mail addresses are included if they were available at the time of writing. The web addresses of these organizations can be found in the list of materials included in the core collection. Some web sites include catalogs and book lists.

Affiliated New Thought Network, P.O. Box 710698, Santee, CA 92072; 619-449-8965; 619-449-8964 (fax). E-mail address: oneness@newthought.org.

Association for Global New Thought, 1331 Mountain Avenue, Santa Barbara, CA 93101; 805-962-9492; 805-962-9493 fax.

Association of Unity Churches, P.O. Box 610, Lee's Summit, MO 64063; 816-524-7414; 816-525-4020 (fax). E-mail address: actop@unity.org.

Christian Science Foundation, P.O. Box 440, Cambridge CB4-3BH, England. E-mail address: heal@ChristianScience.org.
Incorporates the Christian Science Research Library.

Divine Science Federation International, 3617 Wyoming Street, St. Louis, MO 63116; 800-644-9680; 314-664-4143. E-mail address: divscifederation@aol. com.

Foundation for Inner Peace, P.O. Box 598, Mill Valley, CA 94942.

International New Thought Alliance, 5003 East Broadway Road, Mesa, AZ 85206; 480-830-2461; 480-830-2651 (fax). E-mail address: azinta@qwest.net.

Kappeler Institute for the Science of Being, Inc., POB 99735, Seattle, WA 98199; 206-286-1617 (telephone); 206-286-1675 (fax).

Mary Baker Eddy Institute.
See the Web site above; no address is available for this organization.

Religious Science International, P.O. Box 2152, Spokane, WA 99210; 509-624-7000; 800-662-1348; 509-624-9322 (fax).

United Church of Religious Science, 3251 West Sixth Street, Los Angeles, CA 90020; 213-388-2181; 213-388-1926 (fax).

Unity School of Christianity, 1901 N.W. Blue Parkway, Unity Village, MO 64056; 816-524-3550; 816-251-3554 (fax). E-mail address: unity@ unityworldhq.org.

The topic of concern, assembling a core collection of New Thought resources, was outside the immediate purview of the library associations we contacted:

American Theological Library Association, 250 S. Wacker Drive, Suite 1600, Chicago, IL 60606-5384, 888-665-ATLA, 312-454-5505 (fax). E-mail address: atal@atal.com; Web page: (http://www.atla.com).
Church and Synagogue Library Association, P.O. Box 19357, Portland, OR 97280-0357; 503-244-6919; 800-542-0357; 503-977-3734 (fax). E-mail address: csla@worldaccessnet.com; Web page: (http://www.worldaccessnet. com/~csla).

Databases

The following databases were indispensable aids in clarifying citations.

WorldCat. (1997-). [Dublin, Ohio]: OCLC.
Includes over 36 million bibliographic records of any type of material cataloged by OCLC member libraries.

Ulrich's international periodicals directory (41st ed.). (2003). New York: R. R. Bowker.

Library Catalogs

Catalogs of two theological schools we visited in London, Ontario each had only a handful of New Thought titles. Most of the catalog records for these titles did not include "New Thought" as a subject heading. Instead, the books were assigned headings for specific denominations.
The Southern Methodist University catalog has the largest academic collection of New Thought material extant. SMU was the recipient of two large private collections of published and unpublished New Thought materials: the

Charles S. Braden collection on New Thought and Christian Science, and the Arthur Corey collection, which contained many rare Christian Science titles. Besides bibliographic records for published materials from the Corey collection, the SMU online catalog includes the entry, "Corey, Arthur. Archives." This entry represents 19 boxes of archival and manuscript materials from the Arthur Corey collection that are located in Bridwell Library Archives at SMU. The SMU catalog also has a large number of titles under headings for The Unity School of Christianity and other New Thought denominations.

There has been almost no New Thought material added to the SMU collection since 1973. Discussion with SMU librarians indicated that the reasons for this were a combination of budget restrictions and the necessity of purchasing library materials that directly support instructional programs. SMU has not maintained the physical integrity of its New Thought collections. Neither the Corey nor the Braden collections of published materials can be identified as such in the SMU catalog, since no added entries for the collections were made in the bibliographic records for individual titles. Both collections were broken up and allocated among the SMU libraries. No bibliographies, print or otherwise, exist of the original collections. Additional confusion is caused by the fact that Arthur Corey actually contributed two major collections to SMU. Even when Corey collection material is found, it is difficult to distinguish between those items that were part of his New Thought collection and those that were part of his collection on magic. Corey was both a Christian Science practitioner and a well-known magician.

SMU has a specific collection listed as the "New Thought Collection" in other reference sources. Unfortunately this collection is misnamed, since it is a collection of sermons dating from the late 1700s and early 1800s that have no connection with the New Thought movement. SMU would serve its clients better if these materials were identified differently, particularly in reference books to library collections.

There is little use of cross-referencing (i.e., "see" and "see also" references) for New Thought in library catalogs. In this subject area, where boundaries can be drawn in quite arbitrary ways, the absence of cross references often leads to unfounded conclusions about New Thought materials in the larger collection. For example, the SMU libraries have only four titles listed under the subject heading "Jesus Christ–New Thought–Interpretations" even though the libraries hold several hundred Christian "New Thought" titles.

Titles listed in the SMU catalog under the heading "Unity School of Christianity" generally are not cross-referenced to "New Thought." Lack of cross-referencing in library catalogs means, in this instance, that there is no scheme that illustrates the conceptual or organizational development of New Thought. Some bibliographers would argue that the concept of establishing developmental lineage in a subject like New Thought may be as important as the collocation function of the catalog, albeit more subjective and difficult to determine.

We consulted the library catalogs of the following institutions, either in person or online:

Library of Congress Online Catalog (http://catalog.loc.gov/)

Mary Baker Eddy Library for the Betterment of Humanity (http://vtlsweb-p. csps.com/cgi-bin/gw_41_3/chameleon?skin=web&lng=en)
This library, located at 200 Massachusetts Avenue, Boston, is an archive and visitor center as well as a library. It is part of the Christian Science "Mother Church" complex and makes available to researchers selected unpublished manuscripts, published materials and secondary sources on Christian Science and related subjects. Its online catalog, "Book Search," is still in development, and will include 10,000 books, periodicals and audiovisual resources.

Southern Methodist University Libraries, Dallas, TX (http://www.smu.edu/ libraries/)

St. Peters Seminary, London, Ontario, Canada

Truth Lending Library, Santa Barbara, CA

Unity School of Christianity, Unity Village, Lee's Summit, Missouri

Walter Clinton Jackson Library, University of North Carolina at Greensboro (http://library.uncg.edu)

Weldon Library, University of Western Ontario, London, Ontario, Canada (http://www.lib.uwo.ca/newalpha.shtml)
This shared catalog includes the library collections of Huron University College and Brescia University College, also located in London, Ontario.

Publishers' and Distributors' Catalogs

Publishers' and distributors' catalogs we consulted are listed below. Some publishers publish the works of only one author (e.g., the Kappeler Institute); others publish only material dealing with one author (e.g., Emma Publishing); others publish only material approved by certain organizations (e.g., the Christian Science Publishing Society). Some distributors specialize in only specific types of religious material (e.g., DeVorss & Co. specializes in New Thought and related material).

As mentioned earlier, including the Christian Science Publishing Society as a source of New Thought publications could be questioned, since the Boston-based First Church of Christ, Scientist does not identify itself with the New Thought movement. Because we decided to include formative Christian Science among New Thought and mind-healing organizations, some reprints available for purchase from the Christian Science Publishing Society could be of value for this collection. It must be noted that Christian Science Reading Rooms stock only literature authorized for sale by the denomination. The First Church of Christ, Scientist has, in the past, purchased the copyrights to New Thought publications and thereby prevented their dissemination.

None of the catalogs we examined identified copyright or publication dates consistently. Only one of the catalogs offered materials in languages other than English, namely the catalog of the Christian Science Publishing Society. No catalog described the quality of editions (i.e., the binding or paper used), although some of the glossy ads inserted with the print catalogs visually identified the quality level of the covers. Some catalogs, such as The Bookmark, maintained a section for reprints of rare books, usually photocopies of titles in the public domain. No catalog identified both retail and wholesale prices.

Titles listed in many of the catalogs were aimed at a middle-of-the-road reading level and level of philosophical sophistication. Exceptions were the Christian Science Publishing Society, Rare Books, DeVorss & Co., and The Bookmark. Few catalogs contained materials other than monographs written for adults, except for the Unity and Christian Science Publishing Society catalogs, which included materials for children, print materials in Braille, and audio and videocassettes.

The Bookmark, P.O. Box 801143, Santa Clarita, CA 91380-1143; 805-298-7767; fax 805-250-9227.
   The Bookmark catalog includes detailed annotations. It focuses entirely on Christian Science and New Thought materials.

Christian Science Publishing Society, One Norway Street, Boston, MA 02115; 617-450-2000.
   This is the official source for authorized Christian Science materials. Christian Science Reading Rooms carry only materials authorized by the denomination. The web site of the Publishing Society is linked to the official Christian Science web page: (http://www.tfccs.com).

DeVorss & Co., P.O. Box 550, Marina del Rey, CA 90294-0550; 310-870-7478; 800-843-5743; fax 310-821-6290.
   This company is reputed to be the largest distributor of materials related to New Thought. Unfortunately, much of the material listed in the catalog is

syncretistic and/or related only casually to New Thought. The company maintains a web site: http://www.devorss.com.

Emma Publishing Society, P.O. Box 1113, Cuyahoga Falls, OH 44223-0113.
This is the best source for material on Augusta Emma Simmons Stetson. The Emma Publishing Society's web address is: (http://www.emmapublishing.com).

Foundational Book Company, P.O. Box 659, London, England SW3-6SJ; 071-584-1053.
This company seems to have reciprocating distribution rights with the Rare Book Company and The Bookmark in Europe.

Hailsham Book Distributors, 30 Citchling Way, Hailsham, East Sussex, England BN27-3LU; 0323-848061.
A source to approach if the acquisitions librarian cannot locate needed materials in North America.

Kappeler Institute, P.O. Box 99735, Seattle, WA 98199; 206-286-1617 (telephone); 206-186-1675 (fax). See web address above.
This is the best source for Max Kappeler material.

Rare Book Company, P.O. Box 6957, Freehold, NJ 07728; 908-364-8043.
This company has extensive coverage of historical Christian Science and related New Thought materials. It is both a publisher and a distributor, and has reprinted many out-of-print titles.

Unity School of Christianity, 1901 N.W. Blue Parkway, Unity Village, MO 64056; 816-524-3550; 816-251-3554 (fax). E-mail address: unity@unityworldhq. org. See web address above.
Best source of Unity and related New Thought materials. Unity School is both a publisher and a distributor. Older Unity publications are seldom reprinted.

Printed Sources: General Overviews

General theological reference sources were disappointing in their coverage. Very few had specific coverage of New Thought or helpful leads to other sources for these materials. The notable exceptions were the books of Gordon Melton, who can be regarded as the expert in North American religious traditions.

Some source materials showed initial promise, like *Religious Books, 1876-1982*, which had 145 listings under "New Thought" alone. However, these titles were English-language monographs only. Furthermore, the listings were not well balanced. Although the title of the source claims coverage from 1876 to 1982, thirty-four of the New Thought entries were published in the

1960s and another fourteen in the 1950s. Although New Thought began during the American Civil War, only two of the titles listed were published before 1900. The works of one author, Joel Goldsmith, comprised twenty-one of the entries, an over-representation. Few sources included such related subject subdivisions as "New Thought–Bibliography," "New Thought–History," "Jesus Christ–New Thought–Interpretations," and when they did the materials so identified were often of a New Age or occult nature rather than New Thought.

Few sources identified birth and/or death dates of all the authors, which are necessary to know to balance a New Thought collection. Seldom in these sources are Christian Science or The Unity School of Christianity included or referred to under New Thought headings, although these organizations are direct descendants from Phineas P. Quimby, the acknowledged "father" of New Thought. In some key source materials, such as *Index to Book Reviews in Religion*, published by the American Theological Library Association, there are no headings at all for New Thought, Unity School of Christianity, or Christian Science. This source, like many of the rest, has little coverage of small denominational presses.

None of the sources displayed matrices of subjective, relative comparisons among New Thought materials. None of the sources listed below strove to include all formats and subjects of New Thought materials. None had sections devoted to the different levels of New Thought reader (e.g., beginner, advanced, clergy, practitioner, etc.), although some publishers' catalogs do make some such distinctions (e.g., the catalog of The Unity School of Christianity).

None of the following sources gave complete information on New Thought materials, such as price or size of printed volumes, publishers' addresses and contact information, and notes as to whether the item has an index and/or bibliography. None used recognized subject terms.

Treesh, E. (Ed.). (1993). *Index to book reviews in religion*. Evanston, IL: American Theological Library Association.
An author, title, reviewer, series, and annual classified index to reviews of books published in and of interest to the field of religion.

Ash, L. (Ed.). (1993). *Subject collections: A guide to special book collections and subject emphases as reported by university, college, public, and special libraries and museums in the United States and Canada.* (7th ed.). New York: R.R. Bowker.

Atkins, G. G. (1923). *Modern cults and religious movements.* Westwood, NJ: Fleming H. Revell.

Barrow, J. G. (1969). *A bibliography of bibliographies in religion.* Ann Arbor, MI: Edwards.

Bibliographical repertory of Christian institutions. (1992). Strasbourg, France: Cerdic Publications.

Blazek, R., & Aversa, E. (2000). *The humanities: A selective guide to information sources* (5th ed.). Englewood, CO: Libraries Unlimited.

Cornish, G. (Ed.). (1986). *Religious periodicals directory.* Santa Barbara, CA: ABC-CLIO.

Gorman, G.E., & Gorman, L. (1986). *Bibliographies and indexes in religious studies.* New York: Greenwood Press.

Karpinski, L. M. (1978). *The religious life of man: Guide to basic literature.* Metuchen, NJ: Scarecrow Press.

Kepple, R. J. (1981). *Reference works for theological research: An annotated selective bibliographical guide* (2nd ed.). Washington, DC: University Press of America.

Library of Congress. (2002). *Library of Congress subject headings* (25th ed.). Washington, DC: Author.
LCSH is an excellent point of departure for anyone developing a subject collection. It provides recognized subject headings used in library catalogs and printed selection tools, and can be used as an aid to browsing.

Melton, J. G. (1991). *Religious leaders of America: A bibliographic guide to founders and leaders of religious bodies, churches, and spiritual groups in North America.* Detroit: Gale Research.
Melton's books are listed in many bibliographies concerning the development of North American religious organizations.

Melton, J. G. (2003). *The encyclopedia of American religions* (7th ed.). Detroit: Gale Research.
Includes summaries of historical developments in various New Thought organizations.

Reese, W.L. (1988). *The best in the literature of philosophy and world religions* (13th ed.). New York: R.R. Bowker.

Religious and inspirational books and serials in print. (1987). New York: R.R. Bowker.

Religious books, 1876-1952. (1983). New York: R.R. Bowker.
A beginning reference for certain aspects of New Thought. Unfortunately its inherent definition is inaccurate and misleading, since occult and New Age materials appear under New Thought headings.

Reference books bulletin 1999-2000. Chicago, Ill.: Booklist Publications.
"Prepared by the American Library Association Reference Books Bulletin Editorial Board."

Wilson, J. F., & Slavens, T. P. (1982). Research guide to religious studies. In *Sources of Information in the Humanities*; no. 1. Chicago: American Library Association.

Print Sources–Specific

Many of the titles listed in the following subsections would add significantly to the core collection and could be purchased if the collection were larger and better funded.

ANALYSES

The following materials were useful in determining the level of materials needed in the New Thought core collection.

Anderson, C. A. (1993). *Healing hypothesis: Horatio W. Dresser and the philosophy of New Thought*. New York: Garland.
Examines the philosophy of Horatio W. Dresser, here considered to be the father of New Thought.

Holmes, E. S. (1989). *The Holmes papers: The philosophy of Ernest Holmes*. Manhattan Beach, CA: South Bay Church of Religious Science.
Examines the philosophy of Ernest Holmes, founder of Religious Science.

Studdert-Kennedy, H. A. (1961). *Christian Science and organized religion: A plea for an impartial consideration and the examination of a new point of view*. Los Gatos, CA: Farallon Foundation.
An excellent source on the subject of Christian Science, not authorized by the First Church of Christ, Scientist.

Larson, M. A. (1987). *New Thought religion: A philosophy for health, happiness, and prosperity*. New York: Philosophical Library.
Covers the most popular aspects of New Thought: avoiding sickness, gaining wealth, and achieving success.

Clark, M. A. (Ed.). (1982). *The healing wisdom of Dr. P. P. Quimby*. Los Altos, CA: Frontal Lobe.
A readable presentation of Quimby's teachings.

Dresser, A. G. (1895). *The philosophy of P. P. Quimby with selections from his manuscripts and a sketch of his life*. Boston: G. H. Ellis.

Simon, A. M. (1986). *The upward way: The rhetoric of transcendence in the Unity School of Christianity*. Unpublished doctoral dissertation, Ohio State University.
New Thought generally ignores the theological doctrine of transcendence, favoring the doctrine of divine immanence. This is one of the few sources that discusses the concept of transcendence in New Thought.

Apologetics and Criticism

The material in this section was useful in balancing the collection between polemics and outside criticism.

Blavatsky, H. P. (1907). *Some of the errors of Christian Science.* Point Loma, CA: Theosophical Publishing Company.
Critique from a theosophical point of view.

Butterworth, E. (1965). *Unity: A quest for truth.* New York: R. Speller.
Apologetic for The Unity School of Christianity.

Holmes, E. S. (1944). *What Religious Science teaches.* Los Angeles: Institute of Religious Science.
Frequently cited apologetic for Religious Science.

John, D. (1962). *The Christian Science way of life.* Boston, MA: The Christian Science Publishing Society.
Apologetic for Christian Science.

Twain. M. (Samuel Clemens). (1907). *Christian Science.* New York: Harper and Brothers.
Well-known tongue-in-cheek critique.

Bibliographies

Whaley, H.B. (1973). *The collection and preservation of the materials of the New Thought movement, to which is appended a bibliography of New Thought literature from 1875 to the present.* Unpublished master's thesis, University of Missouri, Columbia.
This is an excellent, although dated, source for New Thought material. Unfortunately it is not annotated.

International New Thought Alliance. (1992). *How to build a library of New Thought books.* Mesa, AZ: Author.
This is a misleading source, since the compilers did not arrive at a clear definition of New Thought before making their selections.

Biographies and Autobiographies

The material in this section was useful in constructing the historical and developmental lineage of New Thought leaders.

Bates, E. S. and Dittemore, J.V. (1932). *Mary Baker Eddy: The truth and the tradition*. New York: Alfred A. Knopf.
Includes a catalog of Mary Baker Eddy's personal library.

Gill, G. (1998). *Mary Baker Eddy*. Cambridge, MA.
This 713-page biography combines careful scholarly research with an approachable style of writing and an objective viewpoint.

Hamblin, H. T. (n.d.). *My search for truth*. Chichester. England: Author.

Harley, G. N. (1991). *Emma Curtis Hopkins: Forgotten founder of New Thought*. Unpublished doctoral dissertation, Florida State University.

Holmes, F. L. (1970). *Ernest Holmes: His life and times*. New York: Dodd Mead.

Meyer, D. (1980). *The positive thinkers*. New York: Pantheon Books.

Peel, R. (1977). *Mary Baker Eddy*. Boston. MA: Christian Science Publishing Society.
This major biographical work is authorized and approved by The First Church of Christ, Scientist.

Regardie, I. (1983). *The leaders of fulfillment* (2nd ed.). Phoenix, AZ: Falcon Press.
This monograph covers leaders of Unity, Christian Science, and other New Thought organizations.

Robinson, F. B. (1941). *The strange autobiography of Frank B. Robinson*. Moscow, ID: Psychiana.
Robinson had opinions that others viewed as negative and hate-filled. Many of his followers left without first learning what New Thought was.

Sinkler, L. (1973). *The spiritual journey of Joel S. Goldsmith, modern mystic*. New York: Harper and Row.
Written by a long-time friend of Goldsmith.

Studdert-Kennedy, H. A. (1947). *Mrs. Eddy, her life, her work and her place in history*. San Francisco: Farallon Press.
Objective biography not approved by the First Church of Christ, Scientist, which successfully blocked its publication by larger publishers.

Zweig, S. (1962). *Mental healers*. New York: Frederick Ungar.
Appears in nearly every bibliography of New Thought titles.

Collections

The material in this section was useful in helping to balance the collection across the different aspects of New Thought.

Christian Science: A sourcebook of contemporary materials. (1990). Boston: The Christian Science Publishing Society.
An authorized publication that covers Christian Science theology, organization, and membership.

Peel, R. (1989). *Health and medicine in the Christian Science tradition: Principle, practice, and challenge.* New York: Crossroad.
An authorized publication that covers the healing aspect of Christian Science.

Histories

Resources in this section were useful in developing the personal and organizational lineage of New Thought.

Braden, C. S. (1958). *Christian Science today: Power, policy, practice.* Dallas, TX: Southern Methodist University Press.
An often-cited source.

Braden, C. S. (1963). *Spirits in rebellion: The rise and development of New Thought.* Dallas, TX: Southern Methodist Press.
Braden's writings form the core of New Thought history. Good explanation of conceptual and historical development in the New Thought movement.

Braden, C. S. (1949). *These also believe: A study of modern American cults and minority religious movements.* New York: Macmillan.
A well-regarded work.

Brown, W. G. (1970). *Evolution of the Christian Science church organization.* London, England: Foundational Book Company.

Christian Science Foundation. (1992). *The continuity of the cause of Christian Science.* Cambridge, England: Christian Science Foundation.

Cutten, G. B. (1911). *Three thousand years of mental healing.* New York: Charles Scribner's Sons.

Dittemore, J. V. (1925). *The evolution of Christian Science: A brief summary of its historical development, contemporary attainments, and future destiny.* Washington, DC: Publishing Society of the Christian Science Parent Church.

Dresser, H.W. (1919). *A history of the New Thought movement.* New York: Thomas Y. Crowell.
This was the first history of New Thought and it is still highly regarded.

Freeman, J. D. (1954). *The story of Unity.* Lee's Summit, MO: Unity School of Christianity.

Johnson, W. L. (1927). *The history of the Christian Science movement.* Brookline. MA: Zion Research Foundation.

Kappeler, M. (1970). *The development of the Christian Science idea and practice.* London, England: Foundational Books.

Melton, J. G. (1977). *A reader's guide to the church's ministry of healing.* Independence, MO: The Academy of Religion and Psychical Research.

Orgain, A. L. (1929). *As it is.* New York: Rare Book Company.
This book traces the evolution of Mary Baker Eddy's *Science and health through its many editions.*

Parker, G. T. (1969). *An intellectual history of the New Thought: 1865-1920.* Unpublished doctoral dissertation, Harvard University.
Good tracing of lines of historical development.

Parker, G. T. (1973). *Mind cure in New England: From the Civil War to World War I.* Hanover, NH: University Press of New England.
This title appears in most bibliographies.

Regardie, I. R. (1946). *Romance in metaphysics: An introduction to the history, theory, and psychology of modern metaphysics.* Chicago, IL: Aries Press.

Shepherd, T. (1985). *Friends in high places.* Unity Village, MO: Unity Books.
This books includes a short section on New Thought that provides a concise summary of the major historical events.

Sources of Reviews

Beals, Ann (Ed.). (1993). *The bookmark review.* Santa Clarita, CA: The Bookmark.
This appears to be the only source of reviews of early Christian Science and related New Thought titles, both newly printed and reprinted. It provides explanatory information on authorized and unauthorized Christian Science materials in several formats.

Web Sites

Some web sites we found useful provided information on New Thought and links to other sites:

New Thought Movement Online
http://websyte.com/alan/online.htm

> This site includes links to New Thought discussion groups, bulletin boards, and groups on the Web. These groups are classed as overall organizations; denominational headquarters, including directories to churches and centers; independent local centers, churches, and schools; individuals who maintain New Thought web pages; and groups without web sites that can be contacted by e-mail. We retrieved this information from the site on January 12, 2003 and it had been updated on December 24, 2002, less than three weeks earlier.

New Thought Network (NTN)
http://www.newthought.net/guide/websites.htm

> The NTN site includes links to New Thought, Unity and Religious Science web sites; web sites of other New Thought denominations; independent New Thought churches; denominational schools; "related online centers"; directories of New Thought churches; and a "gateway" to New Thought music sites. When we looked at the site on January 12, 2003, it had not been updated since March 22, 2000.

Society for the Study of Metaphysical Religion
http://websyte.com/alan.ssmr.htm

> This site covers the SSMR organization with links to its bylaws, officers, and committees. It includes links to pages describing the New Thought movement, Quimby's work, New Age, and "metaphysics." Information on membership and on subscribing to an SSMR journal are provided on the site, as well as a contact point for joining an SSMR-sponsored electronic discussion group. When consulted on January 12, 2003, this site had last been updated on August 21, 2002.

REFERENCES

Alt, M.S., & Shields, R.D. (1987). Assessment of library materials on the history of Christianity at the Ohio State University: An update. *Collection Management*, 9(1), 67-77.

American Library Association and Association of College and Research Libraries. (1981). *Notes: College library information packets #2-81 collection development policies*. Chicago: Author.

Stop the Technology, I Want to Get Off: Tips and Tricks for Media Selection and Acquisition

Mary S. Laskowski

SUMMARY. Media selection and acquisition is highly dependent on a number of variables, perhaps the most important of which is changing technologies. New technology is a wonderful and frightening thing, with a high level of impact on media collection development. New technologies can improve sound and visual quality, but can also play havoc with established collections and budgets. Availability of various media formats and titles is a very fluid phenomenon, which poses a unique set of challenges to media librarians and selectors. *[Article copies available for a fee from The Haworth Document Delivery Service: 1-800-HAWORTH. E-mail address: <docdelivery@haworthpress.com> Website: <http://www.HaworthPress.com> © 2004 by The Haworth Press, Inc. All rights reserved.]*

KEYWORDS. Media acquisitions, video collection development, selection aids

Selection and acquisition of media materials presents a number of unique challenges. Unlike print acquisitions, where though vendors and selection tools may change rapidly the format remains fairly constant, the types of media

Mary S. Laskowski is Coordinator of Media Services, Cataloging and Reserves, Undergraduate Library, University of Illinois at Urbana-Champaign, 1402 West Gregory Drive, Urbana, IL 61801 (E-mail: mkschnei@uiuc.edu).

[Haworth co-indexing entry note]: "Stop the Technology, I Want to Get Off: Tips and Tricks for Media Selection and Acquisition." Laskowski, Mary S. Co-published simultaneously in *The Acquisitions Librarian* (The Haworth Information Press, an imprint of The Haworth Press, Inc.) No. 31/32, 2004, pp. 217-225; and: *Selecting Materials for Library Collections* (ed: Audrey Fenner) The Haworth Information Press, an imprint of The Haworth Press, Inc., 2004, pp. 217-225. Single or multiple copies of this article are available for a fee from The Haworth Document Delivery Service [1-800-HAWORTH, 9:00 a.m. - 5:00 p.m. (EST). E-mail address: docdelivery@haworthpress.com].

10.1300/J101v16n31_17

217

available can change dramatically over short periods of time. Documentaries and educational titles in particular are difficult to evaluate and locate for purchase, while feature and mass marketed films on video are easier to identify and acquire. All media acquisitions share a variety of traps and pitfalls for the unwary however. As Gary Handman states in his introduction to *Video Collection Development in Multi-type Libraries: A Handbook*, libraries too often try to emulate print practices to the detriment of media collections.

> In the sorriest cases, they've cut off the head and feet (the diverse needs and wants) of visitors (patrons) to match a bed clothed exclusively in print. In other cases, they've built video collections on a fiscally short-sheeted bed feathered with conservative public service and collections policies. Lop! Off with anything too controversial, too non-mainstream, too expensive or difficult to acquire. (Handman, 2002, p. xiii)

For readers interested in further developing their understanding of video collection development, this book is highly recommended.

COMMON PROBLEMS AND ISSUES IN MEDIA COLLECTION DEVELOPMENT AND ACQUISITIONS

One of the biggest challenges in the selection of media materials is the variety of formats available at any given time, and the ephemeral nature of most of those formats. Preservation and/or replacement costs need to be calculated and assumed up front for each title purchased in a media format. Many people are familiar with some of the basic preservation problems with print materials, such as books printed on acidic paper. What is often less known and harder to predict is the shelf-life of media formats. Standard VHS videotapes, for example, can last for decades under appropriate storage conditions, but on the other hand they can be ruined quite easily with excessive heat, damaged VCRs, demagnetization, etc. In some cases the viewing equipment becomes unavailable before the collection shows great wear and tear. For example, for many years the industry standard was 3/4" U-Matic tapes, but many libraries and other institutions, even those owning a 3/4" U-Matic collection, are hard-pressed to provide working playback equipment for their 3/4" U-Matic collections at this time.

The advent of each new technologically advanced format such as DVD (digital video disc) requires either the purchase of new playback equipment for in-house viewing or a saturation of the public market so that a majority of patrons have the capability to view material in the format acquired. Much as many patrons have problems with various electronic resources, as there are many different types and levels of computer access, it is extremely unlikely that all patrons will at any given time have the same viewing capabilities at home. At the moment it is fairly safe to assume that the majority of the general public have access to a VCR, but recent statistics indicate that DVD is also here to stay and will become increasingly popular for the foreseeable future. Given a choice based strictly on durability of the format, DVD may be the preferred choice, but until the majority of patrons have DVD playback capability, service impact may require a mixed format collection. Aside from durability issues, the DVD industry is currently geared largely towards feature films and mass market titles. Until the industry uniformly adopts DVD as the next video format, marketing educational and documentary titles in DVD as well, the change from one format to the next cannot be complete. There are aesthetic choices to be made as well. DVDs often include many "extras" which are not available on corresponding VHS copies such as commentary by director and cast, alternate endings and eliminated scenes, and multiple language subtitle options.

Aside from the necessity of determining the appropriate format such as VHS or DVD for the individual institution and population served, the plethora of available formats can cause quite a bit of confusion at the time of purchase as well. A VHS tape is a VHS tape, right? Not necessarily. Purchasing international titles, or even from vendors with an international clientele, can result in material that is unplayable in local machines. A fairly common mistake made at the time of order is that though the selector may specify a VHS videotape, they may not realize that they may also need to specify NTSC or PAL format. VHS-NTSC (National Television Standards Committee) is used mainly in North America, Japan and Taiwan, while VHS-PAL (Phase Alternate Lines) is the format in Australia, New Zealand, United Kingdom, Europe, and most other countries. Unfortunately many catalogs and web sites do not articulate the difference, and assume that purchasers are local to their coding region.

It is often attractive to purchase DVDs, particularly for foreign films as they often include numerous language subtitles, but there are coding issues there as well. The various production and home video studios lobbied for a coding system for copy protection which would prevent titles manufactured in the United States from being marketable elsewhere, and vice versa. There are universal DVD players that will play items coded for any region, but they are not the norm, and not all the copyright issues have been addressed. The current DVD regions are as follows: Region 1–The U.S., U.S. territories and Canada; Region 2–Europe, Japan, Middle East, Egypt, South Africa, Greenland; Region 3–Taiwan, Korea, the Philippines, Indonesia, Hong Kong; Region 4–Mexico, South America, Central America, Australia, New Zealand, Pacific Islands, Caribbean; Region 5–Russia (former USSR), Eastern Europe, India, most of Africa,

North Korea, Mongolia; Region 6–China. There are several other possible regional codes that have been set aside for future use.

There are several problems in media acquisitions that are similar to issues in serials acquisitions. The first is the difficulty in replacing individual volumes of series. Quite often one particular volume of a series either receives heavier use or is damaged and needs to be replaced independently of the rest of the series. Many distributors, however, do not price individual volumes, or else price them at a disproportionate rate. In some cases it is actually much more cost effective to purchase the entire series again and store the extra copies against future need, though some distributors do have wonderful replacement policies for material that is damaged. Also similar to problems encountered with serial acquisitions are the various pricing schemes for media. Much as scholarly journals are often many, many times the cost of mass market magazines, educational films and documentaries are usually much more expensive than feature film titles for often much shorter pieces. It is not uncommon for a 20 minute educational title to cost several hundred dollars, which plays havoc if the media budget is built around feature film titles. In addition, there is also the issue of institutional pricing. Many educational films and documentaries are available at one price to the general public and a greatly higher price to institutions on the same theory as journal subscriptions where the institutional subscription may keep individuals from subscribing, thereby driving up the costs and lowering the profits. There can also be an added fee for the purchase of public performance rights, which is sometimes included in the institutional pricing and sometimes not. Depending on the proposed uses of the material, public performance rights may or may not be an issue.

Finally, there are several possible problems related to the identification and acquisition of quality copies of media materials. Oftentimes the same title will be available through several different vendors at different prices, but different distribution companies frequently have very different levels of quality. In some cases, regardless of the distributor involved, it is impossible to get a good quality copy of some material as the copies were printed from old film prints that had already started to deteriorate before transfer. An important aspect of media acquisitions is the viewing of titles upon receipt to ensure that the copy purchased does not have faults with the sound track, image tracking, etc., but the availability of many different copies from differing sources combined with the sometimes unavoidably poor image quality of older titles makes this a less than simple prospect at times. Unlike book ordering, where acquisitions staff can work closely with several major "jobbers" for the majority of requested material, media acquisitions requires dealing with many small distribution companies. Quite often educational films and documentaries are only available from the original producer, who may not have done any other projects.

What that means for libraries is that there are constantly new vendors that need to be set up in the acquisitions system, and they may be used for only one title. Also, if cataloging records are identified at the time of purchase there is often a greater problem for acquisitions staff to correctly identify the appropriate record for the item on order. Videos lack ISBNs, catalog numbers vary from distributor to distributor, and unless the person placing the order is familiar with issues in media cataloging, mistakes are easy to make. For example, there are different cataloging records not only for the same title released in different formats, often simultaneously, but also for different distributors, differences in format such as wide-screen or standard view, different release dates, special editions such as director's cuts, and re-releases as boxed sets, etc.

RECOMMENDED SELECTION AND REFERENCE TOOLS

Bowker's Complete Video Directory

Bowker's Complete Video Directory is one of the more complete video directories on the market. *Bowker's* is published annually in four volumes, and has been in existence since 1990 in its current format. Two of the volumes are dedicated to entertainment videos currently available for home distribution, and two of the volumes are dedicated to educational/special interest titles. The volumes are formatted identically, with ordering information and a short synopsis available in the alphabetical title index, while volumes 2 and 4 have additional cross-referencing indexes. The 2002 edition contains over 67,000 entertainment titles and over 133,000 educational and special interest titles. Additional indexes include (but are not limited to) an awards index, a genre index, a cast/director index, a manufacturer index, and a subject index of over 500 categories. Especially nice and often hard to find information is included in the closed-captioned index. For libraries interested in only entertainment titles, or exclusively educational and special interest, the set can be broken up into two sets and purchased independently. A slightly modified version of *Bowker's Complete Video Directory* is also available in CD-ROM format as *Bowker's Audio & Video Database on Disc*, which is updated quarterly. The CD-ROM version includes information drawn from *Words on Cassette* in addition to *Bowker's Complete Video Directory*. Not only does the CD-ROM version include information relating to over 120,000 audiocassettes (not included at all in the video directory), it also contains over 6,000 full-text reviews from *Variety*, plus the same index access as found in the print version. The major drawbacks of both the print and CD-ROM product are that they are fairly pricey, and, as with all video selection aids due to the nature of the market, must be purchased annually in order to stay reasonably up-to-date.

Video Source Book

Gale's *Video Source Book* is another fairly comprehensive guide to the titles available on the market. The *Video Source Book* is published annually in two volumes; the first edition was published in 1979. Unlike *Bowker's Complete Video Directory*, the *Video Source Book* does not separate entertainment titles from educational and special interest titles. Instead, all video titles are included in the video program listings section by title. In addition to the program listings section, the *Video Source Book* includes six other indices: alternate title, subject, credits, awards, special formats (including closed-captioned), and program distributors. The *Video Source Book* has coverage for more than 130,000 program listings, including over 160,000 videos. The *Video Source Book* is part of the VideoHound reference guides to movies and entertainment. A subset of the *Video Source Book*, roughly 25,000 of the movie and entertainment titles, is published as the *VideoHound's Golden Movie Retriever* guide, which is a great public reference tool. Also available is *Magill's Cinema Annual*, which is geared towards serious film research and provides essay reviews for the "significant" films released each year. Neither of these two smaller titles is nearly as comprehensive as the *Video Source Book* however, and both are better used as public reference tools than selection aids. Like *Bowker's Complete Video Directory*, the *Video Source Book* is fairly pricey, especially for smaller libraries. Unfortunately, accurate and comprehensive coverage is best guaranteed by the purchase of both titles on a yearly basis, and even then there are some things that fall through the cracks.

RECOMMENDED VIDEO REVIEW SOURCES

Video Librarian

Video Librarian, published bi-monthly, is one of the best video review sources around. The reviews are written by a variety of folk including librarians, teachers, and film critics in addition to the *Video Librarian* staff, and are geared towards public, school, academic and special libraries. There are roughly 200 reviews per issue, as well as feature articles on items of interest including new technologies. Reviews are divided up by major subject areas such as Children's, Education, Language, Health & Fitness, The Arts, etc., and there are separate listings for video movies and a DVD spotlight. Reviewed material is current and new to the market within the last 2-3 months in its current format. Each review includes appropriate ordering information and data on the availability of public performance rights and other special features. The *Video Librarian* is also now available online as *Video Librarian Plus!* (http://www. videolibrarian.com/), which adds online access in addition to the print subscription. The online access offers a searchable database of over 12,000 full-text video reviews and roughly 1,000 video distributors. *Video Librarian* is one of the more affordable review resources around, and is highly recommended for libraries of all types with a video collection.

Educational Media Reviews Online

Educational Media Reviews Online (libweb.lib.buffalo.edu/emro/search. html) is another excellent source of reviews for educational and documentary titles. The reviews are written by librarians and faculty in institutions throughout the United States and Canada. *Educational Media Reviews Online* uses a three-tiered rating system; all material is given a rating of Recommended, Highly Recommended, or Not Recommended. The primary intended audience of the database is academic librarians, but there is a fair amount of material included that is appropriate for school and public librarians as well. Originally the *AV Review Database*, part of *MC Journal: The Journal of Academic Media Librarianship*, *Educational Media Reviews* came into existence in its current form after *MC Journal* ceased publication in early 2002. The database is searchable by title, subject, reviewer, year, rating, distributor and format. There are currently over 1,000 reviews accessible through the database, and the cost (free!) makes *Educational Media Reviews Online* a very attractive review source.

Movie Review Query Engine

If you are looking for reviews of feature film titles, a fast, easy and free resource is the *Movie Review Query Engine* (www.mrqe.com). A note to keep in mind is that these reviews are not written for or by librarians for selection. Unlike other sources mentioned, the *Movie Review Query Engine* compiles reviews from various news and web sources such as the New York Times, Chicago Sun-Times, Reel.com and many others. This can prove very helpful though, particularly if a patron mentions a particular review in support of a title purchase.

OTHER RECOMMENDED MEDIA INFORMATION SOURCES

OCLC WorldCat

Online Computer Library Center (OCLC), Inc.'s *WorldCat* is one of the best online reference sources for media materials. Introduced in 1971 as a union catalog for 54 college and university libraries in Ohio, *WorldCat* now houses over 48 million records from libraries around the world. Over 1,476,500 of these bibliographic records are classified as visual materials. This is by far the most comprehensive representation of media materials available, and each title is entered in MARC format, allowing searchability through all the major access points including Library of Congress subject headings. The drawback of the information being entered at the time of cataloging is that the distribution information, price, availability, etc., is often out of date.

University of California, Berkeley Media Resources Center

A great online resource for information relating to a variety of media issues is the University of California, Berkely Media Resources Center web site (www. lib.berkeley.edu/MRC/). Of particular interest is the well-maintained Video Distributor Database, which allows searching by name or partial name of distributor and browsable lists for documentary, educational, performance video distributors/producers, studio producers/distributors of theatrical/feature films, distributors and wholesalers of theatrical/feature films, and used/out of distribution video distributors. The site also maintains bibliographies on a number of film topics and genres, and a compilation of resources for film studies.

Videolib *and* Videonews *Listservs*

The American Library Association Video Round Table (VRT) supports two listservs for active communication among media professionals. *Videolib* is designed as an open forum on a wide range of issues of interest to media librarians and other professionals including collection development, preservation, and copyright. *Videolib* also serves to connect video librarians with distributors and vendors. *Videonews* allows distributors and vendors to advertise new services and products. Subscription information for both listservs can be found at http://www.lib.berkeley.edu/MRC/vrtlists.html.

Video Round Table Notable Videos for Adults

The Video Round Table of the American Library Association selects a number of titles each year considered to be the best releases of that year or the previous year in documentaries, educational and instructional titles, and performance works for adults. Established in 1998, the Notable Videos for Adults lists are intended to provide public and academic librarians with a core list of diverse titles which represent the best currently available on the market. The lists can be found on the ALA Video Round Table web site (www.ala.org/vrt/notable.html).

REVIEWS OF A/V MATERIAL IN STANDARD
LIBRARY SELECTION RESOURCES

In addition to the sources already listed, some media selection information can be obtained in standard library selection resources. *Booklist* and *Library Journal* both include a section of non-print reviews. A nice *Booklist* feature is that every January there is a Booklist Editors' Choice list published which include media broken up into video and DVD, audio, and audiobooks (also available at www.ala.org/booklist). *Library Journal* has separate video review and audio review sections in each issue. Though the quality of the reviews in both of these publications is high, the material being reviewed is often not nearly as current as those reviewed in the *Video Librarian*, and the selection of titles is much smaller.

CONCLUSION

Though it would be wonderful to have one major comprehensive collection development tool for media materials akin to *Books in Print* for books, alas such is not to be. Used in combination, however, the sources identified here provide a wealth of information on the world of available media formats. Perhaps the most important aspect of becoming proficient in media selection and acquisitions is to identify the appropriate formats for the patron population in question and to plan ahead for the inevitable changes in format and playback equipment availability. Being aware of coding differences in various parts of the world, and incompatibilities with local equipment goes a long way towards avoiding the purchase of unusable materials. New innovations continually reform the unique challenges and opportunities presented by media collection development.

REFERENCES AND RECOMMENDED SOURCES

Booklist. http://www.ala.org/booklist.
Bowker's Complete Video Directory. Annual. New Providence, NJ: R. R. Bowker.
Educational Media Reviews Online. http://libweb.lib.buffalo.edu/emro/search.html.
Handman, Gary P. (2002) *Video Collection Development in Multi-type Libraries: A Handbook.* Westport, Connecticut: Greenwood Press.
Library Journal. Monthly. New York: R. R. Bowker. http://www.libaryjournal.com.
Movie Review Query Engine. http://www.mrqe.com.
Online Computer Library Center(OCLC), Inc.'s WorldCat. http://www.oclc.org/worldcat/.
University of California, Berkeley Media Resources Center. http://www.lib.berkeley.edu/MRC/
Video Librarian. Bi-monthly. Seabeck, WA: Randy Pitman. http://videolibrarian.com/.
Video Round Table Notable Videos for Adults. http://www.ala.org/vrt/notable.html.
Video Source Book. Annual. Farmington Hills, MI: Gale Group. http://www.gale.com.
Videolib and Videonews Listservs. http://www.lib.berkeley.edu/MRC/vrtlists.html.

The Approval Plan:
Selection Aid, Selection Substitute

Audrey Fenner

SUMMARY. Approval plans are used by many libraries as an adjunct to title-by-title selection, and sometimes as a substitute for it. The author examines this approach to purchasing library materials, considering positive and negative effects approval plans may have on collection balance as well as on acquisitions budgets and workflow. The article also serves as an introduction to approval plans for entry-level acquisitions librarians, library school students, and paraprofessional library staff. Practical concerns in setting up approval plans are discussed, such as approval plan profiling, plan maintenance, and evaluation. Budget and accounting considerations are introduced. Although approval plans are widely used, new librarians may have learned little about them in library science courses. The approval plan is presented as a useful tool for shaping and maintaining library collections. *[Article copies available for a fee from The Haworth Document Delivery Service: 1-800-HAWORTH. E-mail address: <docdelivery@haworth press.com> Website: <http://www.HaworthPress.com> © 2004 by The Haworth Press, Inc. All rights reserved.]*

KEYWORDS. Acquisitions, approval plan, blanket order, collection development, library budget, library materials, profile, selection, workflow

Audrey Fenner is Head, Acquisition Department, Walter Clinton Jackson Library, University of North Carolina at Greensboro, P.O. Box 26170, Greensboro, NC 27402-6170 (E-mail: fafenner@uncg.edu).

[Haworth co-indexing entry note]: "The Approval Plan: Selection Aid, Selection Substitute." Fenner, Audrey. Co-published simultaneously in *The Acquisitions Librarian* (The Haworth Information Press, an imprint of The Haworth Press, Inc.) No. 31/32, 2004, pp. 227-240; and: *Selecting Materials for Library Collections* (ed: Audrey Fenner) The Haworth Information Press, an imprint of The Haworth Press, Inc., 2004, pp. 227-240. Single or multiple copies of this article are available for a fee from The Haworth Document Delivery Service [1-800-HAWORTH. 9:00 a.m. - 5:00 p.m. (EST). E-mail address: docdelivery@haworth press.com].

http://www.haworthpress.com/store/product.asp?sku=J101
© 2004 by The Haworth Press, Inc. All rights reserved.
10.1300/J101v16n31_18

WHAT IS AN APPROVAL PLAN?

An approval plan is an agreement between a library and a vendor under which the vendor sends specified types of materials to the library as they are published. The library completes a detailed profile that tells the vendor what subject areas, languages, series and formats are wanted, and lists publishers and presses to be included. Price ceilings are stated for single volumes and multi-volume sets. The vendor's staff selects materials that fit the profile and sends them to the library in regular, continuing shipments. The library may return unwanted titles, but most approval plan profiles restrict returns to a small percentage of the volumes sent.

Libraries have used approval plans as a means of acquiring books since the 1960s. Some vendors, such as YBP and Blackwell, have offered approval plans to their customers for many years. For other vendors, such as Emery-Pratt, approval plans are a recent venture. Some vendors, like Book House, do not offer them at all.

HOW IS A BLANKET ORDER DIFFERENT FROM AN APPROVAL PLAN?

Approval plans came into existence as "gathering plans," a type of blanket order. The "Greenaway Plan" was devised in the 1950s by Emerson Greenaway of the Free Library of Philadelphia. Under his gathering plan, trade publishers sent copies of all of their books to the library before publication. Library staff reviewed the books, placed orders, and prepared catalog records. By the time of publication the library had copies of the selected books, and cards were ready for the card catalog (Ford, 1978).

Under a typical blanket plan, a library receives comprehensive coverage of all titles published by particular presses, or all titles published in specified subject areas. Because the library has agreed to accept all or nearly all of the titles sent, the publisher gives a considerable discount from list prices. Because approval plans and blanket orders are closely related, librarians setting up a plan must be sure that they and the vendor are using the same definitions of the terms "blanket" and "approval."

Blanket orders are now most often used to acquire materials in specific, limited subject areas. For example, a blanket plan could cover local history. A blanket plan may also be publisher-specific, such as a plan with a publisher specializing in a subject such as nursing or business management.

HOW CAN USING AN APPROVAL PLAN SUBSTITUTE
FOR TITLE-BY-TITLE SELECTION?

One of the chief purposes of setting up an approval plan is to ensure that a library will receive automatically all newly published titles from mainstream publishers in areas that fall within its subject or publisher profile. When it is working as it should, a good approval plan will bring new materials into the library as soon as they are published. Not only is this timely delivery an advantage in making new materials available to users, it also ensures that the library receives titles that may go out of print quickly. All of this is an advantage for selectors of library materials, whether they are teaching faculty or librarians who work as subject bibliographers. The approval plan furnishes the library with new titles, from one supplier, in timely fashion. Selectors are free to concentrate on acquiring more esoteric or hard-to-find materials.

Approval plans allow a library to reject and return material that is outside the scope of its collection. Selectors have the advantage of examining approval books they can see and hold and are not dependent on reviews, publishers' blurbs or annotated lists. However, the selectors must take the time to review approval shipments, and generally new shipments arrive weekly. If either librarians or teaching faculty responsible for selection have too many demands on their time, evaluation of new approval books may be given a low priority.

With an approval plan, specified areas of a subject discipline are represented in a collection, and the library receives new titles of any significance in those areas. Ideally, the selectors who work for the vendor are subject specialists. A good vendor maintains contact with the library, analyzing returns, answering questions, and working with the library to revise profiles when necessary.

In conjunction with a book approval plan, a library may request notification slips from the vendor. Under a "slip plan," the vendor sends printed slips that provide bibliographic information on new titles. A selector studies the slips, makes selections from them, and the library purchases the books chosen. Like approval plan books, notification slips are supplied according to a profile set up by the library. In recent years some vendors have offered electronic new title announcements rather than multi-part paper slips. In either case, a library can use a notification service to combine the advantages of firm ordering with the approval plan system. The work of selection is done for the library, but no books are sent until the library places individual orders for them.

Selection for many academic library collections is done, at least in part, by teaching faculty. Faculty may be sincerely interested in the campus library and its collection but lack time to be directly involved with collection development. Often both they and librarians are quite willing to leave initial selection work to an approval plan vendor. Selection of individual titles by faculty can then augment the approval plan, adding materials that are of value for particular courses, specific to faculty research interests, or more obscure and harder to locate. Interested faculty should be consulted and involved with the initial setup of the approval plan. Later, their help with reviewing approval books may be invaluable.

WHAT ARE SOME ADVANTAGES TO THE LIBRARY OF USING AN APPROVAL PLAN FOR COLLECTION BUILDING?

Shipments of new approval plan books arrive automatically, saving staff time in searching, verifying and creating orders. Because of the regular shipments, approval plans distribute the receiving of books evenly through the year. This is helpful to staff because the workflow can be more easily predicted and regulated. A good approval plan vendor will further reduce the workload for library staff by dealing with publisher shipping errors before the volumes ever reach the library.

An approval plan vendor may be able to offer the library coverage of a wide variety of publishers and presses, including international coverage. Acquisition of materials from outside the country is made easier, sparing library staff the searching of titles, assigning of vendors, and possible complications with currency conversion and payments. Publications of museums and galleries, small presses and association presses may also be covered by approval plans. This permits a consolidation of ordering that the library could not accomplish by relying entirely on firm orders.

Finally, vendors often offer greater price discounts for books furnished through an approval plan than through firm orders.

IF LIBRARIES USE APPROVAL PLANS, WILL THEIR COLLECTIONS BE TOO MUCH ALIKE?

Setting up an approval plan is a form of outsourcing, since it shifts selection responsibilities from librarians to vendors. Critics of outsourcing ask if a vendor should be given the responsibility for choosing a substantial percentage of a library's materials. However expert they may be as subject bibliographers, a vendor's selectors are working outside the library and apart from its collection. They cannot be as familiar with the collection, its users or its services as are the library staff or the teaching faculty within an academic institution. Instead, the vendor's bibliographers are selecting books for all their approval plan customers. Will the use of approval plans therefore make library collections too homogeneous?

Nardini, Getchell and Cheever (1996) studied approval plan purchases made by four libraries from the vendor YBP during the 1994-1995 fiscal year. Their study paired similar libraries, and collected data on titles in various subject areas shipped on approval to these libraries and subsequently purchased for their collections. Results of the study showed that, overall, the purchases of the two larger libraries overlapped by 51%. The two smaller libraries in the study purchased only 23% of their approval titles in common. Nardini et al. found that overlap among purchases was higher with publications of university presses, and also greater in certain subject areas. "Traces of a common core," they reported, "are most evident in humanities subclasses where overall output is modest and university press publishing predominant" (p. 90). They found less overlap in the social sciences, and almost none in law and the physical sciences.

These researchers point out that some librarians believe that libraries ought to share a common core of titles. They also point out that the word "core" can be defined differently. Does it mean a core of titles that every library ought to own? Does it refer to a core collection vital to the needs of one particular institution? As the definition of "core" changes, the concern with overlapping collections may also change. Nardini et al. found in their study that, "a common approval plan core among all four libraries is barely visible at all, only about 6 percent of the unique titles [being] acquired by the group. What core there was may be found almost entirely in the humanities and social science sections of university press catalogs. Whether this seems about right, as an assertion of local priorities, or seems symptomatic of fractured mission among libraries, would be a matter of opinion" (p. 95)

DOES USING APPROVAL PLANS HAVE DISADVANTAGES FOR LIBRARY STAFF?

Rosann Bazirjian (1996) questioned the assumption that approval plans always and inevitably reduce the workload of acquisitions staff. While approval plans clearly benefit library selectors in reducing the amount of title-by-title selection they need to do, Bazirjian states that "approval plan processing in acquisitions can be extremely labor intensive, as well as disruptive to work flow" (p. 31). Books received on approval must be unpacked, sorted, and searched on a bibliographic utility. Titles expected but not received must be claimed. Where notification slips rather than books are sent, staff sort and distribute the slips and selectors make choices from them. Staff place firm orders for these titles, and for any volumes that are part of a series or set received only in part through the approval plan. Books not accepted for the collection must be packaged and returned. There are approval invoices to process and credits to record. While the sum total of all of this work may be less than that required if the library depended entirely on firm orders, the amount of work associated with approval plans should not be discounted or ignored.

Bazirjian describes other processes connected with approval plans that actually add to the work of acquisitions support staff. Both librarians and clerical staff may be questioned by faculty or librarians about specific approval titles that have arrived: Why has this book been sent to us? What part of the profile applies to this title? Support staff may be required to verify that titles will not be shipped on approval before placing firm orders. Returning books that duplicate library holdings adds to the time required to complete the processing of approval shipments. Staff must alter invoices, make financial calculations, and pack the books to be returned to the vendor. As Bazirjian points out, time saved at the point of selection may be time added for support staff who process approval books.

Reorganizing an acquisitions department to accommodate an approval plan does not necessarily make these plans disadvantageous, but workflow must be taken into consideration before a plan is set up. Some libraries that use approval plans do no selection from approval shipments, accepting everything that arrives. They may use lack of staff time to justify this approach. Rather than adopting such an after-the-fact expedient, it would be better to restructure staffing and workflow before putting an approval plan into operation. Joan Grant (1999) advises examining areas of responsibility of acquisitions support staff while considering such necessary procedures as sorting and searching books received on approval, keeping records of orders placed from notification slips, and managing approval claims, invoices, and credits. Bazirjian's solution for workflow problems is to ensure that an approval plan involves as few exceptions as possible to routine procedures. Bazirjian (1996) recommends consulting acquisitions staff before making procedural decisions. The people most familiar with the work can help to devise the most efficient, most streamlined processes.

WHAT ABOUT DUPLICATION OF ORDERS?

In writing about the interface between firm orders and approval plans, Susan Flood and Barbara Nelson (1996) cite potential duplication as the point where the two types of orders most frequently cross. How can acquisitions staff predict what titles can be expected to arrive automatically? Must they check each firm order request against the vendor's approval plan database before placing an order? Doing that much checking would be time-consuming indeed, and perhaps would cost the library more in staff time than it would cost to accept some duplicates. Should acquisitions staff order rush requests only, and hold other orders to avoid duplication? What if a title that should come through the approval plan is somehow missed, or arrives a very long time after publication? There may be an advantage in placing most firm orders from notification slips provided by the approval vendor. Faculty or library selectors use these slips in requesting that firm orders be made, and they will not duplicate books that the vendor is sending on approval. The library can then stipulate "do not duplicate on approval" whenever placing a firm order.

When a library receives materials through firm orders, approval plans, blanket orders and standing orders, the risk of new materials being duplicated increases. The approval plan profile must exclude the library's standing order titles and blanket order presses, whether or not the same vendor covers all of these plans.

Knowledge of the approval plan profile gives staff a good idea of the plan's coverage. The library also needs to know how the vendor screens titles to avoid sending duplicates. The vendor should check for duplication across all accounts the library may have with that vendor: firm order, standing order, and approval accounts. Screening would include checking for duplicates between cloth and paperback editions, or U.S. and UK editions, or titles with the same ISBN. The vendor should also do duplicate checking when the library places a firm order, when the vendor generates a profiled book on approval, and when the vendor is ready to send a volume of a standing order. In this way duplication can largely be prevented; no duplicate copy should be shipped unless the library specifically requests a second copy of a certain title.

Of course a vendor cannot be expected to check for duplicates against titles purchased from another supplier, or gift volumes donated to the library. Meredith Smith (1996) cautions against possible duplication of standing orders and continuations through an approval plan, suggesting that the library supply the vendor with a title list of its standing orders for monographic series and sets, and annuals or other continuations. The vendor can then block shipment of series titles as long as the library keeps this list current.

HOW DOES USING AN APPROVAL PLAN AFFECT THE BUDGET?

Joan Grant (1999) points out that approval plans began at a time when library budgets were ample, and using approval plans provided a comprehensive range of new publications to libraries. These days, nearly all libraries are expected to do more with less money. Depending on an approval plan to take care of routine selection work is often seen as a way of providing good service without increasing staff. Rather than placing firm orders for hundreds or thousands of individual titles, the library receives many of its books in regular approval shipments, each with a single invoice that can be charged to one approval plan fund.

The simplest and most straightforward approach to bookkeeping for both the library and vendor is to set up one approval plan, with the library charging all approval plan purchases to a single fund. With one large plan the library may be able to negotiate higher discounts and better services with the vendor. However, some libraries opt to set up a number of small plans with one or several vendors, separating them by academic department, subject area, or type of material. The library may want to track the amount of money spent on various disciplines, and approval plan purchases will be charged to individual subject funds. It may be politically necessary to track expenditures in this way, to ensure that every subject area gets a fair share of the approval plan total. In a branch library system, separate plans may be set up for individual branches so that each branch maintains its own plan profiles and controls selection in its own area. Shipments, invoicing and payment in these situations must be tracked separately, increasing the difficulty of record keeping for the vendor and the library. The advantage of this extra work in plan accounting is that expenditures in specific areas can be tracked more precisely.

Grant (1999) recommends asking the vendor for an estimate of annual cost when an approval plan is being developed. As she points out, the library must also budget for additional materials that cannot easily be provided through approval plans: standing orders, some foreign imprints, retrospective selection, and imprints not covered by the plan.

Because vendors often offer greater discounts through approval plans, the plan can help the library control its expenditures on materials. Good discounts are possible because the vendor can depend on a predictable volume of sales to approval plan customers, and can depend on those customers to do much of their book-buying business through their approval plans rather than through firm orders with other suppliers.

Vendor-provided management reports help a library to monitor its budget expenditures. However, using either an approval plan or a blanket order means that total expenditures in any one year are unpredictable. It is not possible to predict exactly how many approval books will be received and added and what they will cost. In academic libraries, when charges for approval books are made against a department's fund allocation, it is difficult to estimate how much of the fund will be used for approval books, and how much will be left for individual title selections. There may be serious dissatisfaction if faculty perceive that the approval plan is drawing from funds they consider their own, previously set aside for title-by-title selection of books. To help to avoid this problem, the library may set an upper limit by fund for expenditures on an approval plan. Any under-expenditure will have to be resolved at the end of the year.

Approval plans require regular infusions of funds, and the outlay to support a plan for a year can be very large. It may be possible for some libraries to make substantial pre-payments to vendors, as is done with serials subscriptions, to maintain an approval plan. State-supported colleges and universities considering doing this need to ascertain whether having money on deposit with vendors for long periods of time is consistent with state regulations.

Often it is larger, better-funded, research-oriented libraries that use approval plans. A small library may be unable to afford the kind of approval plan it would like since its budget may not allow sizeable sums of money to be earmarked for purchases of approval books. Vendors may be reluctant to set up approval plans for small libraries. College libraries that focus on undergraduate instructional needs rather than on research may not want or need comprehensive subject coverage, but an approval plan covering specified, limited subject areas or a few specialized publishers may be successful.

APPROVAL PLAN PROFILING

Developing an approval plan profile requires the input of a number of people. Selectors, whether librarians or teaching faculty or both, should take part in the process as well as collection development and acquisitions personnel. A well planned profile will not bring in everything wanted in a particular library, but it will do an efficient job of bringing in a steady supply of new publications in defined areas. Periodic review of the profile will allow the library to add or reduce coverage, and to take advantage of any new services that may be offered by the vendor.

The publisher-based profile is a relatively simple one, specifying a list of publishers and/or imprints whose new titles are to be shipped by a vendor to the library. Sometimes a plan may be set up directly with a publisher that offers approval plans of its own, shipping books directly to libraries. So many academic libraries purchase the publications of university presses that they frequently set up comprehensive university press plans. Another type of publisher-based profile covers only a specialized format, such as printed music. Receipts from all of these publisher-based plans are easy to predict, and the profiles are relatively simple to update and maintain.

To be of greater use as an adjunct to selection, a more complicated, subject-oriented plan must be put in place. Nardini et al. list three basic components to be included in an approval plan profile: the library's preferred publishers, subject specifications, and non-subject parameters (Nardini et al., 1996). Subject specifications may be organized by a library classification scheme, such as the Library of Congress (LC) classification, Dewey Decimal classification, or the National Library of Medicine (NLM) scheme. Examples of other library specifications (non-subject parameters) incorporated in a subject-based profile are: publishers to be included in the plan, interdisciplinary areas to be covered, per-volume price ceilings, and formats that are or are not wanted. For example, a library may state that paperback editions are preferred if a choice exists between paper and cloth editions, ask that no coil-back books be sent, and require that books be sent in some subject categories and notification slips in others. There may be special instructions regarding series or sets of volumes. A library may specify academic levels desired, languages to be included, and country of publication. Because of their complexity, subject-oriented approval plans require detailed work to set up and can be time-consuming to maintain.

Approval plans covering foreign imprints are available. Book and slip plans can be set up with vendors outside the United States and Canada.

MANAGING AND MAINTAINING AN APPROVAL PLAN

Meredith Smith (1999) believes that the library bears a high degree of responsibility in ensuring that an approval plan operates effectively. The success of the plan should not be left to the vendor. Smith says that both selectors and support staff must be aware of the plan profile and able to recognize what new titles are likely to arrive by way of the plan. The library must clarify with the vendor just what constitutes out-of-scope material and why, whether this means popular treatment of a subject, undesired physical formats such as pocket books, or unwanted reprints.

To maintain an approval plan, selectors must be conscientious in reviewing the material supplied on approval and monitoring the titles they reject. Mary Eldredge (1996) recommends checking publishers' catalogs and reviewing sources against approval receipts, as a "quality control check" that will reveal gaps in coverage and indicate where the profile may need to be changed. The librarian or librarians with chief responsibility for overseeing the plan must request management reports from the vendor, generate in-house reports, and undertake projects or studies that reveal and clarify problems.

Libraries must periodically re-examine their approval plan profiles. In an academic environment courses are added or dropped and faculty research interests change, necessitating changes in plan coverage. Ideally the vendor will make no changes in the profile that the library does not know about, and any changes the library requests from the vendor will be implemented promptly. The library and the vendor must know that they are both working from an up-to-date version of the current approval plan. One of Meredith Smith's strongest points is to solicit the vendor's advice before making adjustments in an approval plan profile. "Most vendor contacts," says Smith, "are both capable of offering and prepared to present suggestions for profile adjustments" (p. 45).

The approval plan vendor should offer management reports to the library, providing such details as numbers of books sent during a specified time period, percentages returned, and expenditures by time period. Often these reports will be available online, on the vendor's web site, making data on approval shipments and purchases quick and easy to obtain. The vendor's management reports can be very useful to the library in collection development. Because they are generated by an outside agency they save time for the librarians who oversee the plan.

IS IT WORTHWHILE TO SEND BOOKS BACK?

Plan profiles should be set up and revised to keep returns within a reasonable limit, often no more than 5% of the material shipped. Returns waste time and money for both the library and the vendor. The vendor incurs initial costs in reviewing, selecting, packing and shipping books to the library. Invoicing is another expense for the vendor, as is maintaining a database that records the status of books with individual approval plan customers. When books are returned, the vendor must re-shelve them or return them to the publisher (if that is possible), update its database, adjust invoices, and issue credits for returns. The library's initial costs for approval books include receiving, processing and reviewing them. When books are returned, there are added expenses for packing and shipping as the library is likely to be responsible for return shipping charges under the terms of the plan. The library must request credit from the vendor and maintain records of credit requests until they are received, all of which costs staff time.

Smith (1996) describes a return rate of 5% to 10% as "acceptable," with a higher rate to be expected for newly established plans. Others, like Eldredge (1996), favor a considerably lower return rate. According to Eldredge, 2% or less is the acceptable limit for returns. In her opinion, it may be less expensive for a library to keep books it does not want than to return them. Flood and Nelson (1996) mention the possibility of returning only books that cost more than a set amount. While positing blanket acceptance as a defensible policy, Eldredge cautions that reviewing and monitoring approval plans is still necessary to ensure that good performance is maintained.

Librarians may question a vendor's assignment of titles to particular subject classifications, or to non-subject specifications of the profile. For example, a university library may specify that no textbooks are to be shipped. Do the library and the vendor define "textbook" in the same way? If high-school or introductory textbooks are excluded, are upper-level undergraduate textbooks acceptable? As such questions arise, it becomes obvious that the approval plan profile must be re-examined and modified over time. If this is not done, the book return rate may become unacceptably high for both the library and the vendor.

Smith (1996) advises analyzing return rates to see what they may suggest about adjusting plan profiles. Statistics can indicate patterns, such as high returns in particular subjects or of certain imprints. If the vendor's reports are not sufficiently detailed for an in-depth analysis, Smith suggests that the library create its own database on approval plan returns. The database could include such data as subject classification, cost, publisher, ISBN, reason for return, type of approval plan, and date returned. Reports generated from this database may help in determining what areas of the approval plan need to be modified.

TECHNOLOGY'S EFFECTS ON APPROVAL PLANS

Approval plan management, like every other facet of library work, has changed rapidly due to application of sophisticated technology. For example, with interactive access to a vendor's website, library support staff can check firm order requests against the vendor's database and avoid ordering duplicate copies of titles ready for shipment through an approval plan. While this would be a time-consuming procedure if carried out with every firm order request, it is convenient when staff are uncertain if a title would be included under an approval profile. It is also possible to obtain status reports of approval shipments online.

Web-based management reporting is now offered by a number of vendors, making it quick and easy for librarians to obtain statistical and budgetary reports on approval purchases through the vendor's website. Such easy access to data streamlines approval plan management and steadily increases the attractiveness of approval plans as alternatives to in-house materials selection.

A vendor may process approval books through OCLC, so that the library's location symbol is attached to the OCLC bibliographic records. Service of this type affects profiling decisions since returning books would necessitate deleting holding symbols from records in OCLC. Also available are vendor-provided bibliographic records, physical processing and cataloging services. All of these services are very likely to make non-returnable plans more acceptable, and blanket acceptance of approval shipments may become commonplace rather than exceptional.

EDI (electronic data interchange) provides for direct transmission of bibliographic records and invoices in electronic format, allowing libraries, vendors and publishers to transfer data quickly and easily. EDI has been used in libraries since the early 1990s and its use is becoming increasingly common. Two standards are currently used for EDI: the North American standard ASC X12 developed by ANSI (American National Standards Institute), and the European standard UN/EDI-FACT. These standards include mandatory and optional data elements, such as ISSN or ISBN, title, purchase order number, price, etc. Certain data elements called "match points" link messages sent by one communication partner to another (Stephens, 2001).

Not all vendors or integrated library systems support the X12 EDI capability for electronic ordering and invoicing. When EDI can be used with approval shipments, it simplifies and streamlines the process. The vendor can transfer bibliographic records for books in the shipments directly to the library's integrated library system. Library staff can download the bibliographic records and invoices for approval shipments, also sent using EDI, avoiding time-consuming manual entry of data.

CONCLUSION

If properly planned and maintained, an approval plan can be an efficient and effective tool in building a library collection. The size of the library and its budget must be taken into account when setting up an approval plan, as well as the degree of involvement and interest of librarians and other selectors in collection development. Before formalizing approval plans, it is important to study staffing requirements and effects on acquisitions workflow. Budget and accounting questions must also be kept in mind. Careful planning and management are necessary to maintain approval plans that work successfully.

REFERENCES

Bazirjian, R. (1996). The impact of approval plans on acquisitions operations and work flow. *The Acquisitions Librarian*, 16, 29-35.

Eldredge, M. (1996). Major issues in approval plans: the case for active management. *The Acquisitions Librarian* 16, 51-59.

Flood, S., & Nelson, B. K. (1996). Interface of approval and firm order. *The Acquisitions Librarian* 16, 5-12.

Ford, S. (1978). *The acquisition of library materials.* Chicago: American Library Association.

Grant, J. (1999). Approval plans: library-vendor partnerships for acquisitions and collection development. In K. A. Schmidt (Ed.), *Understanding the business of library acquisitions* (pp. 143-156). Chicago: American Library Association.

Nardini, R. F., Getchell, C. M., & Cheever, T. E. (1996). Approval plan overlap: a study of four libraries. *The Acquisitions Librarian* 16, 75-97.

Smith, M. L. (1996). Return to sender? Analyzing approval plan returns. *The Acquisitions Librarian* 16, 37-49.

Stephens, J. M. (2001). The impact of EDI on serials management: don't let the ship sail without you! *The Serials Librarian* 40(3/4), 331-336.

Index

Page numbers followed by t indicate tables.

BOOK ORDER FORM!

Order a copy of this book with this form or online at:
http://www.haworthpress.com/store/product.asp?sku=5068

Selecting Materials for Library Collections

____ in softbound at $29.95 (ISBN: 0-7890-1521-8)
____ in hardbound at $49.95 (ISBN: 0-7890-1520-X)

COST OF BOOKS _____

POSTAGE & HANDLING _____
US: $4.00 for first book & $1.50
for each additional book
Outside US: $5.00 for first book
& $2.00 for each additional book.

SUBTOTAL _____

In Canada: add 7% GST. _____

STATE TAX _____

CA, IL, IN, MN, NY, OH & SD residents
please add appropriate local sales tax.

FINAL TOTAL _____

If paying in Canadian funds, convert
using the current exchange rate,
UNESCO coupons welcome.

❏BILL ME LATER:
Bill-me option is good on US/Canada/
Mexico orders only; not good to jobbers,
wholesalers, or subscription agencies.

❏ Signature _____

❏ Payment Enclosed: $ _____

❏ PLEASE CHARGE TO MY CREDIT CARD:

❏Visa ❏MasterCard ❏AmEx ❏Discover
❏Diner's Club ❏Eurocard ❏JCB

Account # _____

Exp Date _____

Signature _____
(Prices in US dollars and subject to change without notice.)

PLEASE PRINT ALL INFORMATION OR ATTACH YOUR BUSINESS CARD

Name

Address

City	State/Province	Zip/Postal Code

Country

Tel	Fax

E-Mail

May we use your e-mail address for confirmations and other types of information? ❏Yes ❏No We appreciate receiving
your e-mail address. Haworth would like to e-mail special discount offers to you, as a preferred customer.
We will never share, rent, or exchange your e-mail address. We regard such actions as an invasion of your privacy.

Order From Your **Local Bookstore** or Directly From
The Haworth Press, Inc. 10 Alice Street, Binghamton, New York 13904-1580 • USA
Call Our toll-free number (1-800-429-6784) / Outside US/Canada: (607) 722-5857
Fax: 1-800-895-0582 / Outside US/Canada: (607) 771-0012
E-mail your order to us: orders@haworthpress.com

For orders outside US and Canada, you may wish to order through your local
sales representative, distributor, or bookseller.
For information, see http://haworthpress.com/distributors

(Discounts are available for individual orders in US and Canada only, not booksellers/distributors.)

Please photocopy this form for your personal use.
www.HaworthPress.com

BOF04